Praise for Charles Derber's previous works:

"This book is joyfully jammed with wisdom, experience, tools and motivation to overcome the ravages of the corporate state. So gripping is *Welcome to the Revolution* you can scarcely put this book down without putting yourself down."
Ralph Nader for *Welcome to the Revolution*

"Charles Derber is one of our most astute and eloquent social critics... His political analysis is persuasive and is enlivened by graceful prose."
Howard Zinn for *Greed to Green*

"In this lucid and informed study, Charles Derber breaks through the necessary illusions and shows how the United States is being turned into a 'sociopathic society.'"
Noam Chomsky for *Sociopathic Society*

"What would Karl Marx think about Lady Gaga, Facebook, and the Wall Street-driven economic meltdown? Derber's gift is to bring Marx alive and engage the worldly philosopher about the great issues of our day."
Chuck Collins for *Marx's Ghost*

"A superb – and superbly readable analysis of the way our ruling elites manufacture their own legitimacy and protect wealth and power...a much needed and optimistic antidote to Trump-inspired gloom."
Jonathan Steele for *Moving Beyond Fear*

"An engaging and provocative book...to encourage ongoing thoughtful discussions among students, scholars, and the general public...presenting panoramic views on democracy, race and corporate power."
G. William Domhoff for *Who Owns Democracy*

"Charlie Derber's new book...is the right message for the Trump era, and it is presented in powerful, moral, and practical terms. A must read."
Gar Alperovitz for *Welcome to the Revolution*

"Fascinating, provocative, and very timely. I found it very hard to stop reading... On every page, there's something startling to be learned about the past that is crucial to understanding our vertigo-inducing present."
Daniel Ellsberg for *Glorious Causes*

Praise for *Bonfire*:

"Derber masterfully traces how the erosion of social bonds and class solidarity has allowed racial division to be weaponized by both political parties throughout American political history to the present day."
Maya Rockeymoore Cummings, Ph.D., Founder, President & CEO of Global Policy Solutions

"Derber has done it again, diagnosing our current malaise by connecting the breakdown of social relations to the rise of authoritarianism."

Michael Burawoy, Professor of Sociology, University of California, Berkeley

"*Bonfire* artfully diagnoses the breakdown of social solidarity, the hollowing out of U.S. democracy, and the impending collapse of public life."

Chuck Collins, Institute for Policy Studies, author of *Burned by Billionaires*

"Derber's new book, *Bonfire*, is just what is needed for the Trump years. Read it and help spread the warmth of resistance and a democratic Reconstruction."

Medea Benjamin, Co-founder of Code Pink and Global Exchange, winner of Ghandi and Martin Luther King peace prizes

"As Trump's Far Right threat looms, this book becomes essential reading to prevent the self-destruction of any kind of real democracy within America."

Yale Magrass, Chancellor Professor Emeritus, University of Massachusetts–Dartmouth

"Derber sends us a stark warning: America is rapidly veering towards sociocide from the loss of trust and solidarity in the economy, family, and community. Yet he finds hope in history of progressive movements.

David L. Swartz, Professor of Sociology, Boston University

"Derber has discovered a key insight into the self-destructive dynamic taking control of America's commanding heights. But Derber refuses to succumb to despair."

Mark Sommer, founder and host of the syndicated radio program, *A World of Possibilities*

"An exceptionally important book. Essential reading for students and the public, to better understand their anxieties and fight for democracy."

Jonathan White and Shelley White, co-authors of *The Engaged Sociologist*

Bonfire

In this book, Charles Derber shows how the US is moving toward sociocide – the erosion of durable, positive social relations in the economy, family, politics, and civil society essential to sustaining society itself – while offering a combination of pragmatic solutions.

Bonfire: American Sociocide, Broken Relations, and the Quest for Democracy examines how new technologies and production and financial strategies are part of broader economic, environment, cultural, and political shifts that create tipping points generating more competition, distrust, isolation, and violence. In doing so, Derber spells out the implications for democracy and social cohesion. Importantly, he explores options that could stop the spiral and reconstruct a sustainable and equitable community, civil society, and democracy via emerging movements against neoliberalism capitalism, climate change, war – and in favor of labor solidarity, human rights, and community.

This book will be of interest to students, scholars and activists with an interest in political sociology, political economy, and social movements in the US.

Charles Derber is professor of sociology at Boston College, USA. A lifelong social justice activist, his work focuses on the crises of capitalism, globalization, corporate power, militarism, the culture of hegemony, the climate crisis, and peace and global justice movements. His recent books include *Turnout!: Mobilizing Voters in an Emergency* (Routledge, 2020), *Dying for Capitalism: How Big Money Fuels Extinction and What We Can Do About It* (Routledge, 2023), *Who Owns Democracy?: The Real Deep State and the Struggle Over Class and Caste in America* (Routledge, 2024), and *How We Win: Energizing Strategies, Voters, and Agendas* (Routledge, 2024).

Universalizing Resistance Series
Edited by Charles Derber and Suren Moodliar

The modern social sciences began in the late 19th century when capitalism was establishing itself as the dominant global system. Social science began as a terrifying awakening: that a militarized, globalizing capitalism was creating the greatest revolution in history, penetrating every part of society with the passions of self-interest and profit and breaking down community and the common good. The universalizing of the market promised universal prosperity but delivered an intertwined sociopathic system of money-making, militarism and environmental destruction now threatening the survival of all life itself.

In the 21st century, only a universalized resistance to this now fully universalized matrix of money, militarism and me-firstism can save humanity. History shows that people can join together under nearly impossible odds to create movements against tyranny for the common good. But when the world faces a universalizing system of madness and extinction, it takes new forms of resistance moving Copyright Material – Provided by Taylor & Francis beyond the "silo" movements for social justice that have emerged notably in the US in recent decades: single-issue movements separated by issue, race, gender, social class, nation and geography. The story of what universalized movements look like, how they are beginning to be organized, how they "intersect" with each other against the reigning system of power, and how they can grow fast enough to save humanity is the purpose of this series.

The series is publishing works by leading thinkers and activists developing the theory and practice of universalizing resistance. The books are written to engage professors, students, activists and organizers, and citizens who recognize the desperate urgency of a universalizing resistance that can mobilize the general population to build a new global society preserving life with justice.

How We Win
Energizing Voters, Strategies, and Agendas
Edited by Charles Derber, Suren Moodliar, Matt Nelson, and Nancy Treviño

Bonfire
American Sociocide, Broken Relations, and the Quest for Democracy
Charles Derber

Forthcoming:
Disrupting Narratives of Deservedness
Changing the Stories that Hold Economic and Racial and Inequality in Place
Chuck Collins

¡Viva Latinx!
How a New Generation of Organized Power Can Win Elections and Transform Culture
Elisa Batista and Matt Nelson

After Midnight
How Modern-Day Abolitionism Can Save the Planet
Charles Derber and Suren Moodliar

Revolution Has an Address!
The Transformative Power of Movement Building Spaces
Suren Moodliar

For more information about this series, please visit:
https://www.routledge.com/Universalizing-Resistance/book-series/RESIST

Bonfire

American Sociocide, Broken Relations, and the Quest for Democracy

Charles Derber

Routledge
Taylor & Francis Group

NEW YORK AND LONDON

Designed cover image: Getty Images

First published 2025
by Routledge
605 Third Avenue, New York, NY 10158

and by Routledge
4 Park Square, Milton Park, Abingdon, Oxon, OX14 4RN

Routledge is an imprint of the Taylor & Francis Group, an informa business

© 2025 Charles Derber

The right of Charles Derber to be identified as author of this work has been asserted in accordance with sections 77 and 78 of the Copyright, Designs and Patents Act 1988.

Library of Congress Cataloging-in-Publication Data
Names: Derber, Charles author
Title: Bonfire: American sociocide, broken relations,
and the quest for democracy / Charles Derber.
Description: New York, NY: Routledge, 2025. |
Includes bibliographical references and index.
Identifiers: LCCN 2025001474 | ISBN 9781032793894 hardback |
ISBN 9781032793634 paperback | ISBN 9781003491798 ebook
Subjects: LCSH: United States–Social conditions–2020- |
United States–Politics and government–2021- | Social conflict–United States |
Civil society–United States | Democracy–United States
Classification: LCC HN59.3 .D47 2025 | DDC 306.0973–dc23/eng/20250409
LC record available at https://lccn.loc.gov/2025001474

ISBN: 978-1-032-79389-4 (hbk)
ISBN: 978-1-032-79363-4 (pbk)
ISBN: 978-1-003-49179-8 (ebk)

DOI: 10.4324/9781003491798

Typeset in Sabon
by Deanta Global Publishing Services, Chennai, India

Contents

List of figures   *viii*

Introduction: The great societal bonfire   1

1   The bonfire of social relations and democracy: The self-destructing
    society, tipping points of social disconnection, and the path to
    sociocide and policide   3

2   The bonfire of the new Robber Barons: Melting down productive
    relations and dissolving the workplace   12

3   The bonfire of the tech revolution: AI and social media, surveillance
    capitalism, and the sociocide of Silicon Valley   26

4   The bonfire of the vanities: The over-heated American Dream, me
    over we, and the culture of social media and the lonely   44

5   The bonfire of environmental devastation: Climate change,
    COVID-19, and the sociocidal shock doctrine   63

6   The bonfire of the armed society: Packing heat, militarized America,
    and the new war system at home   76

7   The bonfire of American fascists: Racial and class policide, the anti-
    Democratic Party, and ballots to bullets in the Trump era   89

8   Beyond the bonfire: Historic lessons, sociophiliac movements, and
    creating deep democracy and community   112

Index   *135*

Figures

4.1 Decline of Marriage   46
4.2 National Trends for Social Connection   50

Introduction
The great societal bonfire

Today, we think of a bonfire as a big outdoor fire, often used for celebration. Bonfire is originally a 16th-century British word meaning "burning bones" or "burned to the bones." The US sociocide discussed here is the burning down of the bones – the personal and social relations in the workplace, household, and civil society – that support democracy and preserve the very existence of social life. Sociocide is an existential threat to the very survival of society itself, breaking down social connections, networks, and associations – forms of social capital – that are the fabric of a society and the foundation of democracy.

Sociocide can lead toward policide, the end of politics as we know it. Policide is rule by the iron fist, an inevitable authoritarian form of governance when the social trust and consensus undergirding elections and peaceful transitions of power break down. It is now marked by the victory of Donald Trump in the 2024 election, which is giving rise to both intensified corporate oligarchy and existential threats to democracy.

The surge of Far-Right populism in the Trump era, and the new constitutional authoritarianism put in place by the Trumpist Supreme Court preceding Trump's victory, reflect the dire threats of sociocide and policide in America. It comes with authoritarian political parties and practices that feed on social isolation and help break down communities not directly controlled by a "Great Leader." Authoritarian leaders such as Trump offer their own cult-like political party and groups that attract people who have lost their social capital and are experiencing a breakdown of their own social ties.

The anthropologist Colin Turnbull wrote a celebrated book, *The Mountain People*, about a displaced mountain tribe called the Ik in Uganda. He called it the loveless society.[1] The Ik were all starving, having been forcibly relocated to a stark and barren area where it was almost impossible to grow food or get enough water. The economic conditions turned each Ik against each other, as helping even another family member would take away the energy and reserves needed to prevent oneself from starving. As a result, the Ik were laser-focused on their own survival, competing for scarce food and too self-focused to offer support or affection to anyone else. There was the me but no we.

The US is not an impoverished starving society, but there are striking parallels with the Ik.[2] The Ik society could be described as a sociocidal bonfire that had burned the bones holding Ik social relations – and IK society itself – together. In the US, we have created a wealthier economy that pits most Americans against each other in our own sociocidal struggle for both success and survival. It is burning down American social relations in the workplace, family, and the polity, eroding social capital among working people and creating an armed society of people who distrust each other and are increasingly atomized. Those most affected – suffering atomization and loneliness from the increased

DOI: 10.4324/9781003491798-1

breakdown of social relations and civil society – are more likely to be working-class people with reduced access to secure jobs and social associations; they are vulnerable to being drawn to authoritarian politics and neo-fascist strongmen who fill the void of their eroding family, friendship, and civil society communities. Nonetheless, we show that sociocidal forces are impacting people of all classes, races, and gender orientations in America, where sociocide has become a universalizing systemic threat.

Large overheated bonfires can burn and kill people, but people can also gather together to admire the flame, warm up, or put it out if it gets out of control. Sociocidal forces can generate opposing forces that actually mobilize people to make new connections and put out the sociocidal fire through economic and social change fueled by solidarity and love.

This book will show that sociocide, catastrophically intensified now by Trump's re-election, is a deep existential threat to democracy and American society but is not irreversible. Even facing threats of violence and neo-fascist opponents, young people, unions, civil rights organizations, women's groups, and pro-democracy movements began to unite before and during the 2024 presidential election around some of the bonfires we describe. Despite Kamala Harris' disastrous defeat, which we explain in later chapters, a new and larger movement for both economic and political democracy is likely to emerge. It will not only resist authoritarian policide but move us beyond American sociocide toward sustainable democracy and community.

We will look throughout this book at the "sociophiliac" forces – those that build humanizing face to face relations and loving solidarity, as well as democracy – that can put out the sociocidal bonfire and light a new sociophiliac one. It invites people to expand what they already have started to do: gathering together to protect themselves, organize politically, and bond around a new flame of democracy, community, and love.

Notes

1 Colin Turnbull, *The Mountain People*. NY: Touchstone, 1987.
2 Charles Derber, *The Wilding of America*. 6th edition. NY: Worth Publishers, 2014.

1 The bonfire of social relations and democracy

The self-destructing society, tipping points of social disconnection, and the path to sociocide and policide

A bonfire can sound inviting. We gather with friends and family to eat, play, or just talk. The warmth can bring us together. But this is not the bonfire we should be discussing today.

The bonfire we need to laser-focus on now is one that is way too hot for comfort – or for company. We are talking about a massive bonfire that is setting fire to our entire society. It is so hot that it is burning our relationships – and beginning to melt down our collective social institutions like the workplace, the family, and the community. Put slightly differently, it is so hot that it is melting down our social connections and relations – in other words, burning down the social bones that keep a society together. The result is sociocide, an increasingly disconnected society lacking a "we" and focused on the survival of the "me." It opens the door wide to political authoritarianism, reflected in the reign of Donald Trump in his second term, a political catastrophe arising from and reflecting the breakdown of social cohesion and civil society essential to democracy.

In an earlier work, *Sociopathic Society*, I argued that a society can be sociopathic, based on values and institutions that are anti-social.[1] Sociopathic values create norms of self-interested, exploitative, violent, or other behavior that weaken social relations and connections. Sociopathy can emerge in multiple sectors of society, including the economy, the political system, and the culture. A sociopathic society tends to generate behavior that weakens the society itself. It is self-destructive in the sense that it targets the social relationships – whether of work, family and friends, or politics – which make society possible in the first place.

Sociopathic societies vary in degree, intensity and scope of sociopathy. Almost all societies generate some sociopathic values or behavior, but most also create other norms that strengthen social connections and build community. The most endangered societies are those creating sociopathic values and institutions that are dominant in the economic system and govern behavior in the cultural sphere and politics. These societies are the most vulnerable to the erosion of strong and sustainable social relations and are the most likely to experience tipping points that accelerate sociopathic forces, putting democracy and the entire society at even more risk.

In the most extreme cases, tipping points can emerge in multiple sectors at such high speed that they push all social relations and society as a whole toward destruction. The great 19th-century sociologist, Emile Durkheim, in a foundational contribution to sociology, warned of the possibility of what he called social "disaggregation … in which the meshes of the social fabric are … dangerously slack." Durkheim argued that the loss of traditional forms of occupational and social solidarity could lead to complete

DOI: 10.4324/9781003491798-2

social breakdown, creating extreme individualism, anomie, and suicide.[2] In such cases, the sociopathic society becomes what I call sociocidal.

A sociocidal society, as I conceive it here, is one whose sociopathy is intensifying into new yet more dangerous forms, with family, friendship, community, and broader civil society breaking down so widely and rapidly that democracy and the actual self-destruction of the society, as Durkheim worried, is possible. As mentioned in the Introduction, the loveless tribe of the Ik demonstrates how a survivalist "me" can destroy the "we" of a loving society – or even break apart any social relationships essential to the survival of any kind of society.[3] While Durkheim does not use the term sociocide, I have drawn on his classic sociological writings on rising economic and cultural threats to solidarity, where a crisis of "egoism" emerges in which the "individual is isolated because the bonds uniting him to others are slackened or broken because the society is not sufficiently integrated."[4]

The politics of a sociocidal society are highlighted in this book, because sociocide is the social breeding ground of what political scientists have called policide, now a looming threat in the US. Policide is the end of politics as bargaining, partisan politics, and democracy itself, emerging when sociocide breaks apart the social bonds and trust essential to compromise, consensus, and acceptance of democratic governance. It is rule by force, typically by a strongman whose coercion and iron fist become the primary instrument for assuring stability and order. As societies become sociocidal, people hunger for the community that authoritarian political leaders offer; the strength of that hunger was reflected in the 2024 victory of Donald Trump for a second term.

Strongmen such as Donald Trump seek to break down all social associations that they do not control. They promise to reconnect people in a community of "true patriots," bonding together to purge others "poisoning the blood" of the great nation. Building a nation of the true people of the nation, with an authoritarian leader uniting them against alien races, is the heart of fascism. The triumphant rise of Trumpism and broader Far-Right populism is the clearest sign of the growing American crises of sociocide and both corporate oligarchy and neo-fascist policide.

* * *

It is important to note that most sociopathic societies are not sociocidal or policidal, but some become so over time. The degree of sociopathic forces is not fixed; it is a historical dynamic that changes over time. Durkheim saw economic and cultural forces in the late 19th century that created sociocide and egoism, but felt they could be countered by new forms of division of labor and identification with modern interdependent occupations creating what he called "organic solidarity."[5] In the first few chapters, I show that the US economy and culture have not evolved benignly in the solidaristic way Durkheim had hoped, but rather reflect the intensification of the "disaggregating" forces that globalizing capitalism and its intensely individualizing cultural transformations could create, something that Durkheim's contemporary, Karl Marx, foresaw more accurately.[6] As Marx well understood, the history of any society is partly a story of the structure and evolution of its sociopathic tendencies.[7] At the heart of this question, as I show later, are the institutionalized forms and scale of the underlying sociopathy. In most societies, sociopathy is contained. But tipping points of vital social connection and disconnection can be historically triggered and turn the sociopathic society toward sociocide and policide, a history that we show in this book is playing out rapidly in our own society.

Two other modern sociologists, Johann Galtung and Keith Doubt, have introduced and used the term sociocide in a related but distinct way. Galtung and Doubt, both peace and conflict scholars, have each discussed sociocide as a specific type of war or aggression by one society against another.[8] They view a war as sociocide if one country attacks and destroys the "social infrastructure" of the other. The "social infrastructure" means the core economic, family, and political relations that are essential to sustaining the social order. Their sociocide is closely related to concepts like genocide or other totalistic wars that annihilate the possibility of any meaningful social life in societies, condemning them to chaos, authoritarian politics, and permanent failed states.

While I view both sociopathic and sociocidal societies as prone to aggression and militarism, I define sociocide as a society engaged in what Galtung or Doubt would likely conceive as an annihilating war against itself. Their concept views sociocide as societal murder: one nation murdering another. My concept defines sociocide as societal suicide: one nation killing – or at risk of killing – itself. My analysis links to that of Galtung and Doubt, as I show that sociocidal societies tend to become hyper-militaristic and policidal; they wage sociocidal wars destroying other nations as a part of their own path toward self-destruction and authoritarianism or tyranny at home.

I have earlier argued that the US is among the most striking cases of sociopathy among affluent Western societies. In *Sociopathic Society*, I argued the US had dominant institutions and norms of individualism and self-interest shaped by our system of corporate capitalism and its creed of the American Dream.[9] I viewed these intertwined economic and cultural systems, tied to our corporate politics, as deeply anti-social or sociopathic. But I did not view America as sociocidal. I viewed the US as one among other highly developed, deeply troubled societies with strong anti-social values and institutions but also strong countervailing forces that could counter sociocidal and policidal forces.

History can change the course of societies very rapidly. I am writing this book because I believe that tipping points in American society from sociopathy to sociocide are accelerating in our economy, culture, and politics. A notable shift toward sociocide has taken place in the last several decades, intensifying in the last five to ten years, threatening American social ties and the survival of democracy in ways that I and many others did not fully anticipate.

This book looks at both the manifestations of breakdown in our social and political relations as well as the multiple systemic drivers of this shift toward sociocide in the US. The change from the "we" of a publicly regulated political economy to the "me" of a hyper-individualistic, neoliberal market capitalism is the most important structural or systemic change fueling the sociocidal transition. In the US, this transition, steered by bipartisan political leaders funded by and closely allied with corporate elites, is generally viewed as rising dramatically in the Reagan Revolution, beginning in the 1980s, when the earlier New Deal forms of regulated capitalism and public investments for common goods were abandoned. They gave way to the neoliberal focus on abandoning the very idea of a society as a collectivity, focusing the economy and politics instead on the individual acting solely for his or her own interest in the market. This would rapidly lead toward the triumph of the me over the we, the cultural bedrock of sociocide. And it would open the door to the seductions of a new "we" trumpeted by hyper-nationalist policidal leaders, such as Donald Trump. They promise to restore a strong community of great Americans while also allying with neoliberal corporate elites and seeking to break down unions and other social ties outside their own control while integrating people into their own cult-like political tribe.

Neoliberalism advanced by Reagan – and evolving over several decades into Trump's own Far-Right political economy – fueled a long sociocidal and policidal transition through a huge array of now familiar economic policies prioritizing deregulated, unfettered markets. This involved universalizing the market and making everything a commodity for sale and profit, concentrating capital in huge monopolistic banks and corporations, shrinking government and all public goods and social services, while weakening unions and other forms of social organization and social solidarity. Existing forms of social relations and solidarity in our culture, politics, and civil society have been drastically weakened as we moved from sociopathy toward sociocide, a transition highlighted in popular culture by the huge hit series and film, *The Hunger Games*. *The Hunger Games* didn't use the term neoliberalism but it offered the mass public a visceral, crash course on the subject, featuring a subjugated population forced to compete violently with each other to survive, designed for the power and entertainment of the authoritarian "Capitol" or ruling oligarchic and fascist regime.

The prime beneficiaries of sociocide are ruling elites since social solidarity in the general population is the essential condition of any challenge to the existing order. The neoliberal revolution of the late 20th century in the US strengthened the power of elites through all the economic and political measures –globalizing the markets, shrinking government, and other neoliberal measures noted above – but it wasn't enough. To fully secure power, elites need to weaken social connections and ensure that relations are not strong enough to build social solidarity that can translate into social movements or popular organizations seeking to displace elites and democratize the ruling system. At the same time, the breakdown of social relations can create openings for new authoritarian elites, often intertwined with existing ones. This is emerging now in the US, as Trump and Vance, allied with conservative corporate elites, promise in Trump's second term to overcome growing social division and isolation; they join in the attack on unions and other social associations they don't control but promise to build a community of "true Americans," coming together in a proud new Far-Right populist and increasingly neo-fascist politics to restore economic prosperity and social relations that sociocide has destroyed.

While the economic system is a central driver, steered and protected in the US by political leaders tied to the business class and corporate elites, I am not offering a single-factor view of the rising sociocidal crisis. In this book, I look at cultural, environmental, technological, racial, and military US systems as intertwined with and partly driven by the economic system. Environmental change, culture, the military, and other sectors of society – most notably the political sphere – give rise to their own partly autonomous sociocidal threats. All are manifestations of hyper-individualism, egoism, and intense competition pitting worker against worker in the markets, trending toward violence and political authoritarianism but idealized in a new extreme American Dream, and radiating throughout US society in the late 20th and early 21st century.

The post-New Deal Reagan period, seen by economic historians as the neoliberal era, was marked by major cultural shifts intensifying individualism, competition, speed-up, and destabilization of attachments to time and place, and social disconnection, all linked to a more extreme American Dream.[10] The rise of high-tech giant firms, AI, and social media involved both economic and cultural forces playing their own increasingly intense role in weakening and endangering face-to-face relations both in the workplace and the family and community. Demographic racial tipping points toward a minority–majority society have given rise to white fear, fueling a sociocidal political transition marked by the authoritarian neo-fascist turn of the Republican Party in the Trump years. As noted above, we shall show that the weakening of social relations and solidarity always threatens democracy itself because force and coercion become the only way of holding together a society sociocidally atomized and polarized; moreover, authoritarian leaders have their own interest in destroying all social organizations they don't control.

* * *

The evolution toward major erosion of social ties and connections became a topic of interest in the 1980s and 1990s when political scientists and sociologists such as Robert Putnam and Robert Bellah published important work on what Putnam would vividly capture in his 2000 book, *Bowling Alone*.[11] Putnam's work documented the weakening of voluntary organizations and other classic forms of American civil society, which had been highlighted more than a century ago by Alexis de Tocqueville as social foundations of American democracy itself.[12] The connection between the breakdown of everyday social relations and civic ties – and how it creates a "lonely society" as well as corporate oligarchy and political authoritarianism – is a central concern of this book. It is prefigured by Hannah Arendt in her renowned work, The Origins of Totalitarianism.

> What prepares men for totalitarian domination in the non-totalitarian world is the fact that loneliness, once a borderline experience usually suffered in certain marginal social conditions like old age, has become an everyday experience.[13]

In the US, the cultural forces creating loneliness and helping give rise to authoritarianism and neo-fascism are rooted in economies with extreme market systems. This is epitomized by hyper-market capitalism, which seeks to market everything, including the self. Karl Marx foresaw this looming capitalist threat to social relations as he discussed the atomizing forces of the market – and alluded to the market bonfire so intense that "all melts into air," burning up the molecules of connection and solidarity among working people while opening up a political tyranny of the rich.[14] Tocqueville from a very different focus, shared Emile Durkheim's concern of modernity's assault on social solidarity, also seeing social isolation and the breakdown of civic ties as destroying democracy.[15]

More than a century later, these themes resurfaced, both from revolutionary Marxists and liberal critics of fascism such as Arendt. As neoliberal forces created hyper-individualistic markets that pitted people against each other, the breakdown of social relations – whether in the workplace, marriage, friendship, neighborhood, or civil society – intensified in the late 20th century. This gave rise to and attention to important works on social capital in the US such as Putnam's *Bowling Alone*.[16] Putnam used the concept of social capital to analyze the eroding social bonds and societal cohesion of the 1980s and 1990s. Putnam documented the scale and dangers of declining social trust and relations, highlighting voluntary associations like bowling leagues. He offered a variety of cultural and generational causes of social capital decline: urban and suburban sprawl, the rise of television, and money-related time pressures. He argued that the breakdown of social capital could help breed political authoritarianism, including Nazism in Germany and Trumpism in the US.[17] Putnam made a major contribution, awakening many Americans to the danger. But he did not dwell at length on what I argue here are the root causes of sociocide, specifically our system of political economy and its forms of structural dominance and class power that I argue here are all integral to the breakdown of social relations and social capital.[18]

Neo-Marxists such as Pierre Bourdieu, David Harvey, Fredric Jameson, and Mark Fisher all offer a stronger basis for locating the erosion of social capital and democracy in the economic system itself.[19] Bourdieu views *social capital* as one of three forms of capital – economic, social, and cultural. It is central to class power and highlights the importance of access to social networks and resources that provide all of us access to economic and personal well-being.[20] Bourdieu's analysis calls attention to the number and strength of our social relations as foundational to both our personal identity and power, as well as to the integrity and social sustainability of society.

The stronger our social relationships and integration into social communities, the higher our level of social capital. Greater social capital strengthens both the individual and society; social capital is thus a key form of capital and class privilege. Bourdieu's theory suggests that the weakness of social relationships is a class attribute and will vary by income and education. This is an empirical proposition that we analyze in Chapter 4, where we show that particular groups – notably working class and poor people – are at distinctly high sociocidal risk. Nonetheless, the sociocidal forces in play now are impacting all major demographic and class groups in the US and represent a threat to the entire population and social fabric.

When social relationships weaken and social capital declines, so too does the cohesion of society. Bourdieu's concept of social capital helps highlight, as does Durkheim, the critical importance of social relations as the essential "social glue" of society and at the heart of sociological and political analysis. The breakdown of social relations that defines American sociocide can be understood in Bourdieu's terms as the weakening and potential destruction of social capital. When social capital erodes in the working classes, the well-being and power of workers weaken drastically. When social capital erodes and disappears across the entire society, all individuals and the entire society are doomed. We show here that both threats now need to be taken very seriously.

Other Marxist theorists offer helpful economic perspectives on the breakdown of social relations as well. While David Harvey does not analyze in depth the breakdown of social relations, his theory of space-time compression, developed in his 1989 book, *The Condition of Postmodernity*, is useful in showing how a globalizing neoliberal capitalism is a core economic driver of potential social and political breakdown. Fredric Jameson, in *Postmodernism*, and Mark Fisher, in *Capitalist Realism*, also offer powerful insights into the ways in which neoliberalism breaks down a culture supporting humanizing and democratic social connections.[21] I offer my own integration of capitalist-fueled economic and cultural forces fueling the transition to sociocide and to policide.

Many Marxists do not give enough attention to the authoritarian and Far-Right populist forces that historically have both fueled and been fueled by breakdowns in social relations and powerful sociocidal forces in American capitalism. In the US, Far-Right populists have operated in covert alliances with corporate elites whose Establishment they claim to challenge. They play their own role in causing sociocide ginned up by capitalism while also gaining political power from it, drawing strong political support from working-class people most deprived of social capital and experiencing erosion of their social relations and networks. Political authoritarians like Trump ally with corporate leaders to destroy unions and other bases of social solidarity that they do not control and can give rise to organized opposition either to corporations or to authoritarian leaders like Trump himself. Trumpism benefits more broadly from neoliberal and other sociocidal forces that atomize and separate people, making them insecure and feeding their hunger for the strong social ties and political community offered by MAGA and built around the direct control of Trump himself.

We now need to focus on American sociocide and policide as both a national and global emergency. Because America is the most powerful nation in the world, a shift toward American sociocide threatens not only the US but much of the world. Corporate neoliberalism and the rise of Far-Right authoritarianism create extreme sociocidal and policidal peril for the US itself. Trump's second term has brought the US to the brink, threatening a political emergency for democracy.

In the short and long-term, we will need support to survive and mount opposition to neofascism. Immigrants, people of color, women, working people, civil servants, election officials, and progressive activists and journalists will all face extreme risks, including loss of basic freedoms and violent repression. Social solidarity will become more important to all Americans because fighting and defeating the short and long-term threats of neofascism will require the mobilization of all our personal, civil society, and political associations. History shows that defeating fascism depends on the capacity to build new communities of solidarity and courageous resistance at every level of social and political life.

American sociocide, though, ensures that the threat to democracy will remain high for a long period. MAGA politicians will continue to rule in at least half of the states in the US. Moreover, the Supreme Court, as shown in later chapters, has created a new constitutionally mandated authoritarianism, making the president effectively a king, as Supreme Court Justice Sonia Sotomayor said in her dissent to the 2024 Trump Immunity decision. The attacks on democracy intensified furiously well before the 2024 election, involving attacks on women's bodily freedom and rising political violence. This is likely to intensify in new forms and on a new scale as Trump's second term unfolds.

***

Despite the serious threats to democracy and existential risks to social solidarity and human survival, they can be fought and defeated. Just as many suicidal individuals do not commit suicide, many sociocidal societies do not kill themselves. The possibilities of self-destruction are rising, but there remains – in America as in most sociocidal societies – the possibility of creating a path away from social destruction and authoritarian politics toward a sustainable and democratic reconstruction.

In July 2024, the surprise Kamala Harris presidential candidacy initially catalyzed an electric surge of collective energy, creating a new social community and political coalition that brought together women, people of color, young people, labor, poor people, and political progressives. As we show later, her campaign lost because of a fatal failure to mobilize mass support by speaking directly to working people and their need for systemic changes to the militarized corporate system, which helps fuel sociocide and Trumpism. Nonetheless, the initial collective excitement and surge showed that the dire threats of sociocide and policide have created a hunger for social connection and change, and there remain new opportunities to confront and overcome the dire threats we currently face.

Along with sociopathic and sociocidal values, there are what I call sociophiliac values. Sociophiliac norms and institutions are those that strengthen and sustain humanizing social relations, typically basing them on free, democratic, and equitable associations and institutions rather than hierarchical, exploitative, and violent systems. In some sociocidal societies, such as Nazi Germany, the sociophiliac forces latent in German society were politically crushed, and Germany had to be reconstructed with the help of the victorious Allies after its destruction in World War II. In sociocidal societies such as the US today, external nations will be important in limiting and reversing American sociocide, but internal democratic reconstruction remains a possibility.

A potential new reconstruction depends on the renewal of the civil society and community ties, tied to anti-fascist and pro-democracy movements and political coalitions of a different kind than Kamala Harris and the Democratic Party have tried to organize through mainstream political agendas that do not address the weakening of social ties and the economic suffering of most working people. Fortunately, sociocidal forces often are deeply contradictory, opening up possibilities for new social and political connections even as they destroy existing relations. Technological innovation related to the Internet, social media, and AI are an obvious example. While they are driven by Big Tech for profit and will eliminate or weaken and corrupt many existing employment, community, and family relations, they also create new social connections, both online and in-person. They even create opportunities for new social movements challenging the corporate titans and new authoritarian leaders, with online resistance growing in importance as repressive state power makes in-person community organizing and street protests dangerous, leading increasingly to firings, arrests, or jail. This contradictory character of many sociocidal forces – which can give rise to sociophiliac forces rebuilding broken relations, social solidarity, and democracy – is a reason to sustain hope even under adverse political conditions.

Historically, the deep sociopathic forces that have always existed in the US have long been challenged by abolitionist, reconstructionist, populist, labor, civil rights, feminist, communitarian, and anti-fascist democratic movements and ideals. Anti-sociocidal and anti-political forces are deeply grounded in US history, and new movements for community and democracy in America are rising to rebuild the US, prevent civil war, defeat prolonged authoritarian rule, and avoid complete social breakdown.

Today, we face a decisive phase of the struggle for an equitable social life and democracy in America. The sociocidal and policidal threats in the second Trump term are greater than they have been in any other period, except perhaps those leading toward the Civil War. When Trump leaves the scene, MAGA politics will be weakened but remain powerful for a substantial period. Indeed, the Trumpist Supreme Court, in its momentous 2024 Presidential immunity and Chevron decisions, put in place the seeds of a deeper constitutionally sanctioned authoritarianism in America, already institutionalizing parts of the Trumpist policidal agenda.

It is almost certain that external as well as internal forces will be necessary to limit and reverse American sociocide and policide. But the stakes are so high – for the US and the world – that failure is not an option. In fact, it is a real possibility, but as we shall detail here, there are paths toward a less profit-driven and more just economy, toward rebuilding and deepening a more peaceful civil society and democracy, and nurturing more loving face-to-face relations that are already being explored, with millions of young people in particular mobilized to bring them to fruition. After all, their lives and social survival hang in the balance.

Notes

1 Charles Derber, *Sociopathic Society*. NY: Routledge, 2013.
2 Emile Durkheim, *Suicide*. 2nd edition. NY: Harper and Row, 2013. Lukes, *Emile Durkheim*. Harmondsworth: Penguin, 1973, pp. 198–207.
3 Colin Turnbull, *The Mountain People*. NY: Touchstone, 1987.

4 Durkheim, cited in Lukes, *Emile Durkheim*. Harmondsworth: Penguin, 1973, p. 206.
5 Durkheim, *The Division of Labor*. Digireads.com Annotated Edition, 2013. See also Lukes, *Emile Durkheim*, Chapter 7.
6 Karl Marx, *Capital Vol. 1*. Harmondsworth: Penguin Classics reprint, 1992.
7 Karl Marx, *Capital Vol. 1*. Harmondsworth: Penguin Classics reprint, 1992.
8 Keith Doubt, *Understanding Evil*. NY: Fordham University Press, 2007. Johann Galtung, *World Politics of Peace and War*. London: Hampton Press, 2015.
9 Charles Derber, *Sociopathic Society*. NY: Routledge, 2013.
10 Charles Derber, *Sociopathic Society*. NY: Routledge, 2013. David Harvey, *A Brief History of Neoliberalism*. NY: Oxford University Press, 2007.
11 Robert Putnam, *Bowling Alone, Revised and Updated*. NY: Simon and Schuster, 2020. Robert Bellah, *Habits of the Heart*. Oakland: University of California Press, 2007.
12 Alexis de Tocqueville, *Democracy in America*. Chicago: University of Chicago Press, 2002.
13 Hannah Arendt, *The Origins of Totalitarianism*. Cited in Samantha Rose Hill, "Where Loneliness Can Lead." *Aeon*, 2022, aeon.com
14 Karl Marx, *The Communist Manifesto*. London: Arcturus Publishing Ltd, 2010.
15 Alexis de Tocqueville, *Democracy in America*. Chicago: University of Chicago Press, 2002. See also Steven Lukes' discussion of Durkheim in Lukes, *Emile Durkheim*.
16 Robert Putnam, *Bowling Alone, Revised and Updated*. NY: Simon and Schuster, 2020.
17 Robert Putnam, *Bowling Alone, Revised and Updated*. NY: Simon and Schuster, 2020. Lulu Garcia-Navarro, "Robert Putnam Knows Why You're Lonely." *New York Times*, July 13, 2024, Nytimes.com
18 Robert Putnam, *Bowling Alone, Revised and Updated*. NY: Simon and Schuster, 2020.
19 Pierre Bourdieu and L.P.D. Wacquant, *An Invitation to Reflexive Sociology*. Chicago: University of Chicago Press, 1992. David Harvey, *The Condition of Post-Modernity*. London: Blackwell, 1991. Frederick Jameson, *Postmodernism, or, The Cultural Logic of Late Capitalism*. Durham: Duke University Press, 1992. Mark Fisher, *Capitalist Realism*. London: ZerO Books, 2022.
20 Bourdieu, P. 1986. "The Forms of Capital," pp. 241–258 in *Handbook of Theory and Research for the Sociology of Education*, edited by J.G. Richardson. NY: Greenwood Press.
21 David Harvey, *The Condition of Postmodernity*. London: Blackwell, 1991.

2 The bonfire of the new Robber Barons

Melting down productive relations and dissolving the workplace

John D. Rockefeller, J.P. Morgan, and Andrew Carnegie, the most famous of the late 19th-century Gilded Age tycoons, created the modern US industrial capitalist system. They are known as the "Robber Barons" because they established a corporate system based on theft and exploitation of workers. While they garnered huge profits and became the country's first billionaires, they overworked and underpaid their mostly immigrant and poor workers who labored in filthy and unsanitary conditions. Workers were harshly treated if they tried to form a union or otherwise demanded better wages or working conditions. Many Robber Barons used their own armed guards and police violence against strikers to maintain control over workers, viewing any form of social solidarity or social capital of workers as a threat to their profits and power.[1]

The term Robber Barons is apt because they were transparently sociopathic. They openly celebrated their greed and bribed top politicians, who protected their exploitative system. There was little pretense of generosity or civility in their relations with employees or their community. Famous early critics of the Robber Barons, such as the journalist Upton Sinclair, described the Robber Baron factory as "The Jungle," in his 2006 best-selling book of that title about the meat-packing industry.[2] The progressives of that era helped create new movements and settlement houses to help the workers and poor but did little to change the fundamentally sociopathic character of what neo-Marxist labor scholars such as Michael Burawoy and Harry Braverman, in the late 20th century, have discussed as the enduring capitalist "labor process" or "relations of production."[3]

But while the founding American capitalists, backed by their wealthy political patrons, were clearly sociopathic, they were not sociocidal. They actually helped create and sustain a new industrial order and society that lasted for more than a century. They essentially founded the modern concept of employment, which represented a new economic and social tie, exploitative but sustainable, between employer and worker. Moreover, to stabilize and manage those relations, they created the modern workplace, bringing together dispersed workers into a collective workplace, which actually created new face-to-face social relations of production that had great importance.

In pre-capitalist societies most tradespeople, craftsmen, and other workers worked from their homes. The early Robber Baron factories brought workers together in one place with new opportunities to develop their own relations or communities. As Karl Marx pointed out, the capitalist introduction of the industrial factory was a tool not only for exploitation but also for liberation. It created a "socialized" space for the development of worker associations that could ultimately become a vehicle for building worker social capital and social solidarity, class consciousness, and reform or revolution.

DOI: 10.4324/9781003491798-3

The new Robber Barons of our own era, backed by billionaire political donors and the MAGA GOP (Make America Great Again Republican Party) Trumpist as well as by corporate Democrats, are beginning to melt down the production relations created by their predecessors and are in the process of dissolving the workplace itself. The new Robber Barons are themselves the creation of a new post-industrial social order, a 21st-century capitalist system dominated by trillionaire companies such as Amazon, Apple, Microsoft, and Alphabet (Google) – and new tycoons such as the world's two richest men in 2024, Tesla founder and X owner, Elon Musk, and Amazon CEO, Jeff Bezos, both worth about $200 billion, with Musk reported by Bloomberg to be on track to become the world's first trillionaire in 2028.[4] The Big Tech tycoons are just one leading sector of the New Robber Barons, joined by CEOs of major trillionaire banks and financial empires such as Jamie Dimon of Morgan Chase and heads of multi-billionaire companies across the entire economy. These include Big Oil's Exxon, Big Pharma's Pfizer, Big Ag's Cargill, Big Industry's General Motors, and the Military-Industrial Complex's Lockheed Martin, all integrating industrial and post-industrial technology, new exploitative anti-union labor and marketing practices, and intertwined online and offline communications.

These practices are all politically supported by a coalition of neoliberal and Far-Right GOP politicians. While Trump often uses anti-corporate and pro-worker rhetoric, his regime strongly supports the new Robber Barons in practice. The global economic and political power of the new Robber Barons is greater than their predecessors, but what distinguishes them most importantly is their shift from sociopathic to sociocidal labor processes, which have helped open the door to authoritarian political leaders like Trump who prey on sociocide as a breeding ground for Far-Right populism and neo-fascist policide.

* * *

The first of several new sociocidal practices by today's Robber Barons involves destroying the social relation of employment. There is still a concept of employment, but its social character is being eroded by legal, technological, and spatial transformations, which lead toward a post-modern workplace in some ways reminiscent of pre-capitalist times. The employment relation that persists remains sociopathic in the overworked and underpaid character of the worker. But the worker laboring in the emerging "contingent worker" order is essentially deprived of the legal and social character or expectation of a sustainable social relationship.[5]

The new worker, often dubbed a member of the "precariat class," is existentially insecure because employment is being redesigned to be ephemeral and socially obsolescent. Legally, the worker is increasingly categorized as contingent, meaning with no expectation of a continuing relation. The language may be one of "temp," "adjunct," "freelancer," "gig," "independent worker," or "contractor," but socially and politically the new legal design is tied to transient conditions that do not assume or permit a sustainable social relation. Contingency is a discreet term for atomization, breaking relationships with and among the working population. In the language of French social theorist Pierre Bourdieu, contingent employment undermines the social capital of the labor force.

Many forces fuel the breakdown of traditional employment, but it is not hard to see the overriding benefit for the new Robber Barons. Transient workers cannot build long-term social relations fostering solidarity – and unions and other collective worker power – to gain higher wages and multiple other benefits, including retirement, health, disability, and power over working conditions won during New Deal era labor struggles. All these legally sanctioned New Deal benefits of the employment contract reduced profits and sparked Ronald Reagan's corporate-fueled neoliberal revolution.

The dismantling of the New Deal employment model and accelerating shift toward contingent work, tied to the corporate and political assault on the New Deal's support of unions and the ability of workers to organize, is one of neo-liberalism's most devastating attacks on social relations, and arguably its most important contributor to sociocide and larger social breakdown; by the end of Trump's first term, the MAGA GOP had quietly embraced much of Reagan's assault on wages, job security and worker social capital or labor solidarity in the misleading rhetoric of Far-Right populism.

The official Bureau of Labor Statistics data – which report 10% "independent workers" and 2% employed by temporary agencies in 2023 – vastly undercount the actual size of the contingent labor force. A widely circulated 2023 study by the leading management consulting firm, McKinsey, reports that contingent workers grew from about 16% in 2016 to represent 36% of the US workforce in 2023.[6] Reports by the Government Accountability Office (GAO) state that a remarkable 40% of the US workforce in 2023 is comprised of contingent workers.[7]

Moreover, the percentage of contingent workers is widely expected to grow in the coming years. In 2023, Sania Khan, the chief economist of Eightfold AI, projected the following increases over the next four years (globally as well as in the US):

- 2023:
  - Global contingent workforce participation: 53% increase
  - US contingent workforce participation: 26% increase
- 2024:
  - Global contingent workforce participation: 34% increase
  - US contingent workforce participation: 16% increase
- 2025:
  - Global contingent workforce participation: 25% increase
  - US contingent workforce participation: 14% increase
- 2026:
  - Global contingent workforce participation: 20% increase
  - US contingent workforce participation: 16% increase[8]

These projections suggest that *between half and two-thirds of US workers will be contingent by 2026.*[9] Researchers such as Khan and corporate-linked researchers offer an optimistic view of this transformation, noting that the new model of work provides flexible hiring strategies that can "close skill gaps without adding full-time workers." Khan and other management strategists argue that workers as well as companies benefit from the new "autonomy and flexibility," and that the contingent model even offers a way of bringing more diversity into the labor force – sunny views widely trumpeted by Silicon Valley Big Tech pioneers of the "independent worker" model during the 2008 crisis.[10] But many of these same researchers show that contingent workers are less well-paid and lack basic security, with many moving in and out of poverty.[11] Moreover, there is rarely discussion of the cost of social disconnection of workers from each other, undercutting vital social relationships and the worker solidarity and unions or other worker associations that can create better wages and working conditions for all workers. Socially disconnecting workers is a way of shrinking their social capital — making them weaker and less capable of challenging the power of the new robber barons that employ them.

Social disconnection is a recurrent theme emerging from periodic interviews I have done over the last twenty years with contingent workers, particularly temps.[12] One temp told me a story of eating lunch alone in a parking garage next to the office where he worked. He wasn't invited to join others and didn't feel welcome in the office itself. His main social connections were to the dispatchers in the temp office, whom he rarely saw face-to-face.

A woman working as a white-collar temp in a police department of a university described her morning anguish of simply walking to her desk behind a few rows of other workers. She described a morning ritual of preparing for that walk, which caused her anxiety because other workers did not greet her or even look at her as she walked past them. She felt invisible, and the sense of being separate from others haunted her through-out her workday.

Beyond isolation, contingent work conditions, at home in the US as well as abroad, often involve such intensive overwork that no worker has time to socialize. Nor are they assumed to be capable, given the physical and emotional stress, of continuing even in a temporary condition; contingency is an invitation to be exploited since the exhausted or debilitated worker will soon be replaced. Amazon warehouses constitute a continu-ing social workplace, but workers are deliberately overworked and "sped up" with the assumption that they will soon be gone. This new worker is "burnt out" of work con-nections by virtue of the toxicity of the labor process itself, tied to short-term profit gains and the sociocidal new norms of transient work. The remaining full-timers are working alongside new transient workmates, who are not able to stay long enough to become friends and organize across or within the traditional versus contingent divide.

The intensified exploitation and overwork inherently tied to transient and contin-gent labor are hardly restricted to Amazon warehouse workers or other low-educated workers. Even the many college graduates rushing to work in Wall Street financial or consulting firms – who are often replaced in a few years by other more recent college graduates – find themselves buried in the amount of work dumped on them by their bosses. One young woman in a prestigious financial consulting firm told me that she was exhausted by the volume of data analysis and audits that were part of her daily routine. She described the pressure she was under as relentless and overwhelming, with little time to connect and socialize with her fellow employees. The dream of finance majors headed toward New York for six-figure jobs becomes, for many young employees, a nightmare of endless work with little broader social meaning and short-term employment in the dream firm, either because of not performing up to the unattainable expectations or deciding to leave for a less toxic workplace.

* * *

It is easy to see the spiral of tipping points that fuel more contingency, exploitation, and social disconnection. As more workers become contingent, employers have more incen-tives to overwork and exploit them because the short-term profits they gain continue with new workers, while they won't bear the cost of damaged workers who will soon be replaced. As contingent numbers grow, worker resistance and unionization erode, since temps or short-termers cannot build long-term relations and hope to organize. GOP corporate and Far-Right politicians, from Reagan to Trump, passed legislation and executive policies supporting assaults on workers and unions. When a significant fraction of the workplace is contingent, a tipping point arises as the majority of workers expect to be leaving, and either lack the motive or capacity to come together to fight.

Prior to the Biden Administration, this all helped undermine unions and labor organization, the crucial source of social capital and countervailing power that workers have desperately needed since the Reagan revolution to prevent the rise of contingent work relations and the breakdown of secure jobs and good wages. Reagan's first major act as President was to destroy PATCO, the union of air traffic controllers on strike in 1981. That signaled Reagan's commitment to destroy unions, a commitment that the GOP largely made good on in the four decades from Reagan through Trump. When Reagan became president, about 20% of the labor force was unionized. By the end of Trump's first term, only about 10% of American workers – and 6% of private sector workers – were in unions, an astonishing collapse of American unions that would intensify under Trump.

The Reagan revolution unleashed four decades of a fierce corporate and political anti-union crusade – breaking down worker solidarity and creating the sociocide of the new contingent workforce. Unions are the central way in which workers build social capital and their capacity for collective power against corporations. Trumpism intensified the attack on unions and worker social capital in the name of pro-worker Far-Right populism. As Hillary Clinton was embracing Democratic identity politics, and furthering Bill Clinton's abandonment of New Deal labor and class politics, Trump won his first term by mimicking Bernie Sanders' pro-worker politics. Sanders had won a substantial part of the working-class votes in the 2016 Democratic primaries with his democratic socialist appeal to working-class voters in Michigan, Wisconsin, and Pennsylvania. With Sanders out and Left populism fading, Trump exploited the vacuum in his presidential campaigns, building Far-Right populism with his rhetoric of saving the blue-collar "forgotten man" that would transform Republican politics.

His new populist rhetoric resonated with workers in the Rust Belt who were the target of the corporate great shift toward contingency and labor sociocide. Thirty-five years after the Reagan revolution, Trump made the anti-union, corporate-allied Republican Party appear as the new political champion of workers. His populist rhetoric disguised his covert coalition with the corporate Republican Establishment he was attacking and helped him win major victories in both 2016 and 2024.

The new Robber Barons' sociocidal burning down of employment relations all rested on breaking unions. Trumpism provided the politics to strengthen the corporate anti-union crusade. As workers began to flock to Trump and elect him, they believed that his populism and pro-worker rhetoric was their last hope as they were losing the social capital of unions and secure jobs to actually protect themselves against the new precariousness of their jobs, rising costs of living, and economic futures, even as Trump was leading a crusade against unions and against broader government worker and social protections.

Trump's war against unions in the name of supporting workers against the global corporate establishment is one of the under-reported stories of American society and politics, fueling the breakdown of social capital among working people and the rise of American authoritarianism supported by many workers themselves. We tell many chapters of this story in this book, including the changes wrought by the recent Democratic attack on neoliberalism and the catastrophic rise of Trumpism. But we introduce it here by making clear the deep damage done by 40 years of Reagan–Trump corporate neoliberalism – and Trump's continuing ruthless attack on unions. Union leaders like Shawn

Fain of the UAW, campaigning against Trump in 2024, proclaimed that "every fiber of our union is being poured into fighting the billionaire class and an economy that enriches people like Donald Trump at the expense of workers."[13]

Trump refused to support Fain's 2023 epic strike against the Big Auto companies, flying instead to address a Michigan non-union auto plant and claiming that the UAW would do nothing for workers. In his first term, Trump appointed what many consider the most anti-labor National Labor Relations Board (NLRB) in US history. The NLRB is the government agency setting the rules for union elections and oversight as well as protecting workers under existing law. The NLRB that Trump appointed during his first term, with a board led by the attorney who helped engineer Reagan's destruction of PATCO, drastically rolled back union protections and workers' rights to organize:

> the Trump NLRB has advanced an anti-worker, anti-union, corporate agenda that has undermined workers' ability to form unions and engage in collective bargaining. Through a series of decisions, rulemakings, and general counsel initiatives, the agency has systematically rolled back worker protections and betrayed its statutory obligation to administer and enforce the NLRA. The Trump board has faithfully acted on a top-10 corporate-interest wish list published by the Chamber of Commerce in early 2017 – taking action on 10 out of 10 items on this list.[14]

Trump's own political actions and executive orders attacking unions in his first term – and intensified in his second term built around corporate oligarchy despite his surprise appointment of a Labor Secretary, Lori Chavez-DeRemer supportive of unions – were all disguised as a defense of workers only he as a great leader could bring. He told workers that their strikes were meaningless; he said "it doesn't make a damn bit of difference what you get because in two years you're all going to be out of business."[15] Only his protectionism and tariffs on China could save the workers, Trump said, cloaking his anti-unionism as part of a populist defense of the workers that he alone could deliver. Some pundits suggested that J.D. Vance might bring a more union-friendly approach to Trump's second term, but Vance's Far-Right record offered little support for this, reflecting the type of deeply misleading labor-friendly rhetoric that Trump himself spewed. Warning workers of the catastrophe of a second Trump term, the AFL-CIO summarized Trump's past anti-labor record in 2023:

> Donald Trump told us in 2016 he would stand with workers. He lied. The difference now is that he has a record he can't hide from. And that record was catastrophic for workers. Former President Trump spent four years in office weakening unions and working people while pushing tax giveaways to the wealthiest among us. He stacked the courts with judges who want to roll back our rights on the job. He made us less safe at work. He gave big corporations free rein to lower wages and make it harder for workers to stand together in a union.[16]

Trump covertly allied with the corporate establishment that his right-wing populism attacked, reflecting the interest of authoritarian leaders in breaking down social organizations and solidarity they don't directly control. This coordinated corporate and political anti-union assault by corporate elites and their Far-Right allies created weaker opposition that allows bosses to overwork their employees and make an even a larger percentage of their workers contingent, while also helping their political allies rake in more money from billionaire donors. The second Trump term will help consolidate this anti-labor and anti-union sociocidal regime, creating a new sociocidal crisis in the US labor force.

* * *

It is not surprising that the rise in contingent and over-worked labor is reported globally as well as in the US since globalization and contingent labor are intertwined. Indeed, outsourcing can be understood as a second major sociocidal assault by neoliberal globalizing corporations on employment relations, disconnecting workers from each other by eliminating some of them and weakening connections that are likely to be discontinued in the future. Globalization creates a mass of surplus workers by outsourcing jobs.[17] Since the Reagan revolution of the 1980s, neoliberalism inaugurated a revolution of globalization that skyrocketed the numbers of both outsourced and contingent labor. This occurred most dramatically in manufacturing industries, particularly in the Rust Belt, where many millions of American jobs in auto, steel, and other industrial plants were outsourced, sometimes destroying entire communities. Outsourcing workers or making them contingent has the same basic aim: to reduce costs and increase profits while pitting workers within and across countries against each other.

They also have the same sociocidal consequence, disconnecting workers from each other and from any firm hope of a long-term relationship with either workers or the company. Supported by both Reagan Republicans and corporate Democrats, globalization effectively made all workers part of the "precariat," or a disguised form of contingent workers or "temps," since even those still legally defined as conventional employees can be replaced through outsourcing.

CNBC's John Schoen wrote that outsourcing "is what millions of Americans fear most about their jobs."[18] Schoen was summarizing the results of a Pew Research study based on 5000 workers. It showed that 80% of US workers see outsourcing as a threat to their job security, potentially sabotaging both their income and their social connections.[19]

Meanwhile, it is not just manufacturing or blue-collar workers who fear outsourcing, since outsourcing is growing most rapidly among white-collar workers. This is intertwined with yet another sociocidal threat we discuss later in more detail: the shift toward remote labor. In 2022, journalist Andrew Van Dam headlined a story called "The remote revolution could lead to offshoring Armageddon," reporting that:

> When offshoring methodically disemboweled the Rust Belt, white-collar Americans thrived, free to enjoy the spoils of globalization safe in the knowledge that their jobs could not be outsourced easily to cheap foreign rivals. Now, some economists say the remote-work revolution may have changed that almost overnight.[20]

Van Dam cites economist Richard Baldwin, in a forum sponsored by the Center for Economic and Policy Research, speaking of white-collar workers, "If you can do your job from home, be scared. Be very scared. Because somebody in India … or wherever is willing to do it for much less."[21]

The profits and scale of US corporate outsourcing are growing, as discussed in a 2023 study:

> With roughly 66% of American companies outsourcing jobs, the country generates an impressive $62 billion of the outsourcing market's $92.5 billion global value.

Although outsourcing often equates to losing American jobs, it also significantly helps U.S. businesses. Today, it's estimated that approximately only 300,000 U.S. jobs are outsourced every year, with more than one-fifth of occupations having the potential to be outsourced in the future.[22]

The scale of globalization and outsourcing has been large enough to create political earthquakes, connected with the sociocidal costs of broken social relations among workers. Trumpism is a response by US workers to a Democratic Party that catastrophically failed to take decisive action to prevent massive job losses and growing job and social insecurity, especially in the Rust Belt manufacturing-base swing states such as Michigan, Wisconsin, and Pennsylvania.[23] The right-wing anti-globalist rhetoric under Trump helped disguise his anti-union assault as well as his own continuing personal global empire-building and anti-government agenda aiding corporate globalization. But Trump's vocal right-wing populism, in the absence of Left populism abandoned by Democrats, strongly resonated with workers hit with the intertwined double whammy of contingency and outsourcing. Trump has fueled, as we show in later chapters, a deep worker resonance to MAGA authoritarianism, papering over Trump's covert alliance with the globalizing corporate establishment that he rails against.

Both de Tocqueville and Arendt foresaw authoritarianism as an inevitable consequence of people hit by atomizing sociocidal forces, leaving them facing survival crises on their own and fearful of losing workmates and family who could offer them help. Only a strongman can now protect them. Lacking other political choices, and without other sources of social relations, the appeal of a strong relation to a would-be dictator becomes cult-like and absolutist; to lose the leader is to lose one's last social support.

Another new sociocidal Robber Baron employment innovation, closely related to outsourcing and with similar far-reaching sociocidal consequences, is new technology designed to replace workers with robots, artificial intelligence (AI), or other computer-based innovations. While developed initially in high-tech and the military, AI is spreading through all sectors of the economy. Such technologically fueled sociocide is a key component of the movement toward the elimination of the social relations of work, unions and other labor associations, and of employment altogether – evolving potentially toward a systemic firing of the human workforce.

AI is already a major job-killer: 1.7 million US jobs in manufacturing alone were lost to automation by 2023.[24] Beyond blue-collar factory and assembly jobs, areas hard hit already include retail, automotive, marketing, and logistic workers. Globally, 2.25 million industrial robots are currently in use, with 1.6 manufacturing jobs lost for every new industrial robot in production; studies show that increases in robots between 1990 and 2007 significantly reduced the employment-to-population rate and significantly reduced wages in highly automated sectors.[25]

The data shows that most of the millions of robots building cars, delivering goods, or clearing restaurant tables are performing jobs once done by human workers. It is thus not surprising that by 2023, 37% of US workers said they were worried about losing their jobs to robots or AI. And, in fact, they have good reason to worry, even taking into account that robots and AI create many new jobs as they sweep away millions of old ones, with 375 million industrial robots in use by 2023.[26] In early 2024, the head of the International Monetary Fund announced that AI would impact 40% of jobs worldwide, while worsening global inequality.[27]

Experts are projecting eye-popping numbers of potential future job losses due to robots, AI, and other automation. The most drastic losses are predicted for non-college workers, both in manufacturing and the service sector. In 2024, the Brookings Institute projected that up to 55% of jobs that require less than a bachelor's degree may be eliminated by 2030. Specific jobs for non-college workers like food preparation and serving could be virtually wiped out by 80% by 2030. Jobs requiring a college education are at lower risk, but Brookings predicts that 24% of these educated workers could be replaced by 2030. By 2030, 25% of US jobs are at high risk of automation, while another 36% of job positions are at medium risk since many of the components of these additional millions of jobs can be automated.[28]

Consider the following probability of job replacement by robots or AI as estimated by researchers:

Waiters: 73% probability of being automated
Shelf fillers: 72%
Bar staff: 71%
Higher education teachers: 20%
Dental practitioners: 21%
Medical practitioners: 18%[29]

Note that while blue-collar workers, long vulnerable to outsourcing, have the greatest reason to worry because of robots, they are hardly alone. Virtually all truckers report worry that they will be replaced by self-driving vehicles. But the fact that about 20% of college teachers and medical practitioners face replacement by 2030 by robots and AI is a striking marker of how universal and dire the sociocidal threat of 21st-century automation has become, even though it breeds contradictory sociophiliac possibilities that we consider later.

* * *

Potentially the most fundamental sociocidal assault on workers, intensifying the impact of all the neoliberal labor strategies discussed above, is this: the new Robber Barons, without major political pushback from either the Democrats or Republicans, are beginning to melt down the institution of the workplace itself. Relying on the evolving technology of the internet and computers – and reaping big profits by eliminating high costs associated with building, operating, and maintaining brick-and-mortar physical structures – there is decreasing reliance on gathering workers in a single collective space and simultaneous reliance on both outsourced and remote workers. This shift away from the office accelerated with COVID-19, but it began before and continued with greater intensity after the peak of the pandemic. We now have the ghosted workplace, often in office buildings with lighting and heating and moving escalators, as I once witnessed in a big office building in downtown Seattle, but no people in the office. We note the sociocidal threats involved, but also, contradictorily, the sociophiliac possibilities often latent in sociocidal forces that could emerge from the creation of a new mode of work and workplace.

The destruction of the workplace carries deep sociocidal threats because, in tandem with destroying traditional employment with temporary or contingent labor, it eliminates the space where human workers can associate and develop solidarity. The post-industrial

Robber Barons are returning us to a new 21st-century version of the pre-industrial era where workers are dispersed and work in their homes. As Marx would observe, this undermines the social conditions under which unions can form and help build community and solidarity.

The shift from the original industrial capitalist sociopathic system to the sociocidal system of neoliberal global post-industrialism is a historical work in progress. It is in relatively early stages, but as more workers become remote, we are beginning to see fully remote companies, that is, companies that have no physical collective office or workplace at all, as well as a much larger number of hybrid workplaces combining office-based and home-based work.

As of 2023, 66% of US employees were working remotely at least part of the time.[30] Remote labor analyst, Jeff Herd, reports that remote work exploded 400 percent between 2004 and 2014, even before COVID-19 arrived (2020).[31] COVID-19 massively increased the numbers of remote workers, going from 5.7% of US workers in 2018 to 24% in 2019 and 41.7% in 2020 as COVID-19 peaked.[32] As COVID-19 weakened in the following years, remote workers decreased to 26% in 2022 and increased gradually to 27% in 2023.[33] But Herd reports projections across the US and Europe that there will be *80 million* full-time remote workers by 2030; by 2030 there will be 255 million remote workers globally.[34] Another study reports that automation has the potential to eliminate *76 million US jobs* by 2030, a staggering *46%* of current jobs.[35] Up to *375 million* jobs worldwide could be lost to automation by 2030. As Herd puts it, "Remote work will eat the world."[36]

The explosive projected growth of remote work is closely tied to dramatic increases in "ghost" companies, that those which are fully remote and have no physical office or collective workspace. While this comprised only 16% of workplaces in 2023, the projections indicate significant expansion of remote companies. This growth is partly fueled by private equity firms and other investors who are reaping big profits by eliminating the rapidly growing costs of maintaining a physical workplace; such investors buy up firms and sell them off after transforming them into remote companies.

Herd argues that "companies who adopt remote work will replace every company that doesn't."[37] He adds that "remote companies drive out traditional office-based competitors because of cost savings, efficiency, and employee preferences who like the flexibility of remote work." He summarizes "The cost saving in real-estate at scale will be eye-watering. The productivity will be the final nail in the coffin for the office."[38]

The major trend right now is toward hybrid workplaces rather than fully remote companies, but that could change as AI kicks in more rapidly. The 16% of fully remote companies – which have no physical workplace – is quadruple that in 2000. Current projections suggest that in 2024 and beyond, we are likely to see 20% of fully remote workplaces and 60% of hybrid models, with only 20% fully office-based.[39]

Both employers and workers are adapting to the shift away from conventional employment and the physical office. As technology evolves and the percentage of remote worktime escalates rapidly, we are currently seeing the perpetuation of some form of physical office in the majority of companies, but with a majority of hybrid workers working at 50% or more of the time remotely. These trends are emerging most rapidly in high-tech industries, companies and professions linked to high-technology and IT, and are spreading widely into other white-collar and service sectors.

* * *

The general trends toward temporary, gig, outsourced, automated, and remote labor are driven by profit incentives exploited by the new Robber Barons operating with the political support of both political parties, though Biden pushed back modestly to help rebuild unions and provide more good jobs. The breakdown of traditional labor and the partial disappearance of the workplace itself weaken the ability of workers to organize and protect and take control of their basic job security, wages, and benefits. But while the breakdown of traditional employment and the dissolving of many workplaces are sociocidal forces, they are not irreversible and, contradictorily, open up sociophiliac possibilities. A majority of workers, for example, say they prefer the flexibility and increased time at home that remote and hybrid labor offer, as well as savings in commuter time and costs. Flexible work has become the watchword of technophiles, who tout the Silicon Valley mantras, discussed in the next chapter, that work-at-home and remote labor are freedom-enhancing, family-building life-savers. But there is also a different story: more remote workers report increases in loneliness and feelings of being cut off or disconnected from their companies and other workers.[40]

This is a reflection of the contradictions latent in many sociocidal forces. There have been few sociophiliac benefits to becoming outsourced, automated, or turned into "temps." But remote labor is a more complex and contradictory development. It tends to break down or weaken social relations among employees, but it may strengthen both work and home life. Working remotely allows the potential building of online relations within "teams of remote workers" that may enable new worker organization and solidarity, starting online but spilling into offsite dispersed centers away from any central physical workplace. The high percentage of workers who say they prefer hybrid work – because it offers more freedom, flexibility, needed time at home, or other benefits than full-time office work – points to potential ways in which a freer and more equitable work and workplace might develop. The greater disconnect from the company might fuel stronger connections at home or in the community, although we are not seeing that materialize at scale now.

Nonetheless, sociocidal practices and tipping points can be reversed. Countervailing social organizations and movements are emerging both offline and online, within labor and progressive democratic political movements, including the coalition of Bernie Sanders and other progressives and democratic socialists inside and outside the Democratic Party. The new sociocidal system is systemically contradictory. Profitability itself may be threatened by the declining purchasing power and numbers of working people. A burnt-out and replaced workforce is, at minimum, a surplus population that will become more desperate to survive, potentially through new sociophiliac movements – both in the workplace and in politics – targeting the new Robber Barons and their corporate Trumpist allies.

We see more than traces of such workplace movements today, notably in the mass 2023 "summer of strikes" led by the United Auto Workers, the Screen Writers and Actors Guilds of Hollywood, successful bargaining by unions in health care, education, air traffic, and the USPS, as well as new labor organizers among Amazon and Starbucks workers. We are seeing new and growing forms of union and other labor solidarity – leading to more workers on strike in 2023 than in any year since 1963.

They are mobilizing partly through the very online technologies that are designed to destroy worker association and power. This leads to unexpected possibilities, including the call by UAW labor leader Sean Fain for the first general labor strike in American history in 2028. Fain's aim is to bring all US workers into a new solidarity that combats the sociocide at the heart of the neoliberal economy. The general strike would seek to create new and strong connections among a highly unionized working population with the political power to create a more just and community-centered economy and society.

The awakening of the labor movement partly reflected political changes in the Democratic Party, with the Biden Administration being the first since Reagan to reject neoliberalism and to actively support unions. Biden was the first president in America to walk a picket line with striking workers. Biden helped introduce a 21st-century pro-union, pro-labor agenda, only partially enacted and poorly developed by Harris in her 2024 presidential campaign, a fatal flaw that doomed her campaign in the crucial blue-collar "Blue Wall" states of Michigan, Wisconsin, and Pennsylvania.

A few days after Harris announced her candidacy for President in July 2024, many of America's biggest and most powerful unions announced that they were endorsing her. This included the American Federation of Teachers, the Service Employees International Union (SEIU), the United Steelworkers, the United Food and Commercial Workers International Union, the Federation of State, County and Municipal Workers (AFSCME), the International Brotherhood of Electrical Workers, and the AFL-CIO, America's biggest federation of unions. These organizations brought funds, organizational clout, and turn-out skills to her candidacy, beginning to unite thousands of paid and volunteer workers in labor halls, town meetings, and street rallies. The 2023 "summer of strikes" appeared to be evolving into a new class politics uniting unions and the Democratic Party. The Harris campaign initially seemed to have the potential to bring workers back into a Democratic Party fighting simultaneously against neoliberal sociocide and Trumpist authoritarianism and policide. But declaring herself "a proud capitalist," and aligning with anti-Trumpist Republicans and militarized corporate politicians like Liz Cheney, she never embraced the kind of class politics and bold anti-corporate agenda that might have defeated Trump and the new Robber Barons.

The new labor politics hinted at by Harris at the start of her candidacy did not develop into a credible class politics that could have helped the Democratic Party become the 21st-century party of the working class. The Harris campaign appeared initially to have the potential to lead a sea change in American politics, countering right-wing populism with a left populism genuinely devoted to workers. Indeed, in her August 8, 2024, talk to the UAW in Detroit, Harris explicitly endorsed unions as the key forces bringing isolated and demoralized workers together. She described a "perversion" in the GOP, where:

> where there's a suggestion that somehow strength is about making people feel small, making people feel alone, but isn't that the very opposite of what we know, unions know, to be strong? It's about the collective. It's about knowing that no one should ever be made to fight alone.[41]

This kind of discourse shows how sociocide can breed its own political contradictions. Harris and Walz made initial hints that they would work to unite American workers and the larger public back into close relations and a movement for democracy. They did not fulfill that promise, in ways we show later, that help explain their defeat. But some of the labor activism and political dialogue that initially emerged show that the contradictions of sociocide and policide are real, and that there remain possibilities of moving beyond the bonfires even when they grow hotter and more dangerous and more atomizing in Trump's disastrous second term.

Notes

1 Charles Derber and Yale Magrass, *Who Owns Democracy?* NY: Routledge, 2024.
2 Upton Sinclair, *The Jungle*. CreateSpace Independent Publishing Platform, 2019.
3 Michael Burawoy, *Manufacturing Consent*. Chicago: University of Chicago Press, 1982. Harry Braverman, *Labor and Monopoly Capitalism*. NY: Monthly Review Press, 1989.
4 "Bloomberg Billionaires Index." *Bloomberg News*, September 7, 2024. bloomberg.com. See also Mamishah Maurf, "Jeff Bezos Dethrones Elon Musk to Become the Richest Person on Earth Again." *CNN*, March 5, 2024, cnn.com
5 Charles Derber, *Corporation Nation*. NY: St. Martin's Press, 1998.
6 McKinsey and Company, "Freelance, Side Hustles, and Gigs." *McKinsey*, August 23, 2023, mckinsey.com
7 Charles Goretsky, "The Rising Contingent Workforce and the Role of HR." *Wowledge*, October 22, 2023, wowledge.com
8 Sania Kahn, "The Contingent Workforce Is About to Skyrocket – Here's What You Need to Know." *Eightfold AI*, February 2, 2023, eightfold.ai
9 Sania Kahn, "The Contingent Workforce Is About to Skyrocket – Here's What You Need to Know." *Eightfold AI*, February 2, 2023, eightfold.ai
10 Sania Kahn, "The Contingent Workforce Is About to Skyrocket – Here's What You Need to Know." *Eightfold AI*, February 2, 2023, eightfold.ai
11 Juliet Schor, *After the Gig*. Berkeley: University of California Press, 2020. Derber, *Corporation Nation*.
12 I started these interviews in 2000 and continued them until the present, reporting some of the stories discussed below in Derber, *Corporation Nation*; and Derber and Magrass, *The Surplus American*. NY: Routledge, 2012
13 David Goldman, "UAW President Has Some Harsh Words for Trump." *CNN*, September 19, 2023, cnn.com
14 Celine McNicholas, Margaret Poydock, and Lynn Rhinehart, "Unprecedented: The Trump NLRB's Attack on Worker Rights." *EPI*, October 2019, epi.org
15 John Nichols, "Trump Just Showed How Little He Actually Cares About the Working Class." *Nation*, September 28, 2023, thenation.com
16 AFL-CIO, "Donald Trump's Catastrophic and Devastating Anti-Labor Track Record." September 27, 2023, aflcio.org
17 Charles Derber, *People Before Profit*. NY: Picador, 2003; Charles Derber and Yale Magrass, *The Surplus American*. NY: Routledge, 2012.
18 John Schoen, "Here's What Millions of American Fear Most About Their Jobs." *CNBC*, October 6, 2016, cnbc.com
19 Pew Research Center, "The State of American Jobs." October 6, 2016, Pewresearch.org
20 Andrew Van Dam, "The Remote Revolutiton Could Lead to Offshoring Armageddon." *Washington Post*, August 26, 2022, washingtonpost.com
21 Andrew Van Dam, "The Remote Revolutiton Could Lead to Offshoring Armageddon." *Washington Post*, August 26, 2022, washingtonpost.com
22 TalkSource, "Outsourcing Statistics." *LinkedIn*, March 29, 2023, linkedin.com
23 Charles Derber and Yale Magrass, *Who Owns Democracy?* NY: Routledge, 2024.
24 Darina L. "Rise of Robots – Jobs Lost to Automation Statistics in 2023." *Leftronic*, March 7, 2023, leftronic.com
25 Daron Acemoglu and Pascual Restrepo, "Robots and Jobs: Evidence from US Labor Markets." *National Bureau of Economic Research*, March, 2017, nber.org
26 Daron Acemoglu and Pascual Restrepo, "Robots and Jobs: Evidence from US Labor Markets." *National Bureau of Economic Research*, March, 2017, nber.org
27 Dan Milmo, "AI Will Affect 40% of Jobs and Probably Worsen Inequality, Says IMF Head." *The Guardian*. January 15, 2024, theguardian.com
28 Mark Muro, Robert Maxim, Jacob Whiton, "Automation and Artificial Intelligence." *Brookings*, January 2019, brookings.edu
29 TeamStage, "Jobs Lost to Automatic Statistics in 2024." *TeamStage*, 2024, teamstage.io
30 Jack Flynn, "25 Trending Remote Work Statistics (2023)," *Zippia.com*, June 13, 2023, zippia.com/advice/remote-work-statistics/

31 Chris Herd, "Remote Startups Will Win the War for Top Talent." *Future*, August 23, 2023, future.com. See also Chris Herd, "Equipping Global Teams," @Firstbase March 17, 2020, linkedin.com

32 Jack Flynn, "25 Trending Remote Work Statistics in 2024," *Zippia.com*, June 13, 2023, zippia .com/advice/remote-work-statistics/

33 Jack Flynn, "25 Trending Remote Work Statistics in 2024," *Zippia.com*, June 13, 2023, zippia .com/advice/remote-work-statistics/

34 Chris Herd, "Equipping Global Teams," @Firstbase March 17, 2020, linkedin.com

35 Jack Flynn, "25 Trending Remote Work Statistics in 2024," *Zippia.com*, June 13, 2023, zippia .com/advice/remote-work-statistics/

36 Chris Herd, "Equipping Global Teams," @Firstbase March 17, 2020, linkedin.com

37 Chris Herd, "Chris Herd's Post." Linkedin.com/posts/chrisherd_ive-spoken-to-200 companiies

38 Chris Herd, "Chris Herd's Post." Linkedin.com/posts/chrisherd_ive-spoken-to-200 companiies

39 EY, "Future workplace Trends: Are You Putting Your Office to Work?" *EY's Future Workplace Index 2023*, February 1, 2023, ey.com/en_isreal-estate-hospitality-construction/future-work place—trends-are-you-putting-your-office-to work

40 Lindsay Ellis, "The Disconnect Between Remote Workers and Their Companies Is Getting Bigger." *Wall Street Journal*, August 24, 2023, wsj.com/life-style/careers/the-growing-disconnect

41 Alice Herman, "Kamala Harris and Tim Walz Boost Union Credentials in Event at UAW Local." *The Guardian*, August 8, 2024, theguardian.com

3 The bonfire of the tech revolution

AI and social media, surveillance capitalism, and the sociocide of Silicon Valley

Silicon Valley has cast a magical spell on millions of Americans. For many, it is a dream place to work and live. It is the American Dream reborn. In 2016, journalist Neil Howe wrote:

> The past few years in Silicon Valley can be likened to a gold rush. Job and income growth have exploded ... Newly minted MBA graduates from elite schools are increasingly choosing these companies over Wall Street ... Silicon Valley has acquired the look and feel of a fairytale, a place where dollars flow and world-altering break-throughs spring to life.[1]

Americans have always had a love affair with technology. Silicon Valley's high-tech revolution has taken the American passion for technology to a new high. But as the new love affair blooms, another understanding of Silicon Valley and its magical technology is beginning to take root. In this chapter, we show that there are very real benefits of the tech we are now are building our identity around – and spending hours of our day glued to the screen and social media. But the Silicon Valley future may become more of a nightmare than a utopian fantasy dream. It finds support among both corporate and some progressive Democrats and GOP Trumpists who have their own ideology reinforcing Silicon Valley's libertarian techno-future. In that nightmare, workplace and broader social solidarity are threatened with a sociocidal revolution, where face-to-face relations become weak and begin to break society apart. This is the path I call the shift from we to me, offering the door to the cult-like appeal and high-tech propaganda tools of Far-Right Trumpist politics. Silicon Valley, a traditional Democratic-leaning corporate sector, has strong mutual interests with Trumpism; major figures like Elon Musk, Peter Thiel, David Sacks, and Mark Andreessen moved to lavishly fund Trump as the 2024 election approached. Musk became a pivotal figure helping cement the oligarchic relation between Trump and the new tech titans.[2]

***

The rise of modern capitalism created and reflected the industrial technological revolution. The technology of the steam engine, coal, oil and gas energy grids, and machinery, the railroads, automotive technology, and the telegram and telephone were all essential technological changes enabling the creation of the factory and industrial mass production. The new industrial technology shaped the nature of productive relations in the machine age, making possible both industrial production itself in the factory and the

DOI: 10.4324/9781003491798-4

distribution of supplies and goods that sustained productive and market relations. As discussed in Chapter 2, vast concentrations of capital and corporate power crystallizing in the Robber Baron era of the late 19th century took ownership of industrial technology and used it to shape the sociopathic, exploitative productive relations and factories that defined the Gilded Age and most of the 20th century.

Toward the end of the 20th century, a new technological revolution began and has accelerated rapidly in the 21st century, intersecting with and intensifying the rise of neo-liberalism. Early forms of this new technology were bred in the US military, where the modern computer was invented in the 1950s and related "high-tech" electronic innovations were pioneered in succeeding decades and spread into the civilian economy. By the 1970s, social theorists such as Daniel Bell were announcing the rise of post-industrial capitalism and a society based on knowledge, with online technology and communications replacing antiquated, earlier industrial and social relations.[3]

The shift to post-industrialism was associated with the rise of a powerful new set of capitalist elites and new corporate centers of production, finance, and communication. In the 21st century, Silicon Valley became the symbol of the new post-industrial high-tech world. It would become the showcase of the new high-tech companies, such as Microsoft, Amazon, and Apple, which were becoming the first trillion-dollar companies, led by tycoons such as Bill Gates, Jeff Bezos, Steve Jobs, Tim Cook, Mark Zuckerberg, Elon Musk, Sam Altman, and Peter Thiel, all fabulously wealthy members of the Big Tech power elite.

Silicon Valley introduced itself as a modern miracle, bringing unprecedented new productivity and prosperity that would benefit both owners and workers, and contribute to the betterment of the general population with magical new products such as the personal computer, the iPhone, and the new internet-based world of online culture and communication on social media. This new world revolutionized the economic and social spheres, while also having major uses and implication for politics and the military. Because billions of people globally now have iPhones or personal computers, with access to the new online universe of the internet and social media, Silicon Valley seemed to open up not only a transformative new economy for entrepreneurs and knowledge workers but a transformed newly connected world of online social communication and relationships.

This is not entirely an illusion. The online world does open up new social connections and political connections, with social media being a powerful new tool for the younger generation to build new friendships, communities, and politics, as seen in the electric and unprecedented online surge for Kamala Harris when she announced her ultimately failed candidacy for President 110 days before the 2024 election. But Silicon Valley's fantastic new array of electronic communications and online connections may also prove to be a gateway to weak social relations and ultimately the end of strong face-to-face social relationships as well as democracy itself. We face a sociocidal transformation fueled by high tech, with Silicon Valley also proffering the surveillance technology and their own politics of authoritarianism. The selection of Silicon Valley venture capitalist, J.D. Vance, as Trump's 2024 Vice President is a sign of the rising political affinity between "New Right" sectors of high-tech capital and Trumpism. Vance, a protégé of Far-Right tech billionaire Peter Thiel, was a Silicon Valley venture capitalist himself, and brought the authoritarian perspective shared by Thiel and Elon Musk. Musk led other Far-Right corporate billionaires to fund and welcome Trump to a second presidential term that is a new 21st-century oligarchy, with many Silicon Valley moguls right at the center of it.[4]

* * *

Silicon Valley symbolizes the danger of concentrating enormous new financial and technological power in a tiny corporate elite. High-tech corporate giants such as Apple, Alphabet (Google), and Microsoft have come to dwarf in capitalization and assets the legendary Gilded Age corporate giants such as Rockefeller's Standard Oil or Carnegie's US Steel. Their financial infrastructure includes both huge equity and venture capitalist firms underwriting Silicon Valley and other high-tech companies. Their power diffuses across societal sectors from the economy itself to culture, politics, and social life. While their technology erodes sustainable face-to-face social relations among employees in the workplace, it also infuses Big Tech money and corporate power deep into the political world and disrupts trust and truth in family, friendships, civil society, and broader social life.

The corporate powerhouses of the high-tech world have been dubbed "the Magnificent Seven."[5] All household names, they include the six largest US companies – all worth at least *a trillion* dollars – ranked below by market capitalization in early 2024:

1. Microsoft $3.02 trillion
2. Apple $2.62 trillion
3. NVIDIA $2.30 trillion
4. Amazon $1.84 trillion
5. Alphabet (Google) $1.67 trillion
6. Meta (Facebook) $1.3 trillion
7. Tesla $570 billion (rising to over $1 trillion right after Trump's re-election).[6]

The Magnificent Seven dwarf the traditional corporate giants of the US economy in terms of market capitalization. Compare them with the relatively "puny" size, again measured in market capitalization, of some of America's most storied, legendary banks and companies, founded by Rockefeller, Morgan, and Carnegie:

JPMorgan Chase $541 billion
Exxon Mobil $425 billion
Bank of America $280 billion
Chevron $277 Billion
General Electric $180 billion
Goldman Sachs   126 billion
Ford $49 billion
General Motors $40 Billion
US Steel $10 Billion[7]

Much of the meteoric rise in the tech giants came as late as the early 2020s. Between October 2022 and January 2024, the Magnificent Seven rose more than 60% in value. By 2024, the Magnificent Seven represented almost *one-third* of the total market capitalization of US companies.[8] When investor doubts about the ultimate profitability of AI surfaced in August 2024, a sell-off of Big Tech stocks created massive tremors throughout US and global markets, a sign of how central Silicon Valley is in both the US and world economy.[9]

The concentration of so much money in such a tiny number of firms is an intensification of wealth in an American economy already famous since the first Gilded Age for its concentration of capital, initially among capitalist legends like J.P. Morgan, Andrew Carnegie, and John D. Rockefeller. These early tycoons would merge to create and control the giant banks and companies, such as J.P. Morgan Chase and US Steel, that dominated the US economy through most of the 20th century. As we move deeper into the 21st century, the astonishing growth of the Magnificent Seven, other Big Tech firms often partnering with them, and the financial firms investing in them is translating into a far greater amount of concentrated wealth and the all-important shift from sociopathy toward sociocide.

Several sociocidal forces emerge directly from the economic restructuring created by the Magnificent Seven and other huge Big Tech firms. One is the interest of these corporate high-tech elites, much like their corporate counterparts in other spheres, in eroding the face-to-face workplace and social ties that can challenge their power. In the workplace, that translates into the intensified attack on secure employment, unionism, and a collective physical workplace, discussed in Chapter 2. The intent is to weaken the social relations of workers in the workplace – and more broadly to subvert the solidarity and face-to-face connections of people throughout society that can challenge authoritarianism both in work and politics.

Focusing first on the workplace, the Magnificent Seven play a special role here by creating and developing the technology – including the personal computer, iPhone, internet apps, AI, robots, and social media — that allows corporate elites to create a precariat of dispersed and contingent workers, increasingly separated from each other, while also replacing millions of workers and transferring their jobs to robots and other AI inventions. The reality hit me when I was sitting in a restaurant with my wife in Seoul, South Korea, eating breakfast. Seoul is very high-tech, melding Silicon Valley tech with its own national advanced tech companies. As we were eating, we saw something I hadn't seen before. They looked like rectangular cabinets on wheels rolling past our table. They turned out to be self-moving and self-directing robots loaded with dirty dishes and glasses. They then joined a line of look-alike robots all moving to deliver the dirty plates and glasses down aisles of the restaurant into the back room, where they unloaded their cargo and redirected themselves back into the dining room to do another round.

There were relatively few waiters or other human workers in the restaurant. It was clear that the robots were stealing their jobs. We are learning now that AI-generated robots – and other forms – can do many of the workplace and home jobs that low-skilled or semi-skilled workers do. But other workers are not safe either.[10] As mentioned in Chapter 2, the most rapid replacement of workers by robots and AI is in high-skill jobs. Matt Sigelman, president of a Human Resources Institute, summarized his Institute's widely circulated report on AI, saying "There's no question the workers who will be most impacted are those with college degrees, and those are the people who always thought they were safe."[11] He indicates that:

> Companies in finance, including Goldman Sachs, JPMorgan Chase and Morgan Stanley, have some of the highest percentages of their payrolls likely to be disrupted by generative A.I. Not far behind are tech giants like Google, Microsoft and Meta.[12]

Tech workers, talented and highly trained, are developing the tools allowing their companies to eliminate many of their own jobs. Meanwhile, employers are also using robots to replace low-skill workers.[13] The sociocidal tech impulse of Silicon Valley, as in other sectors, is embraced because of its profit-saving capacity. And the fastest way to increase profit is to reduce wages, usually by weakening relations among employees or busting unions. The Magnificent Seven have used their overwhelming economic power to directly undermine unions, the most effective form of worker social relations and organization. In January 2024, Elon Musk, now legendary for his anti-union and broader right-wing views, filed a lawsuit in federal courts to declare unconstitutional the National Labor Relations Board – which protects and regulates workers' right to organize. In August 2024, just before his re-election, Trump joked with Musk about firing workers, complimenting Musk during a two-hour conversation on X for firing Tesla workers who wanted to strike. "They go on strike," Trump said to Musk, "and you say, 'That's OK, you're all gone.'" Trump then added, "You're the Greatest!""[14] The UAW filed labor charges against both Trump and Musk for the unfair labor practices that the two had celebrated; Musk's Tesla had clashed with union activists for years, and the NLRB in 2021 had found that the non-union Tesla violated labor laws when it fired a union organizer.[15]

One of Musk's Magnificent Seven compatriots, Jeff Bezos, CEO of Amazon, quickly joined in Trump and Musk's union-busting party, filing a copycat suit to make the NLRB and unions unconstitutional. Here, we see the world's two richest men, leaders of the High-Tech Robber Barons, exploiting economic size to reap the fruit of their technology's economic power. They are seeking a revolutionary breakdown of workplace social relations, moving from the sociopathy of the first Gilded Age to the sociocide of today's Gilded Age.

The Magnificent Seven's power undercuts workplace social relations and fiercely attacks union solidarity in the name of free-spirited libertarianism running rampant in Silicon Valley. As noted in the last chapter, the broader corporate success in drastically weakening unions is key to sociocide in the entire US labor force and has been achieved not only by the anti-union fervor of corporations since the New Deal but also by the zeal of the Republican Party from Reagan through Trump to make the destruction of labor solidarity and unions a top political priority.

As documented in Chapter 2, Trump's anti-unionism has been fierce, with his pro-worker populist rhetoric and rare pro-labor Cabinet picks remarkably effective in disguising his hatred of unions. Trump's populist anti-unionism and libertarianism won the favor of conservative top Silicon Valley moguls such as Thiel and Musk, who endorsed Trump in July 2024 and have been huge MAGA donors, with Musk largely taking over and funding his turnout campaign at the end of the race and donating a remarkable $125 million to Trump in the final weeks. A 2024 International Trade Union Confederation (ITUC) report, summarized by Michael Sainato in *The Guardian*, highlighted the role of huge tech companies, such as Amazon, Tesla, and Meta, in busting unions and supporting broader Far-Right anti-democratic politics.[16] Sainato's summary of the ITUC report, reinforcing and going beyond our observations above about the anti-unionism of Bezos and Musk, notes that Amazon "has become notorious for its union busting and low wages on multiple continents."[17] Similarly, regarding Tesla, the ITUC highlights

> anti-union opposition by the company in the US, Germany and Sweden … and Elon Musk's personal opposition to unions and democracy, challenges to the NLRB in the US, and his support for the political leaders Donald Trump, Javier Milei in Argentina and Narendra Modi in India.[18]

Regarding Meta, the ITUC also highlights the company's huge support for anti-democracy and Far-Right forces, characterizing many of the Silicon Valley companies and their financiers:

> The report cites Meta, the largest social media company in the world, for its vast role in permitting and enabling far-right propaganda and movements to use its platforms to grow members and garner support in the US and abroad. It also cited retaliation from the company for regulatory measures in Canada, and *expensive lobbying efforts* against laws to regulate data privacy.[19]

The Trumpist Big Techies add a new flavor to the traditional neoliberal rhetoric of Reaganism that appeared to benefit and liberate many workers – particularly on the campuses of Silicon Valley.[20] As public concern and distrust of online commercial content and influencers grew, public demand for regulation of social media and online content began to grow. Despite traditional Democratic political leanings in Silicon Valley, and many of its executives staying politically neutral or endorsing Kamala Harris, many others in Big Tech began to see in Trump an extremely powerful and useful political ally, who helped usher in not only steep reductions in taxes on big corporations and wealthy corporate moguls but the most powerful anti-regulatory politics and judiciary in modern US history.[21] The landmark 2024 Chevron decision of the Trump-appointed Supreme Court stamped a stunning constitutional imprint on extreme deregulation, enabling Trump's purging of thousands of "liberal" or "Marxist" career civil servants in the Executive Branch, drastically weakening all government regulatory agencies, including the Federal Communications Commission and other agencies with power to regulate their technology, including AI and cryptocurrency. In that same spirit, the Project 2025 agenda created by the conservative Heritage Foundation has been embraced by Trump in his second term to destroy the "deep state" and eliminate its powers of regulation, increasing Big Tech's attraction to Trumpism. Government regulation of business and technology, especially high-tech, creates public control of the most powerful technological tools for transforming our world that the Magnificent Seven seeks to control itself. The enormous controversy over public regulation of AI – an ongoing saga that has not gotten enough public attention beyond some of the concerns about who controls ChatGPT and the role of the tech wunderkind, Sam Altman – is seen by close observers as a test of whether an unfettered AI could lead to unprecedented human destruction as Silicon Valley seeks to ward off any government regulation.[22]

While Trump's deregulation is a huge gift to Silicon Valley, he gets a lot in return. Beyond the huge multi-million dollar political donations of Musk and other Big Tech moguls, high-tech tools are the dream of authoritarian leaders, who can exploit AI and social media to control the population through online propaganda, lies and conspiracy theories, deep fakes, monitoring of ordinary citizens' preferences, and mobilizing isolated online users into tight political communities and political violence, as noted earlier regarding META's online platforming of Far-Right anti-democracy propaganda. As modeled by Orwell's Big Brother in his classic dystopian novel, 1984, Far-Right authoritarians can mislead and manage the public by breaking down their face-to-face relations and exploiting "tele-screens" to control information and build fevered support among a more isolated and fearful population. The symmetry between the authoritarianism of Silicon Valley's surveillance capitalism and Far-Right authoritarianism is mutually reinforcing and deeply anti-democratic. Peter Thiel, the Silicon Valley billionaire who personally introduced J.D. Vance to Donald Trump, is famous for his authoritarian views, saying that "democracy and freedom are no longer compatible;" Thiel also wrote that women gaining voting rights "rendered the notion of 'capitalist democracy' into an oxymoron."[23]

The neoliberal anti-union, anti-trust, and deregulation religion of Silicon Valley melded with Trump's priorities not only to increase authoritarianism but also to intensify extreme economic inequality, already fueled by Trumpist anti-trust policies and significant reductions in taxes on corporations and the rich. That inequality of income and wealth is dramatically increasing in the 21st-century new Robber Baron economy, with Silicon Valley oligarchs like Musk, Bezos, Thiel, Mark Zuckerberg, and other mega-billionaires concentrating an unprecedented amount of wealth in the top 1% – and, indeed, the top 1% of the top 1%. Eight of the wealthiest 10 billionaires in the US are Silicon Valley super-plutocrats.[24]

With a few hundred billionaires now owning a dominating share of the entire US economy, a growing majority of the rest of the population falls into the precariat discussed in Chapter 2. Living paycheck to paycheck, and fearful of falling into poverty with the loss of an insecure job or one illness, they are vulnerable to isolation and the survivalist mentality seen in the loveless Ik tribe discussed earlier. This economically driven and politically supported sociocidal breakdown, atomizing more and more of the workforce, leads to widespread and intense distrust, fear, and anger, underlying the manic buying of personal guns and the right-wing authoritarian movements that are characteristic of sociocidal societies.

* * *

While focusing so far on workers and production, the sococidal economic revolution triggered by Silicon Valley also extends powerfully into consumption, targeting the social relations among consumers and between sellers and buyers. Exploitative consumption – with corporations jacking up prices and imposing junk and other fees on consumers – is the consumer-exploitation face of neoliberalism. Market and consumer relations have long been sociopathic, but neoliberalism is turning consumption, like production, toward sociocide. The role of Silicon Valley is especially important here as its online technologies enable the consumption of virtually everything online. This offers conveniences but may be moving us toward a consumer world devoid of the face-to-face relations long an important foundation of social life.

The consumption story can start with the ancient role of markets in building social relations and community. For centuries, people have congregated in public markets, often in village centers, to trade and exchange or buy and sell. Prior to modern capitalism, markets were centers of sociability, where different strata could intermingle, chat, and make stronger connections. Moreover, without socializing in markets, it was hard to survive because the markets were a source of food, tools, and other essentials, and the social connections and relationships nurtured in the markets established one's place in the community.

As capitalism emerged and developed, markets expanded geographically and economically, taking on a more commercial and predatory role, while moving deeper into the fabric of social life. Western capitalism began with the trading markets of mercantilism, which transformed the local village market into a global center of trade, empire, and profit. While profit became the dominant force fueling markets, they remained a major underpinning of social life and face-to-face relations.

By the time of the 1890s Gilded Age in the US, American capitalism took shape around the first national markets made possible by the railroads. As the Robber Barons built their companies, they needed new ways to expand their market and turn Americans into mass consumers. Workers would buy from corporate producers and retailers the things they used to either make themselves or buy in familiar local public markets. In the 1920s, the retail sector exploded as it taught a post-war generation to buy products using new Sears and other mass consumer catalogs, and by going to large stores that were replacing the local markets. Nonetheless, while commercially driven, consumption remained largely a sphere of face-to-face social relations, whether in large department stores or small specialty shops, where the face-to-face relation between the buyer and salesperson or owner remained an important part of social life.

By the time of the neoliberal revolution in the 1980s, consumption became a global affair, with local public markets taking a back seat to the big box (think Wal-Mart) and large department stores (think Macy's) that subordinated community building to just another sphere of corporate profit. As with the worker, the consumer was subjected to newly sociopathic institutions that had the feeling of a consumer assembly line. Consumer relations became more transient and less personal, as salespeople and marketers dealt with a mass audience of largely anonymous buyers. But despite these changes, an element of the communal functions of the ancient public markets was sustained. Consumers continued to leave their homes, go into familiar retail stores, and often build face-to-face relations with the sellers in the stores that they made part of their lives. While more anonymous, it is important to recognize that face-to-face encounters with what sociologists, such as Georg Simmel and Stanley Milgram, have called "familiar strangers" can be an important part of social life and community,[25] maintaining a flavor of the personal connection of the early public market as part of the larger consumer system.

This thread of face-to-face social life was acutely threatened by the rise of Silicon Valley and its new model of consumption. The corporate symbol of this transformation is Amazon. Jeff Bezos, Amazon's founder and CEO, made himself the richest man in the world by realizing that virtually all products and a huge array of services can be marketed and sold online. It started when Bezos launched his online bookstore in July 1994 from his garage.[26] Bezos was thirty years old and, to make his first sales, mainly generated by word-of-mouth, he and his workers drove down to the post office to deliver the goods to be sold. In 1996, he reincorporated the company in Delaware with an annual revenue of $16 million. In 1997, Barnes and Noble sued Amazon, claiming it was not a real bookstore, but the suit was settled out of court, and Bezos took Amazon public as it issued its one-millionth order.[27]

By 1998, Amazon started selling music and computer games as well as books, and by 1999 was selling video games, home-improvement goods, and consumer electronic software. In 2002, Amazon started selling clothing and made a partnership with several clothing companies, offering more than 400 brands online. Amazon began selling thousands of products and services online. It also expanded in 2003 into e-commerce and leased its platforms to other physical stores, such as Target and Borders. In 2012, Amazon bought Kiva Systems, which produced robots in Massachusetts; the robots began to work alongside human workers doing delivery out of Amazon warehouses. By 2015, Amazon passed Walmart as the world's most valuable retailer, a symbol of the consumer revolution it had helped launch. By 2019, Amazon was selling nearly 50% of all online sales, a sign that the Silicon Valley moguls like Bezos would be just as monopolistic and cut-throat as the first generation of Robber Barons like Rockefeller and Morgan. And Amazon has proved that virtually everything could be sold online; it also secured control of significant sectors of the remaining non-virtual consumer economy. In 2017, it bought all 471 stores of Whole Foods, paying $13.7 billion. Bezos and Amazon could afford it, as Bezos was named the world's richest man in 2017 and again in early 2024.[28]

The triumph of Amazon symbolizes the end of the traditional village market and its long role in sustaining community relations. The "Amazonization" of everything involves virtually all marketing, advertising, and consumer practices being revamped online. This is proving a pivotal change in already precarious market-based consumer and social relations, drastically weakening both production and consumption as foundations of solidarity or community.

Social media – including TikTok and Instagram – play a major role in this shift toward the sociocidal market. Social media operate through "influencers" and the dissemination of images that subtly promote insecurity, competition, or greed, influencing purchases of everything from clothes to cars to food. Images on social media send viewers messages about what is attractive, healthy, or enviable to buy. The viewer may have no idea about the true source of the post and whether the poster is being paid by a company; they may also not know whether friends or people in their online communities or audiences are being paid to sell products or political messages. Students in my classes tell me that they are living in a world of constant online bombardment that is full of suspect information and subtle marketing that makes them insecure. The sociocidal dimension here is the sense of being captured by an online world they don't fully understand or control, leading to anxious and stressful interactions or relations that are fleeting and toxic. What appears to be new social communities are actually fragmenting and dividing people while driving them toward consumption patterns largely beneficial to influencers who themselves are caught in marketing relations that young people find difficult to understand or resist.

* * *

This moves us from the economic story to the larger sociocidal story of how high-tech Robber Barons' economic revolution is intertwined with broader Silicon Valley cultural and social transformations. It is creating an unprecedented transformation of the way people communicate with each other in all spheres of their lives. In the workplace itself, by 2023, one-third of employees worked remotely.[29] But neoliberalism is extending virtual communication into schools and universities, news and entertainment, and networks of friends and family. In all cases, the relationship is shifting from face-to-face human contact toward online electronic connections, mediated through the internet and social media under the rules and power of the giant Silicon Valley tech companies. The tech algorithms and apps that help shape people's online world – including who is in one's online networks, the personal information that is posted and spread, and the surveillance of the relations themselves – are now suddenly embedded within a new digital world managed by high-tech behemoth corporations and marketers whose interests rest more with profit than with humanizing social relations.

Analyst and author Evgeny Morozov has written on "technological solutionism" as a subtle but crucial expansion of a Silicon Valley-led corporate strategy to mediate all our social relations and solve our social problems with the same market-driven, neoliberal algorithms of our economy applied to all aspects of the self and society.[30] Silicon Valley, Morozov argues, is persuading the public that the miraculous possibilities of AI and ChatGPT prove that market-driven innovations and social relations, ironically heavily subsidized by government and the military, are proving far superior to public investments and public goods.[31]

This helps capture the thesis of his 2013 book, *To Save Everything, Click Here: The Folly of Technological Solutionism*, which argues that the Silicon Valley narrative of a technological solution can be applied to creating our new social brands or identities while solving all our political, cultural, and relationship problems.[32] In fact, Morozov writes, while there are indeed social and personal benefits of the internet, AI, and social media, Silicon Valley is promoting market solutions through which Big Tech will now assume a quasi-governing role in society at large. He doesn't discuss sociocide, but the implication is that social relations are destined to become extensions of neoliberal market relations in which reciprocity and solidarity are replaced by egoism and Big Tech-managed social relations.

Silicon Valley is not politically monolithic, and many Big Tech capitalists have traditionally been Democrats, with most supporting Hillary Clinton in 2016. But in the Trump era, and especially in the run-up to the 2024 election, as Vance became the Vice Presidential Trump pick and Musk endorsed and massively funded Trump, the politics of many Silicon Valley moguls were already shifting toward Trumpism. As Ryan Silkis, the CEO of a crypto research firm, wrote, "The Blue Wall of tech is crumbling before our very eyes."[33]

Morozov's analysis hints at the mutual interests between Silicon Valley and Far-Right populism. Trumpism promotes the libertarian ideology favored in Big Tech that identifies government with coercion and views regulation and unions as the enemies of freedom. Both Trumpism and Big Tech view technology in market capitalism as the savior of liberty. This is all consistent with traditional corporate ideology and neoliberalism, but Trumpist Far-Right populism places this seductively within a new "pro-worker" politics. Implicitly, if not explicitly, Trumpism aligns with technological solutionism that claims to shield workers themselves from the tyranny of big government. Libertarians and conservatives in Silicon Valley bask in a Trumpist image that implicitly identifies high tech as the best ally and tool that working people can have against liberal elites, including journalists and the entire globalizing corporate Establishment itself, offering ordinary people the tools to build their own economic futures and protect their freedom. As New York journalist Max Fisher, has noted:

> People need to understand how mainstream it has become in some tech vulture capitalist circles to argue that journalism itself is dangerous as an idea and should be abolished and that it will be up to the tech world to carry this out.
>
> It comes out of a [Silicon] Valley utopianism that has said since the 90s that all legacy institutions are ultimately barriers to progress, but that the enlightened minds of the tech world, guided by the pure science of engineering, will one day liberate us by smashing the old ways.
>
> The idea of rejecting institutions to build a purer society on the internet, in vogue in tech in the 90s, by the 2010s had become a mandate to abolish and remake those institutions in big tech's image.[34]

Behind a growing alliance between sectors of Silicon Valley and Trumpist Far-Right populist politics are the political benefits reaped by Trumpism itself. The sociocide fueled by Silicon Valley intensifies economic precariousness, social isolation, and fear among working people, providing red meat for populist politics. As the Democratic Party abandoned the New Deal and other forms of Left populism, working people have turned to

Trumpist populism as their best hope. The more sociocide created by Silicon Valley, the more Far-Right populism can thrive, making the cult of Trump a seductive antidote to the loss of community elsewhere in millions of people's lives who flocked to find like-minded allies in Trump rallies.

* * *

A new generation of sociologists and analysts of social communication, in the spirit of Morozov's critique, argue that Silicon Valley's magical new online technology is actually endangering the survival of humanizing face-to-face social relations, as well as increasing corporate powers of control and surveillance. Leading sociologists and communications scholars are deeply concerned about the inherent dehumanizing character of social media and other electronically mediated social connections. MIT analyst Sherry Turkle argues that social media are taking away the "raw human part of being with each other." Along with other analysts, such as Shoshanna Zuboff, she argues in her book, *Alone Together,* that as social media expands, we are witnessing a rise of real-world isolation, loneliness, and personal and social disconnection, accompanied by a loss of skills in talking to each other face-to-face that can be remedied only by limits on online additions or monopolies, and the rebuilding of face-to-face social relations.[35]

In her book, *The Age of Surveillance Capitalism*, Zuboff has powerfully dissected some of the core interests driving the creation and design of the internet and social media for corporate profit while breaking down both face-to-face communities and democracy. The paradise of Silicon Valley is exposed by Zuboff as a nightmare creation by Big Tech of surveillance capitalism.[36] The latest model of neoliberal capitalism, relying on the internet, AI, social media, and all digital technology, turns all of us into 24-hour objects of corporate exploitation and profit extraction. She writes:

> Digital connection is now a means to others' commercial ends ... At its core, surveillance capitalism is parasitic and self-referential. It revives Karl Marx's old image of capitalism as a vampire that feeds on labor, but with an unexpected turn. Instead of labor, surveillance capitalism feeds on every aspect of every human's experience.[37]

Zuboff argues that Silicon Valley feeds off the failures of the "real-world" non-digital neoliberal capitalism to meet our needs. She argues that as we become increasingly atomized and isolated in front of our screens, we have become increasingly vulnerable targets of Silicon Valley's seduction, where online information and services appear to provide us with the resources we need to survive and even thrive.[38]

Zuboff argues that in surveillance capitalism it is not just that our search for information and connection on the web and social media makes all our preferences and needs transparent and accessible to Big Tech for profit. She shows that:

> It is a more profound subjugation of the human brain and body into the digital world reshaping our behavior through the algorithms of AI and social media; we become both the supply and demand of the new economy, simultaneously raw material and constantly refinished product that consumes itself ... Industrial capitalism transformed nature's raw materials into commodities ... Now it is human nature that is scraped, torn and taken for another century's market project.[39]

Zuboff highlights not only the profit but also the social and political control that Big Tech gains in its surveillance capitalism project, as we are glued to our screens and increasingly lack face-to-face solidarity to challenge our new controllers:

> the essence of the exploitation here is the rendering of our lives as behavioral data for the sake of others' improved control of us … the remarkable fact is that our lives are rendered as behavioral data in the first place; that ignorance is a condition of this ubiquitous rendition; that decision rights vanish before one even knows that there is a decision to make[40]

Zuboff is clear about who is taking power:

> Two men at Google who do not enjoy the legitimacy of the vote, democratic over-sight, or the demands of shareholder governance exercise control over the organiza-tion and presentation of the world's information. One man at Facebook who does not enjoy the legitimacy of the vote, democratic oversight, or the demands of share-holder governance exercises control over an increasingly universal means of social connection along with the information concealed in its networks.[41]

Zuboff is one of the few "communication experts" who puts together the economics, culture, and politics of an increasingly hegemonic Big Tech. As we show in Chapter 7, her surveillance capitalism is receptive to and profits from authoritarian politics. It has the potential to access and control all personal information, map and weaken our social con-nections, and create algorithms that shape our behavior online and offline – and benefits from the protection of a strongman whose political appeal rises greatly among fearful and disconnected people.

Indeed, surveillance capitalism is building its own new authoritarian system which resonates with and reinforces the political authoritarianism of Trumpist politics. The log-arithmic dictators of an Orwellian society that Zuboff profiles are fostering the author-itarian social and communications infrastructure that can be exploited by dictatorial leaders to build and solidify their own authoritarian politics. When Orwell wrote about the centrality of the "tele-screen" in his novel, *1984*, he anticipated the real-world online communications devices that would help enable and empower contemporary political "Big Brothers" like Trump.

Silicon Valley's virtual technologies are potent instruments of authoritarian power. Trump has built a social media echo and propaganda chamber, enabled by alliances with billionaire Silicon Valley tycoons such as Thiel and Musk, who provide platforms such as X that can reach a fact-free universe of billions of people. Social media and online communication are perfect communication tools of authoritarian leaders like Trump, who specialize in spreading lies and propaganda, breeding distrust based on fear, misin-formation, and conspiracy theories. X, once it was bought and owned personally by Elon Musk, became a huge platform for Trumpist propaganda, with Musk personally sending his 800 million followers endless pro-Trump tweets, many misleading or outright lies. X offers Trump and his other allies, like former Fox anchor Tucker Carlson, an audience of hundreds of millions to spread lies about the Great Replacement of whites by people of color and build populist fury against immigrants.

The social distrust bred among most users of social media is a special gift to authoritarians like Trump. Users of social media are assaulted by commercial and political influences who plug into the receptive audience that the Silicon Valley logarithms provide. When they hear false narratives and conspiracy theories from populist leaders like Trump, it can become a reassuring source of truth and community. The inherent difficulty of identifying and proving lies offered by online sources makes the internet a paradise for authoritarian movements and leaders.

Silicon Valley technologies have greatly facilitated the spread of Trump's lies and propaganda about elections and related issues. Russian intelligence services, specializing in stealing and distributing online Democratic election strategies and emails, helped him win the election in 2016. FBI Director James Comey's investigation of Hillary Clinton's emails, hacked and distributed by Russian operatives, may have caused her loss in the 2020 election. After his loss to Biden in 2020, Trump's war on democracy was bolstered by a global army of foreign and domestic propaganda leaders, including Trump aides Steve Bannon, Paul Manafort, and Michael Flynn, all linked to powerful online influencers abroad and at home. Trump's own authoritarianism could not be more powerfully mirrored and fueled by the authoritarianism of surveillance capitalism.

Zuboff may not be fully capturing the extreme authoritarianism of major sectors of Silicon Valley elites, including Musk, Thiel, John Case, and others. Their New Right network openly supports autocracy and rallied around the anti-free press views of people like Thiel, who helped school J.D. Vance. When Trump picked Vance as his Vice President, journalists and attorneys began looking deeper into the Far-Right network of Thiel and fellow tech billionaires, who write about their open opposition to democracy and support a free speech absolutism, giving full rein to Trumpist-style disinformation and lies:

> People who don't want democracy don't have many alternatives, which is why Peter Thiel and friends support the idea of an elected autocrat. A person who prefers an autocrat doesn't want freedom of the press. Freedom of the press is protected in the constitution precisely because the first thing an autocrat wants to do is control the press.
>
> In banning journalists while declaring himself a "free speech absolutist," Musk was demonstrating that "free speech absolutism" is just another name for a Russian propaganda technique known as "noise."
>
> The notion that all voices, including "dissenting" voices, must be heard makes sense if the dissenters agree on the basic facts (like "up is up" and "Biden won the 2020 election"). In an intact public sphere(which is required for a working democracy) people agree on the facts but disagree on the best way forward. But if the "dissenting voices" amount to conspiracy theories and lies, the "all voices deserve equal consideration" policy becomes a way to elevate and legitimize lies and conspiracy theories. This elevates and legitimizes lies. It also crowds the airways, jams the signals, and confuses people with noise.
>
> Insisting that lies share a platform with truth under the guise of "all voices must be heard" is thus a technique for spreading and giving credence to disinformation, which creates confusion and undermines factuality, which in turn destroys democracy.[42]

Zuboff's notion of surveillance capitalism is thus being reinforced by more recent perspectives on the political authoritarianism of Silicon Valley and its growing political connection with Trump's and Vance's tight relation with New Right "libertarian" Big Tech billionaires like Musk, Thiel, John Case, David Sacks, Marc Andreessen, and others.[43] Zuboff's work anticipated this, and along with other critics of Big Tech and social media, she showed how social media and the moguls of Silicon Valley are breaking down humanizing face-to-face relations and threatening truth and democracy. The social media world, as I show in the next chapter, becomes a new and leading instrument for breeding a new culture of hyper-individualism, social distrust, and the extreme self-interest of what I call the sociocidal culture of "wilding"; a culture that breeds extreme receptivity to authoritarian politics and leaders.[44]

Sociocidal culture is partly fueled by the economic and political interests of Silicon Valley itself. Social disconnection is the playground of both Big Tech and authoritarian politics. The more disconnected people are, the more likely they are to seek out the "connecting" technology created and managed by Big Tech – and the political communities offered by authoritarian movements like Trumpism. Like all other sectors of the economy, Big Tech not only gets more clients as people become more isolated from face-to-face relations, but, like all other companies, benefits from the inability of its workers, consumers, or clients to build solidarity that can contest the power of either Big Tech or its technology. Social solidarity always lurks as the largest threat to the profits and power of large corporations. Isolation and atomization, whatever their social costs, create large benefits for Big Tech, which makes money off the needs of an atomized, socially disconnected population. Likewise, authoritarian movements like Trumpism fear and seek to break down social organizations that Trump himself cannot control, recognizing that fevered online political communities can provide the funding and solidarity to fuel Trump's political successes.

This calls attention to the other sociocidal and policidal dimensions of social media, which massively amplify the ability of individuals and both commercial and political groups to express both disinformation and lies, often tied to racial or other messages of social hate, as well as to target individuals or organizations with death threats and political or other forms of social violence. Social media amplifies the ability and audience of individuals, companies, marketers, and Trumpist Far-Right groups, as already noted, to reach large numbers of people with doctored and falsified information, to achieve profit, power, or revenge, breakdown of trustworthy social communication and the very possibility of truth itself.

This undermining of trust and truth profoundly serves Big Tech corporate interests along with the political interests of authoritarian leaders like Trump. An increasingly isolated, fearful, and angry tech-dependent population, desperate for connections and information, turns more and more to social media and other Silicon Valley products for "connecting," thinking it will bring more safety and control when its algorithms are so often designed to do just the opposite. Millions also turn to Trump, skilled like most authoritarian leaders in the uses of propaganda and lies, as a major source of connection and truth.

While Trump is largely a political ally, he shows that Silicon Valley is not unified politically, with the Trumpist New Right allies such as Musk and Thiel opposed by other elites nervous about Trumpist populist rhetoric. Moreover, Trumpism shows that Big Tech is not in total control of its own creations. Broader sociocidal assaults on trust and truth serve other economic and political actors with their own agendas. Trumpist political disinformation and lies, racial, gender, and class slurs, hate messages, and invocations toward violence do not represent the views of much of Silicon Valley, despite the authoritarian parallels and ideological alliances between Trump and leaders of Silicon Valley's surveillance capitalism. While there are contradictory political trends, online communications technology is interacting with political mobilization on the neo-fascist Far-Right to threaten and bring violence against entire groups of the population.

* * *

Despite the formidable sociocidal high-tech instruments of Silicon Valley, the same forces also create new forms of sociophiliac relationships and pro-democracy movements. High technology, including social media, is deeply contradictory, not only breaking down face-to-face relations but also fueling new online and offline movements that can contest Big Tech and help challenge authoritarianism and build a deeper democracy. One of the many sources of hope to combat both sociocide and authoritarian policide is that sociocidal technology is, by an exquisite contradiction discussed in the last chapters of this book, giving rise to a movement for the very social solidarity and democratic community that it is attacking. Ironically, this can help avoid a technologically based gloom that is as unfounded as the Silicon Valley notions of technological paradise.

A hint of this possibility exploded into view when Kamala Harris announced she would run for President in July 2024. Less than a week after her announcement, Harris's campaign had sparked the largest and fastest popular mobilization for a presidential campaign in US history. Millions of people rallied together, raised millions of dollars, and volunteered in the hundreds of thousands to call friends, knock on doors, and turn out the vote for Harris and Tim Walz, her popular pick for Vice President. This all became possible only because of social media and the internet, with the Harris very brief but magical moment proving that Silicon Valley's high-tech promise of a new socially connected world was not completely illusory.

Despite the catastrophic failure and loss of the Harris campaign, its first few weeks proved that social media and the online world are, indeed, deeply contradictory, not only fueling the sococide and authoritarianism discussed in this chapter but also offering future potential for a new world of civil society mobilization, new social relations, and democratic social movements. Within the first 24 hours of her campaign, Win With Black Women created a Zoom call joined by 90,000 people dedicated to talking and working together to elect Harris. They raised $1.5 million in three hours. The next day, Win With Black Men held their own Zoom meeting, attracting 200,000 participants and raising $8.5 million for Harris. Four days later, activist Shannon Watts organized a "White Women: Answer the Call" Zoom meeting that attracted an astonishing 200,000 people. This was reported as the largest Zoom call in history, "breaking the internet." The call was shut down temporarily because the donation link was too flooded by thousands of people trying to give their contribution.[45]

This was just the beginning of this online anti-sociocidal pro-democracy movement powered by the internet and social media. The following week, Harris delivered a virtual talk to a huge Gen Z summit called "Voters of Tomorrow." The same week, another group dubbed "White Dudes" organized another huge Zoom meeting with 190,000 white men calling in. Zoom meetings for Harris organized by unions such as the Teachers Unions also began growing.

This all followed up on recent years of intensified earlier online progressive mobilizations. In 2020, a group of swing voters called "Zoom moms" also began to organize online.[46] For several years, online politics of all persuasions – including anti-war and anti-corporate labor politics among unions and the young – had flourished on social media sites such as X, TikTok, Instagram, and Facebook. But the mobilization for Harris marked a new era of online mobilization, not only among young people but rural voters and even "Republicans for Harris." Imani M. Cheers, a media professor at George Washington University, said a week after Harris started her campaign with such an electric online spark, "I have never seen this level of virtual support." He said, "What we're seeing now at the moment is a beautiful intersection of concerned citizens utilizing digital media and virtual technology to campaign, to gather, to organize …"[47] Her campaign raised over $200 million in the first week, mostly online from small contributors who had never donated politically to anyone.

All this early celebration by Democrats of Harris' online surge helped mask her profound failures to connect with voters on core issues of the economy, corporate power, and war which helped doom her. It also disguised the fact that Trump was fueling perhaps more powerfully his own online campaign. In the last few months, his interviews in podcasts and other internet forums directed especially at young and middle-aged men, became more and more widely viewed, ultimately reaching hundreds of millions of followers.

This goes well beyond the interviews on X with Trump's most important tech supporter and mogul, Elon Musk; as noted earlier, Musk's onslaught of posts for Trump in the last weeks of the campaign reached hundreds of millions of Musk's 800 million followers on X. Just as important, on October 29, 2024, just days before his re-election, Trump had a three-hour podcast interview on the Joe Rogan Experience, described by *Newsweek* as "the world's biggest podcast." Rogan's marathon podcast with Trump was seen by more than 33 million viewers on YouTube, was liked 1.7 million times, and garnered more than 400,000 comments. And this is just one part of Rogan's audience, which also reaches an estimated 11 million people on Spotify and millions more on Apple.[48]

Rogan's final huge podcast with Trump capped months of Trump's strategic courting of the "manoverse," the online world communicating mainly with millions of young men and many of their fathers. Described by the *New York Times* as part of an online "testosterone-fueled orbit," it overlaps with but dwarfs the more conventional Fox News and other right-wing traditional media. Rogan is the older avatar of the younger set of manoverse online stars like the Nelk Boys, YouTubers like Jake and Logan Paul, popular podcasters like Theo Von, and streamers like Adin Ross.[49] In the final months of his campaign, Trump dived deep into online campaign conversations and podcasts with all these manoverse stars, recruiting what many view as a decisive margin of supporters among young people who never watch TV news and were never reached by Harris or the Democrats who saw them as inaccessible low-propensity voters or apolitical nonvoters.[50] In fact, the manoverse is a highly politicized universe that Trump galvanized as a symbol of how powerful the online world created and managed by Big Tech may prove to be in building a base for 21st-century authoritarianism and Far-Right populism.

Trump's success in exploiting the MAGA online base and propagating lies and anti-democratic propaganda shows that Silicon Valley's new virtual technology is unquestionably one of the great sociocidal and policidal dangers of our era, poised to help Trump consolidate authoritarian rule in his second term. On the other hand, the flame of the doomed Harris campaign's brief magical moment online, at the same time as the surge of Trump's online manoverse, hints that, as Karl Marx famously argued, the most important force of history is contradiction. The same technology that can bring us a new Big

Brother might eventually truly help bring a new sister, helping us connect with her and each other for new relationships, solidarity, and democracy.

Notes

1 Neil Howe, "Why Do Millennials Love Silicon Valley? It's Not Just the Tech," *Forbes*, August 17, 2016, forbes.com
2 Nicole Narea, "Why Tech Titans Are Turning Toward Trump." *Vox*, July 17, 2024, vox.com
3 Daniel Bell, *The Coming of Post-Industrial Society*. NY: Penguin, 1976.
4 For a focus on Thiel and the "New Right" circles that grew up partly among young tech people in Silicon Valley, though they would also critique elements of the high tech world and politics, see James Pogue, "Inside the New Right, Where Peter Thiel Is Placing His Biggest Bets." *Vanity Fair*, April 20, 2022, vanityfair.com
5 Karl Russell and Joe Rennison, "These Seven Tech Stocks are Driving the Market." *NYT*, January 22, 2024, nytimes.com
6 "Largest American Companies By Market Capitalization." companiesmarketcap.com
7 "Largest American Companies By Market Capitalization." companiesmarketcap.com.
8 Karl Russell and Joe Rennison, "The Seven Tech Stocks Are Driving the Market." *NYT*, January 22, 2024, nytimes.com
9 Dan Milmo, "Why Have the Big Seven Tech Companies Been Hit By AI Boom Doubts." *The Guardian*, August 3, 2024, theguardian.com
10 Kevin Roose, "Meet My A.I. Friends." *NY Times*, May 9, 2024, nytimes.com
11 cited in Steve Lohr, "Generative AI's Biggest Impact Will be in Banking ad Tech, Report Says." *NYT*, February 1, 2024, nytimes.com
12 Steve Lohr, "Generative AI's Biggest Impact Will be in Banking ad Tech, Report Says." *NYT*, February 1, 2024, nytimes.com
13 Steve Lohr, "Generative AI's Biggest Impact Will be in Banking ad Tech, Report Says." *NYT*, February 1, 2024, nytimes.com
14 Aila Slisco, "Donald Trump Cheers Elon Musk Over Firing Workers: 'You're the Greatest.'" *Newsweek*, August 13, 2024, newsweek.com
15 Rebecca Picciotto and Lora Kolodny, "UAW Hits Musk, Trump with Federal Labor Changes Over Union-basting Comments." *CNBC*, August 14, 2024, cnbc.com
16 Michael Sainato, "Amazon, Tesla and Meta Among World's Top Companies Underming Democracy – Report." *The Guardian*, September 23, 2024, theguardian.com
17 Michael Sainato, "Amazon, Tesla and Meta Among World's Top Companies Underming Democracy – Report." *The Guardian*, September 23, 2024, theguardian.com
18 Michael Sainato, "Amazon, Tesla and Meta Among World's Top Companies Underming Democracy – Report." *The Guardian*, September 23, 2024, theguardian.com
19 Michael Sainato, "Amazon, Tesla and Meta Among World's Top Companies Underming Democracy – Report." *The Guardian*, September 23, 2024, theguardian.com
20 Dana Mattioli, Emily Glazer, and Khadeeja Safdar, "Elon Musk Has Said He Is Committing Around $45 Million a Month to a New Pro-Trump Super PAC." *Wall Street Journal*, July 16, 2024, wsj.com
21 John Naughton, "Silicon Valley's Trump Supporters Are Dicing with the Death of Democracy." *The Guardian*, August 3, 2024, theguardian.com
22 Gary Marcus, "OpenAI's Sam Altman Is Becoming One of the Most Powerful People on Earth. We Should Be Very Afraid." *The Guardian,* August 3, 2024, theguardian.com
23 Erin Mansfield, "Peter Thiel and J.D. Vance." *USA Today*, July 17, 2024, usatoday.com
24 Chuck Collins and Omar Ocampo, "Total U.S. Billionaire Wealth: Up 88 Percent over Four Years." *Inequality*, March 18, 2024, inequality.org
25 Georg Simmel, "The Stranger," in Kurt Wolff, *The Sociology of Georg Simmel*. NY: Free Press, 1950. See also Stanley Milgram, "The Familiar Stranger," *Division of Personality and Social Psychology, American Psychological Association*.
26 Groww, "From Bookstore to Superstore: Amazon Through the Years." May 17, 2022, grow.in. See also Colby Hopkins, "The History of Amazon and its Rise to Success," *Michigan Journal of Economics*, https://sites.lsa.umich.edu/mje/2023/05/01/the-history-of-amazon-and-its-rise-to -success.

27 Groww, "From Bookstore to Superstore: Amazon Through the Years." May 17, 2022, grow.in. See also Colby Hopkins, "The History of Amazon and its Rise to Success," *Michigan Journal of Economics*, https://sites.lsa.umich.edu/mje/2023/05/01/the-history-of-amazon-and-its-rise-to-success.

28 Groww, "From Bookstore to Superstore: Amazon Through the Years." May 17, 2022, grow.in. See also Colby Hopkins, "The History of Amazon and its Rise to Success," *Michigan Journal of Economics*, https://sites.lsa.umich.edu/mje/2023/05/01/the-history-of-amazon-and-its-rise-to-success.

29 Emma Goldberg, "All That Empty Office Space Belongs to Someone." *New York Times*, September 1, 2023, nytimes.com

30 Natasha Dow Schull, "The Folly of Technological Solutionism: An Interview with Evgeny Morozov." *Public Books*, September 9, 2013, publicbooks.org; see also Evgeny Morozov, *To Save Everything, Click Here: The Folly of Technological Solutionism*. NY: Public Affairs, 2014.

31 Evgeny Morozov, *To Save Everything, Click Here: The Folly of Technological Solutionism*. NY: Public Affairs, 2014.

32 Evgeny Morozov, *To Save Everything, Click Here: The Folly of Technological Solutionism*. NY: Public Affairs, 2014.

33 Nicole Narea, "Why Tech Titans are Turning Toward Trump." *Vox*, July 17, 2024, vox.com

34 Fisher, cited by Teri Kanefield, "Elon Musk, Fox News, and Free Speech Absolutism." December 17, 2022, terikanefield.com

35 Sherry Turkle, *Alone Together*. NY: Basic Books, 2017.

36 Shoshana Zuboff, *The Age of Surveillance Capitalism*. NY: Public Affairs, 2019.

37 Shoshana Zuboff, *The Age of Surveillance Capitalism*. NY: Public Affairs, 2019.

38 Cited in Sam Biddle, "A Fundamentally Illegitimate Choice: Shoshana Zuboff on the Age of Surveillance Capitalism." *The Intercept*, February 2, 2019, theintercept.com

39 Shoshana Zuboff, *The Age of Surveillance Capitalism*. NY: Public Affairs, 2019.

40 Shoshana Zuboff, *The Age of Surveillance Capitalism*. NY: Public Affairs, 2019.

41 Shoshana Zuboff, *The Age of Surveillance Capitalism*. NY: Public Affairs, 2019.

42 Teri Kanefield, "Elon Musk, Fox News, and Free Speech Absolutism." December 17, 2022, terikanefield.com

43 Andrew Ross Sorkin et al. "Inside Silicon Valley's Political Rift." *Dealbook, The New York Times*, July 30, 2024, nytimes.com

44 Charles Derber, *The Pursuit of Attention*. 2nd edition. NY: Oxford University Press, 2000.

45 Jacob Knutson, "Zoom Is the New Political Rally." *Axios*, July 27, 2024, axios.com

46 Alexi McCammond, Margaret Telev, "2020's Newest Swing Voters: Zoom Moms." *Axios*.

47 Jacob Knutson, "Zoom Is the New Political Rally." *Axios*, July 27, 2024, axios.com

48 Flynn Nichols, "Joe Rogan Showed Donald Trump 'Unedited.' Millions Adored It." *Newsweek*, October 29, 2024, newsweek.com.

49 John Branch, "Donald Trump Courts the Manoverse." *New York Times*, September 1, 2024 nytimes.com.

50 John Branch, "Donald Trump Courts the Manoverse." *New York Times*, September 1, 2024 nytimes.com.

4 The bonfire of the vanities

The over-heated American Dream, me over we, and the culture of social media and the lonely

We turn now from the last two chapters' focus on the rising sociocidal economy – and its authoritarian political threats – to closely intertwined issues of a looming cultural sociocide. American culture has long been based on individualistic values that prioritize the self over others. Self-interest is the fundamental principle of the US market economy. The American Dream, which is a creed of freedom to pursue one's own interests above all else, is the cultural script of American capitalism. That Dream helped culturally sustain our market-based society for two centuries, in ways that weakened but did not destroy community and our social relationships or our democracy.

In books such as *The Wilding of America* and *Sociopathic Society*, I have shown that American individualism evolved in the late 20th century toward "wilding," the pursuit of self-interest that involves increasingly severe harm to others and weakening of the social fabric.[1] While sociopathic individualism had long threatened American social bonds and communities, major forms of labor and social solidarity survived. In *The Wilding of America*, I pointed to the rise of a more extreme form of individualistic culture that one of the founders of modern sociology, Emile Durkheim, warned of as a looming social disaster under circumstances of a breakdown of traditional solidarity and social integration.[2] A century after Durkheim, in the late 20th century, a new crisis of cultural individualism would surface in the US with the breakdown of the New Deal political economy and the emergence of the neoliberal era, leading to a much deeper breakdown of the social bond. America began to move from sociopathy to sociocide.[3]

As discussed earlier, anthropologist Colin Turnbull discovered a sociocidal broken society of displaced people in Uganda called the Ik, who had to spend all their hours searching for food to survive.[4] The values of care and love for others became incompatible with staying alive. Turnbull called this the "loveless" society where people were so obsessed with bare survival that they had lost the capacity to care or feel for others. Social ties, including friendships and the family itself, had broken down into arrangements of convenience and instruments of exploitation by which one would turn against one's own family members or acquaintances to steal food and other resources required for survival.

The US has not moved nearly as far as the Ik model of sociocide, but the domestic "regime change" of the neoliberal Reagan Revolution, now championed by Trump's Far-Right populism, helped usher in a more extreme American Dream that began to edge the nation from sociopathy toward sociocide. In his Inaugural Address, Reagan proclaimed that his goal was to create "morning in America" where everybody could not just prosper but open his or her own business and get rich. Shortly thereafter, a Bostonian named

DOI: 10.4324/9781003491798-5

Charles Stuart killed his pregnant wife for $300,000 insurance money, dreaming, as the public later learned, of opening a new business and getting as wealthy as his affluent clients he catered to while working in an upscale clothing store on tony Newbury Street.[5] Relatives believed that the permanent commitments of marriage and children were burdens to Stuart that conflicted with his sense of entitlement and freedom to pursue his own dreams, a theme highlighting America's current cultural contradiction between committed relationships and freedom.

In Reagan's new neoliberal America, Stuart symbolized a hyper-individualistic and unfettered model of the American Dream, in which people began to normalize the view that pursuit of one's own interests and freedom was morally acceptable even if it involved harming others, including friends and family.[6] A new genre of true crime books featured people like Stuart who murdered their spouses or other relatives to get ahead. While such individuals had always existed, the popularity of these books and other data about more troubled, egoistic, and violent social relationships hinted at a broader change in the stability, egoism, and sustainability of social relations, both in the family and other social networks.

An unprecedented number of Americans are now are never married, divorced, separated, living in single households, childless, without close friends, and report feeling lonely and isolated. More than 40% of all Americans say that they have either nobody or only one other person with whom they can share important personal feelings – and 43% say their relationships are not meaningful, 43% feel isolated, and 39% are not close to anyone.[7] In a July 2023 summary of polling data by analyst Steven Zauderer, between 52% and 60% of Americans report feeling lonely on a regular basis;[8] 47% report their relationships with others aren't meaningful; and 57% of Americans report eating all meals alone.[9] These data are associated with more social violence, higher rates of depression, a rise in suicide, and lower life expectancy, all trends associated with separation or disconnection from others.[10]

As workplace relations become more competitive and frayed, families, friendships, and communities are also weakening, leading millions of Americans to feel more fearful and distrustful of others, needing to focus more on themselves simply to survive. This is especially acute both among working-class people most atomized by corporate economic forces breaking down secure work, as well as young people of all classes facing extreme competitive economic pressures and reduced access to strong neighborhood and community or civil society networks. The intertwined economic and cultural changes move all Americans toward greater egoism and distrust, making people less capable of mutualistic ties, which then triggers yet a faster breakdown of solidaristic relations in the economy, neighborhood, and civil society, spreading yet more isolation, fear, and egoism. This sociocidal spiral downward moves America toward a 21st-century version of what Durkheim called "social disaggregation" and a cultural crisis of extreme individualism, "egoism," isolation, and suicide.[11]

These hyper-individualistic cultural shifts are mirrored and accelerated by the rise of political leaders whose personalities reflect the culture of the new era. Far-Right political populism, led by Donald Trump, is fueled by the atomization, fear, and anger of a society becoming more Ik-like and socialized into more self-interested, egotistical, and anti-social values. Political leaders who reflect the emerging anti-social and narcissistic culture become models for the population. Perhaps the most sociopathic, purely self-interested, and narcissistic president in the history of the nation, Trump's character becomes an appealing model to much of the public. He reflects the triumph of egoism and narcissistic culture in politics and political leaders, who typically reflect ruling social values and the psychology essential to survive and succeed in the existing social order.

***

Marriage, long considered the most important social relationship, has been eroding dramatically for many decades. Consider the chart shown in Figure 4.1:[12]

This data from the Pew Research Center shows that the percentage of aged 40 and older adults who have never married increased 400% from 7% in 1980 to 25% of Americans in 2021, a record high. In a related 2021 survey, Pew found that this drastic increase is reflected in new cultural attitudes and values that Americans express about the

One-quarter of U.S. 40-year-olds have never married, a record high

% of 40-year-olds who had never married

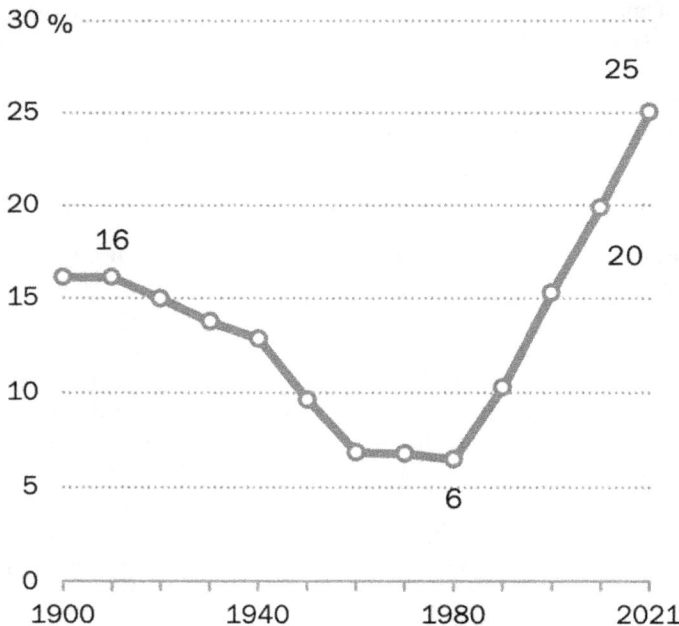

Note: Data labels shown for 1910, 1980, 2010 and 2021.
Source: Pew Research Center analysis of 1900-2000 decennial census and 2010 and 2021 American Community Survey (IPUMS).

PEW RESEARCH CENTER

Figure 4.1 Decline of Marriage

declining value of marriage compared to other factors making for a fulfilling life. While 71% say having a career is extremely or very important for a fulfilling life, only 23% say this about being married and only 26% say this about having children.[13]

This disenchantment with marriage shows up in equally dramatic rises in the percentage of single-person American households. In 1960, only 13% of US households were single-person. By 2022, that number had more than doubled to 29% of all US households being single-person.[14] This is sometimes dubbed the "solo-living" movement, with books emerging like Bella DePaulo's best-selling *Single at Heart*.[15] The eroding collective household is happening along with the eroding collective workplace and are two major foundations of the "we" succumbing to the atomized "me."

Looking at the Pew chart of never married individuals, two things are noteworthy. The spike begins in 1980, the year that President Reagan was elected and ushered in the neoliberal capitalist revolution. In his Inaugural Address, Reagan highlighted that his dream was for every American who worked hard to get rich quickly – a dream that was picked up by millions, like Charles Stuart, the Bostonian wife-killer who felt he had to get out of his marriage and prevent having a child to get ahead and succeed.

Stuart's case illustrates the cultural contradiction emerging between a committed relationship and the sociocidal focus on the self. All social relationships place limits on one's freedom to do whatever one wants. A highly committed relationship like marriage places strong burdens on individual freedom, with children adding to the set of obligations created by marriage and family. In Stuart's case, the curbs on his egoistic need to do what he wanted, which was to spend more time on starting a restaurant, were becoming increasingly intolerable to him. The "we" of the marriage was suffocating Stuart's "me."

Donald Trump's personality and marriages suggest how the egoism and inability to commit to a relationship that also charactterized Stuart have become more normalized and widespread. Trump could never accept the limits of marriage, as a multiple-divorcee who cheated by sleeping with a porn star and indulging in other affairs while his third wife was pregnant. His conviction in the 2024 New York hush-money case involving Stormy Daniels, as well as his salacious quotes in the earlier *Hollywood Access* tapes about his ability as a celebrity to grab women's private parts, made clear his narcissistic personality. But none of this undermined the adoration of Trump by the millions of people in his base. The fact that his family did not come to his 2024 New York trial to support him also did not weaken him with the public, nor did his repeated betrayal of his wife, Melania. His inability to accept any limits on his freedom tied to his marriage – and Trump's long-term popularity and re-election to his second term in 2024 – is another signal that our politics is sending about our collective culture and psychology. Narcissism rules.

Marriage has always brought contradictions between social relationships and the free, unburdened self. But in our hyper-individualistic culture, the contradiction becomes more severe. The values of love and romance that are a major part of American culture exist uneasily with the idea that to be American is to enjoy maximum freedom to do whatever one wants. Marriage prevents such perfect freedom. Love and freedom are in tension.

After 1980, this largely neglected cultural tension exploded into a bonfire of a new, intensely individualistic American Dream. With the rise of the Reagan Revolution, Americans across the board focused intensely on "making it" economically and getting rich fast, which Reagan proclaimed as his dream for everyone. The fear of falling behind one's peers, something that Stuart felt acutely, intensified the economic and cultural contradictions of all committed social relations, including marriage. Stuart wanted love, but he didn't want the obligations that came with it, which he found suffocating. The only economically viable and psychologically tolerable escape for him involved ending the marriage itself, in his case through the horrifying act of killing his pregnant wife.[16]

The idea that Stuart was playing out his own version of a sociocidal American Dream is suggested by a decline in all kinds of committed social relationships. The drastic rise in the percent of single Americans after 1980 is also associated with a decades-long rise in the divorce rate and those not having children.[17] This is tied to a broader breakdown of relationships in recent decades, including erosion in friendships and belonging in civil associations and community or religious groups. This is brewing even among young people whose multiple online relations, as we show later, are the new sociocidal model of what social media analyst Sherry Turkle, has called living "alone together."[18]

* * *

While the data on friendship is not entirely consistent across different studies, Vivek Murthy, the US Surgeon General, issued a 2023 report called "Our Epidemic of Loneliness and Isolation" that offers a sobering analysis.[19] Based on an overview of multiple surveys, the Surgeon General, who views social isolation as arguably the most important public health crisis in the US today, summarizes the decline in friendship. He writes that the number of Americans with close friends has drastically "declined over several decades … almost half of Americans (49%) in 2021 had three or fewer close friends – only about a quarter (27%) reported the same few friends in 1990."[20]

This doubling of the percentage of Americans with few friends since the Reagan years is striking. Murthy shows that face-to-face time spent with friends is in steep decline, "with the amount of time respondents engaged with friends socially in-person decreased from 2003 (60 minutes/day, 30 hours/month) to 2020 (20 minutes/day, 10 hours/month). This represents a decrease of 20 hours per month spent engaging with friends." [21]

This decline in friendship is, again, symbolized in the political sphere by Donald Trump. Supported by a cult of followers, Trump is noteworthy not only for his marital failures and infidelity but also for his inability to make and keep close personal friends. Journalists have commented repeatedly on the specter of Trump being isolated and lacking long-term friends. Indeed, Trump is purely transactional not only in his politics but also in his social relationships. He connects with people for money or political gain and breaks with them when they are no longer useful to him. Again, the leader's personality sends a message of how our collective culture of narcissism is evolving and how deeply self-interest and egoism have become dominant in US social life.

Along with the decline in family and friendship, Murthy documents a marked decline in connections with voluntary associations and civic groups, highlighting the breadth of uncoupling forces across virtually all types of social relationships. Regarding voluntary associations, religious groups, and civil society, as documented famously by Robert Putnam in Bowling Alone, the historical decline since the Reagan years is once again on full display:

> Although the concept of community has evolved over time, many traditional indicators of community involvement, including with religious groups, clubs, and labor unions, show declining trends in the United States since at least the 1970s. In 2018, only 16% of Americans reported that they felt very attached to their local community.

Membership in organizations that have been important pillars of community connection have declined significantly in this time. Take faith organizations. In 2020, only 47% of Americans said they belonged to a church, synagogue, or mosque. This is down from 70% in 1999 and represents a dip below 50% for the first time in the history of the survey question.[22]

The Surgeon General's report concludes that only 16% of Americans reported a strong attachment to their local community in 2018, a number that continued to decline during the COVID-19 years. When combined with the decline in marriage and friendship over the same period, the pattern of sociocidal unraveling becomes even starker. To introduce his report the Surgeon General wrote a letter to the US public summarizing his personal reaction and deep concerns:

> When I first took office as Surgeon General in 2014, I didn't view loneliness as a public health concern. But that was before I embarked on a cross-country listening tour, where I heard stories from my fellow Americans that surprised me. People began to tell me they felt isolated, invisible, and insignificant. Even when they couldn't put their finger on the word "lonely," time and time again, people of all ages and socioeconomic backgrounds, from every corner of the country, would tell me, "I have to shoulder all of life's burdens by myself," or "if I disappear tomorrow, no one will even notice."
>
> It was a lightbulb moment for me: social disconnection was far more common than I had realized.[23]

The Surgeon General then summarizes the data documenting the dramatic increases in social isolation and time spent alone, and feeling lonely:

> In recent years, about one-in-two adults in America reported experiencing loneliness. Social networks are getting smaller, and levels of social participation are declining … measures of social exposure obtained from 2003–2020 find that social isolation, measured by the average time spent alone, increased from 2003 (285-minutes/day, 142.5-hours/month) to 2019 (309-minutes/day, 154.5-hours/month) and continued to increase in 2020 (333-minutes/day, 166.5-hours/month).64 This represents an increase of 24 hours per month spent alone.[24]

Murthy summarizes the data in the chart shown in Figure 4.2, noting a precipitous decline well before COVID-19:

Social disconnection is rising across all major forms of social relations, and the Surgeon General is not including here the decline in workplace social relations that adds to the acute sense of breakdown in relationships and social life. While this is taking place across the whole population, certain large sectors are most impacted and report the most isolation and loneliness. These include the old, the young, racial minorities, and working-class and lower-income people, making it clear that the breaking of social relations is intertwined with economic and political inequalities unleashed by neoliberal capitalism as well as by new technologies.

This helps connect the bonfire of our culture and social life with the neoliberal and Far-Right populist bonfires raging in the economy since the late 20th century and surging

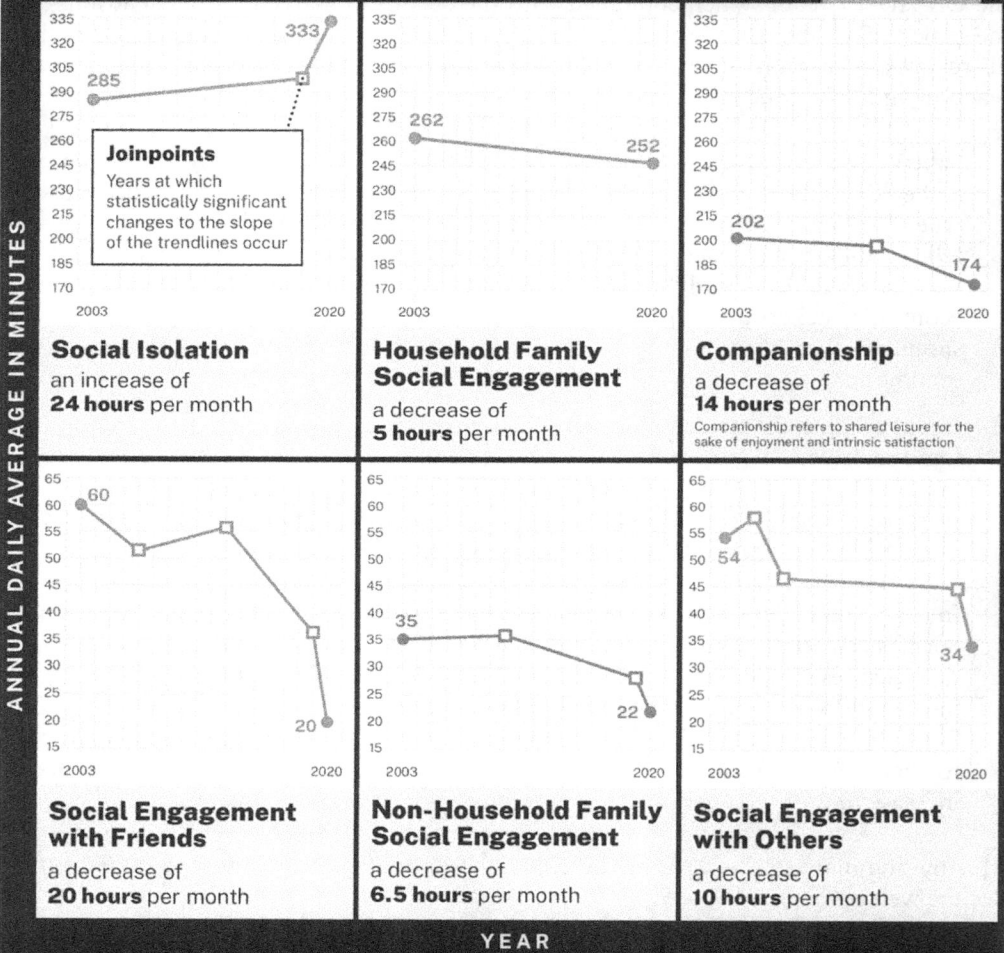

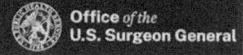

Figure 4.2 National Trends for Social Connection[25]

in our politics under Trumpism. Working people, minorities, and young people most hurt by the concentration of wealth and power are the same groups suffering the most from deteriorating social connections and social isolation. Social relations are eroding in and outside the workplace, increasing the attractions of authoritarian politics that promise a new community centered around its great leader. As Robert Putnam predicted in 2000, *Bowling Alone* is a symbol of the looming breakdown of civil society and voluntary associations that is the foundation of authoritarianism and helps explain Trump's re-election in 2024.

* * *

This hints at the class basis of social isolation, which Murthy documents but does not highlight enough. As the work on social capital by Pierre Bourdieu suggests, and as the corporate forces featured in the last two chapters support, the breakdown of social relations is fueled by neoliberal capitalist economic and class forces that put working-class people most at risk. A 2024 survey called the American Social Capital Survey, sponsored by the conservative American Economic Institute, makes the class dimensions and the distinctive vulnerabilities of working-class people a central concern. As summarized in a report by Daniel Cox and Sam Pressler called "Disconnected: The Growing Class Divide in American Civic Life," the data reinforce the notion of a US "Loneliness Epidemic" described by the Surgeon General but make clear that it is a class-related disaster:

> Americans have smaller social networks and fewer friends, and they spend less time with their friends, neighbors, and family members. This state of affairs has led Surgeon General Vivek Murthy to declare the United States is facing an "epidemic of loneliness and isolation."

But America's civic decline has not affected all groups equally. Americans with college degrees often reside in communities with abundant civic opportunities and thriving civic cultures. They participate in associational life at high rates and have robust social and friendship networks. In contrast, the relational lives of Americans without college degrees have contracted dramatically – compared to Americans with these degrees today and without them in the past. Two institutions that were formerly crucial sources of civic connectedness for less educated Americans, unions and churches, are now more likely to serve college graduates.

Other civic opportunities are becoming stratified along educational lines. Americans with a high-school education or less are more likely to live in civic deserts, lacking commercial places (e.g., coffee shops) and public places (e.g., community centers, parks, and libraries) that are hubs of community connection. Partly as a result, these Americans are less likely to participate in associational life and more likely to be socially isolated. As Timothy P. Carney writes in *Alienated America: Why Some Places Thrive While Others Collapse*, associational life has apparently become "a high-end good" that most people can't access. America's civic decline has not affected all groups equally.[26]

The Social Capital Survey, whose language of social capital and focus on the class basis of social disconnection is evocative of Pierre Bourdieu, offers interesting new insights into the ways that social disconnection operates across society with acute force against working-class people. It shows that part of the reason that working-class people are suffering more disconnection is not only the corporate attack on workplace relations and solidarity described in the last two chapters but the broader corporate assault on public space and public institutions such as public parks and gardens, public libraries, and community centers. The Social Capital Survey shows that the availability and use of these public facilities – where Americans have traditionally been able to make new connections and relations – is eroding, especially among non-college-educated working-class people. They note that public libraries and parks are vital parts of American social infrastructure where Americans connect and make friends but that "College graduates take advantage of them far more than anyone else."[27] They show that about half of college graduates meet and socialize in public parks and libraries while less than one-fourth of high-school graduates regularly do; indeed, among non-college-educated working-class Americans, at least a third say they never go to a public park or public library.[28] The report shows that in contrast to a majority of college-educated Americans, about one-third of working-class Americans say they have no access to at least ten types of public or community gathering spots where they could gather and meet with family, friends, or neighbors. It also documents that those with access to more public or community centers have more friends and social ties. Moreover, the same class differences play out in percentages of those who attend or host local meetings, volunteer in service organizations, or get involved in religious or civic associations. The majority of working-class Americans are in "civic deserts," where they do not engage in any community or local political associations or volunteer activities; in contrast, the main American "civic superheroes" are college-educated parents, with half of college-educated mothers and 42% of college-educated fathers volunteering in their community at least several times a year, making more friends and connections to fellow community members in the process.[29]

New York Times journalist, David French, summarizes the importance of the AEI Social Capital Survey and other surveys documenting similar class-based accounts of atomization, isolation, and loneliness:

> millions of working-class Americans experience a social reality different from that of their more educated peers. The lack of common spaces and common experiences means that isolation can become self-perpetuating.
>
> The friendship numbers are just as sobering. Americans of all stripes are reporting that they have declining numbers of friends, but the decline is most pronounced among high school graduates. Between 1990 and 2024, the percentage of college graduates who reported having zero close friends rose to 10 percent from 2 percent, which is upsetting enough. Among high school graduates, the percentage rose to a heartbreaking 24 percent from 3 percent.
>
> The news just keeps getting worse. In 1990, an impressive 49 percent of high school graduates reported having at least six close friends. By 2024, that percentage had been cut by more than half – to 17 percent. The percentage of college graduates with that many friends declined also, but only to 33 percent from 45 percent.
>
> The disappearance of friendship has profound consequences. According to the A.E.I. report, there is a class divide in the percentage of Americans who can rely on someone to give them a ride to the doctor, lend them a small amount of money in an emergency or offer a place to stay. Another way of putting this is that the Americans who are most vulnerable to losing the informal social safety net of friends and relatives may be the people who need it the most.
>
> It should be no surprise, then, that Americans at lower income levels report a far lower sense of belonging than those who are more prosperous. The Center for Inclusion and Belonging at the American Immigration Council, an immigration advocacy group, and Over Zero, an organization that studies and seeks to prevent identity-group-based violence, have created a comprehensive Belonging Barometer that measures the extent to which Americans feel a sense of belonging in their families,

among their friends and in their workplaces, their communities and the nation as a whole. In every category, those with fewer resources reported less belonging.[30]

This breakdown of social relations and growing loneliness creates anger and a sense of desperation, with dangerous political as well as personal consequences. A growing number of Americans, especially among working-class people, are experiencing societal and class-based isolation that breeds rage, grievance and a feeling of abandonment. This, in turn helps breed an Ik-like culture of survivalism, where people focus on themselves and view others as threats. This is a malignant narcissism and self-interest long normalized in America's individualistic culture and glamorized in the neo-liberal executive suites of Wall Street and Silicon Valley.

All of this normalizes political leaders like Trump, who biographers describe as sociopathic, self-interested, and bereft of mutualistic and caring personal relations. After the 2024 assassination attempt on his life, Trump was seen by his base as a martyr sacrificing himself for others, but Trump more accurately models the self-interested American tough guy, whose narcissistic personality and own grievances and self-centeredness reflect values that many ordinary people feel they need to embrace, Ik-like, to survive. The social disconnections documented by the Surgeon General also create the foundations for authoritarian politics, since the culture no longer supports the trust and bonds of civil society that political theorists such as de Tocqueville and Arendt have argued are required to support democracy and peaceful transitions of power. The monomaniacal egoism of an authoritarian like Trump promising to unify the population in a political community centered on himself, much like a king, appeals to people who are disconnected socially to the degree that Murthy documents, hungering for the strong populist ties to the community cementing around the great leader that they ultimately turned out for in large numbers to re-elect Trump.

Indeed, Trump's biggest supporters, those who travel around the country to see each rally during a campaign, make clear that they just love being with a big group of people who think like they do. A "front row Joe," as he described himself, says:

> I've been to a couple of rallies six days early but now I'm more like I get there 24 hours early. I don't have to be the first one in line because I know if I get there a day early I'll still get a good seat and possibly the front row.

> A Trump rally is fun. There's no violence. You're there with like-minded people. It's hard to explain unless you've been to one.[31]

Two sisters, who are called by fellow Trump fans the "Trump girls," went all over the country to attend as many rallies as possible. They also talk about the joy of just being with people like themselves:

> A Trump rally is always exciting. When you get a group of like-minded people together you can feel it in the air, the energy that he's bringing. People are happy. I've seen people stand in the rain all day long. I've seen them stand in snow and cold all day long just to see him. Cold that I couldn't even stand in – I had to get in the car, I was freezing to death.[32]

Washington Post journalist Michael Bender, has immersed himself for several years in Trump rallies. He highlights the social isolation that so many "Front Row Joes" experience – and writes about how their travel to one Trump rally after another not only helps quench the anger generated by their social condition but also salves the pain. The rallies "made their lives richer"; they "gave the Joes a reason to travel the country, staying at one another's homes, sharing hotel rooms and car-pooling. Two had married – and later divorced – by Trump's second year in office."[33]

Bender's observations square with the disconnection that Murthy describes among working Americans – and how it helps explain the intense attraction of Trump followers to Trump's rallies and to Trumpism itself. Many have characterized the hardcore Trumpist base as a cult. In his book, *The Cult of Trump*, leading cult analyst Steven Hassan, himself a former "Moonie" cult member, makes a powerful case that the Trump base demonstrates the key features of a cult, sacrificing their beliefs, autonomy, and entire minds to the control of the great leader.[34] Much of this, Hassan argues, is based on cultish influence strategies exploiting fear and social disconnection among Trump followers, who find in Trumpism part of the cause and much of the solution to the forces of disinformation and atomization that are engulfing them.

Extreme social disconnection is hitting kids and teenagers hardest today. This is centrally related to the rise of the Internet and social media, which have had a unique effect on the socialization and both economic and social life of young people. The sociocidal impact of social media is revolutionizing not just economic life, as discussed in the last chapter, but also social life. It breeds hyper-individualism and egoistic "look-at-me" virtual relations. As I discussed in Chapter 1, the great sociologist Emile Durkheim, living long before social media, warned of a whole generation – indeed, people of all generations across the whole society – being isolated, at greater risk of suicide and survival.[35]

Before documenting further the sociocidal threat of social media and young people, we should note that the Surgeon General has highlighted the breakdown of social relations because of its devastating effect on both physical and mental health, precisely what Durkheim predicted as a result of a breakdown in social bonds and a collapse of social solidarity.[36] Murthy is not a sociologist, but he captures one of the key findings highlighted by Durkheim: that social disconnection can lead to a panoply of illnesses that corrode quality of life and reduce life expectancy. In his famous book, *Suicide*, Durkheim wrote that social isolation and failure to be socially integrated into the community are major causes of suicide.[37]

As a public health physician, Murthy focuses on the dire health effects that social disintegration and isolation are now having. He notes that:

> Loneliness is far more than just a bad feeling – it harms both individual and societal health. It is associated with a greater risk of cardiovascular disease, dementia, stroke, depression, anxiety, and premature death. The mortality impact of being socially disconnected is similar to that caused by smoking up to 15 cigarettes a day, and even greater than that associated with obesity and physical inactivity.[38]

Those most at risk are experiencing a crisis of survival, evoking the perils of the Ik society discussed in the Introduction. Most Americans are not literally starving for food, like the Ik, but are suffering a kind of social starvation. As they lack the adequate economic and social support essential to both physical and mental well-being, they are vulnerable to the culture of the Ik, which anthropologist Colin Turnbull called "loveless." As noted earlier, the Ik had so little food that if they cared for others and tried to help them, they would exhaust the energy needed to find food for themselves and survive. In the US, the lack of relational or social food breeds the same egoistic focus on the self – and lack of capacity or desire to give to others – that is evocative of the loveless Ik.

* * *

In the last chapter, we discussed the work of scholars like Sherry Turkle and Shoshanna Zuboff, who have pioneered the analysis of social media as a new world of surveillance, dehumanization, and social disconnection. We now look at how the cultural bonfire of egoism, self-interest, and survivalism is fed by social media. As young people grow up glued to TikTok, Instagram, and other social media platforms, they are already experiencing a disproportionately high erosion of face-to-face social relations and are destined for a life built around social media with intense sociocidal threats that dispose them toward "me over we."

The irony here is that a whole new generation has grown up on social media, with parents and kids flocking to it as a cure for isolation and a magical way to build new social relationships and connections. As shown in the last chapter, this ideology, heavily underwritten by Silicon Valley, is not entirely wrong. Social media gives virtually every young person the promise of reaching out to thousands of new connections and friends, and staying in touch with them at any time of day or night and at great distances. This is, after all, built and sold as a new communications technology that revolutionizes our ability to "stay in touch" and to sustain social connections unimaginable before social media.

Moreover, it is true that social media does, in fact, open up doors to a communications transformation that connects millions of people with each other. Under democratic control, it may, in the end, prove a partial but potent remedy to sociocide. This illustrates one of the great contradictions in the sociocidal revolution: some of the key technologies and social forces fueling sociocide today could ultimately help save us from the disaster.

But the current corporate-controlled social media system is proving to be a recipe for disconnecting people. In my own conversations with college students, a growing number tell me that they are looking to limit or find ways to stop using social media altogether, despite the power of the screen addiction. Some say social media makes them feel bad or insecure because they are not certain of who reads their posts, how to interpret social media responses, and who is sending them feeds. Competition to get noticed or get responses that make them feel validated is part of their online world. Many have said their trust in people has declined, feeling that they are an online target of corporate influencers or AI deep-fake generated messengers that could get them into trouble or risk their reputation.

Many students say these concerns are moving them away from posting to relatively anonymous large groups of "friends." They now send mainly text messages on social media to a small group of "real" friends whom they know personally and communicate with offline as well. Many do this to try to fulfill the promise of real social relationships that are reciprocal and emotionally nourishing – and it works for some of them.

It is easy for anyone to get caught up in the chase for endless online friends on traditional social media – and hard to disengage. One of the nubs of the problem is what it means to be a "friend" on social media. On a platform like Facebook, one can be connected with scores – or hundreds or thousands – of friends one hardly knows. and with whom one never communicates offline. On Instagram, one can post images or videos, largely of oneself, that are affirmed by "likes" of one form or another and growing followers. But since one does not know personally many in one's online feed, this can easily become a confusing and self-defeating chase for attention, often increasing deep insecurity, that never translates into the growth of meaningful relationships or real friends.

While Facebook helped inaugurate the language of "friends" and "likes" on social media, it appropriated the vocabulary of real offline social life. But the structure of such relationships, by virtue of their technologically structured quantity and quality, guided by algorithms produced by the corporate platform, made them fundamentally different. In traditional posts on Facebook or Instagram, the user sits alone with his or her computer or phone, frequently sending short messages, pictures, or videos mainly about oneself. The response can be some form of comment or "like," of various lengths, or silence. But posting does not routinely elicit a reciprocal conversation normalized in face-to-face talk. The message of such posts is structured by the technology to be "look-at-me," a communication often designed to share information about oneself and elicit affirmation, approval, envy, or envy and admiration of oneself, or perhaps elicit sympathy for one's problems. Such egoism is the nature of the beast of traditional posts, structuring social media as a vehicle for turning attention to oneself and gaining a sense of security or social worth.

Of course, in offline social life, relationships can take a similar egoistic form. In my book, *The Pursuit of Attention,* I discussed the rising tide in the late 20th century of "conversational narcissism," a form of conversation in which people pursue attention rather than give it.[39] Conversational narcissism uses "shift-responses" in conversation rather than "support-responses." A shift-response is a statement about oneself; a support-response is a rejoinder to the other person that keeps the attention on them rather than shifting the conversation back to oneself. If I say to you, "I had a tough time at work today," and you respond by saying "Yeah, it's terrible, I had the same problem" – and then go on to talk about your own problems, you are triggering the classic narcissistic shift-response, which the other party responds to with his or her own shift-response, setting up a nuanced jockeying for who can turn the conversation toward oneself. This brute turn of conversation to oneself, where I do the talking and you have to listen, is done with polite face-saving rituals. People appear to offer a truly nourishing gesture, while deftly turning attention back to the self. Conversation becomes a means not of building a relationship but rather building the self or ego, a cultivation of the "me" rather than the "we."

In conversational narcissism, both parties use shift-responses and avoid support-responses. It is the offline version of the look-at-me relation on social media, and it has been normalized in the individualistic culture that I saw emerging in the economic and cultural revolution of the late 20th century. Other analysts, such as Christopher Lasch in his book, *The Culture of Narcissism,* and Phillip Slater in his work, *The Pursuit of Loneliness,* were making a similar argument about a more extreme individualistic, narcissistic culture.[40] But normalizing the pursuit of attention, whether online or offline, to alleviate the insecurity and hurt of isolation and lack of real relationships simply fuels more narcissism and breakdown of nourishing relationships. By embracing conversational narcissism, people are learning newly accepted cultural tools for gaining social support that actually disconnect them further from others, making them more alone.

An economic analysis helps frame this new sociocidal culture in the context of the market. Neoliberalism emerged as a corporate system for extending the ideal of the market as the perfect form of all social relationships. From Adam Smith to Milton Friedman, the neoliberal economic founders sought, with great success, to portray the self-interested behavior of people in the market as the basis of the common good. In this context, it is not surprising that conversational narcissism and the culture of the egoistic pursuit of attention would explode as part of the neoliberal triumph of the late 20th century. People were learning to view social relationships as a way to brand and affirm themselves by pursuing attention, socialized to the ideal that egoistic market behavior was the instrument for both economic success and social connection and worth. Social media provided a new technological vehicle for normalizing self-interest and the pursuit of attention in every form of both social and political relationships.

The pursuit of attention is now not only structured into the economy but also modeled in the political world. No political personality or leader has displayed the naked pursuit of attention as aggressively and successfully as Donald Trump. He is the ultimate political narcissist and the political leader capturing more celebrity and public attention than any of his predecessors. Trump reveled in being perhaps the world's most famous man, the perfect politician for the age of social media, celebrity, and cultural narcissism. Trump has reaped more attention on social media and in the larger culture than any political leader in US history.

Trump's rallies are all about himself. He talks about his "luxurious" hair, his perfect golf game, his endless business success, his toughness, his martyrdom, his grievances against everyone who is disloyal to him, his passion for revenge and retribution, and his unprecedented celebrity. Trump's politics are the unabashed, unashamed politics of narcissism, delivered nakedly on Truth Social, his own social media, and on X, the favored mass platform owned by Trumpist ally and endorser, Elon Musk, reaching hundreds of millions around the world.

Trump's model of political communication thus fully embodies the look-at-me relations of social media and the larger culture of narcissism. It is a one-way turn of political attention from constituents to the great leader and his own ego and power. Trump has literally turned politics into the pursuit of attention. Trumpism is the new hyper-individualistic American Dream run wild in the political sphere. Yet, it should be clear that his fans' shared adoration and love of him bring them together in a shared giving of attention to the great man; ironically, Trump's narcissistic pursuit of attention in his rallies became the basis of a fervent community – happy to join together to give all their attention to him.

The invention of social media became the perfect technological instrument for transforming social connections and relations into a dominant and institutionalized culture of "me" over "we." The sociopathic pursuit of attention that I chronicled in the 1980s was becoming widespread, modeled on the spread of the market and the "marketing of the self."

Leading analysts of social media, such as the communications scholar Sherry Turkle has argued that online relations are stripping "the raw human elements" out of social relationships.[41] The Surgeon General, Vivek Murthy, spotlights the crisis of youth, the demographic most deeply engaged with and shaped by social media. Murthy reports that "(the) percentage of teens ages 13 to 17 years who say they are online 'almost constantly' has doubled since 2015."[42] Among teens ages 13 to 17 years, 95% report using social media as of 2022, with more than half reporting it would be hard to give up social media.[43]

Young people aged 15 to 24 spent in 2023 a remarkable 70% less time with friends in person than in 2003. Other research shows that young people today are more isolated and lonely than any other age group.

• According to a study by Cigna, nearly half of all Americans report feeling lonely some-times or always. The same study found that Generation Z (ages 18–22) is the loneliest generation, with 79% reporting feelings of loneliness.[44]

Murthy focuses especially on the rising rate of young people with mental health prob-lems, including high levels of depression, anxiety, phobias, insomnia, distrust of others, and loneliness. But it is a trend across all age groups in the population, and he reports that the social disconnections and loneliness of youth, as well as among other age groups, have been linked by many studies to the rise of social media and other online Silicon Valley technologies, noting that:

> In a US-based study, participants who reported using social media for more than two hours a day had about double the odds of reporting increased perceptions of social isolation compared to those who used social media for less than 30 minutes per day … Additionally, targets of online harassment report feelings of increased loneliness, isolation, and relationship problems, as well as lower self-esteem and trust in others.

Murthy suggests different ways that social media, while seeming to help people con-nect and sometimes succeeding in doing so, is a technology that seems to create forms of connection that resemble disconnection. His view that the younger online generation is at high risk of a rising epidemic tide of loneliness has been confirmed by a multitude of other studies, as summarized by tech journalist Brian Chen, in the *New York Times*.

> Over the summer, Laura Marciano, a researcher at Harvard, interviewed 500 teenag-ers for a continuing study investigating the link between technology and loneliness. The results were striking.
>
> For several weeks, the teenagers, who were recruited with the help of Instagram influencers, answered a questionnaire three times a day about their social interac-tions. Each time, more than 50 percent said they had not spoken to anyone in the last hour, either in person or online.
>
> To put it another way, even though the teenagers were on break from school and spending plenty of time on social media apps, most of them were not socializing at all.
>
> Americans now spend more time alone, have fewer close friendships and feel more socially detached from their communities than they did 20 years ago. One in two adults reports experiencing loneliness, the physiological distress that people endure from social isolation.[45]

Reviewing a spate of other studies on the same subject, Cheng found strong correlations between the amount of time spent online and feelings of disconnection and isolation among young people. Cheng concludes that the studies mostly show how social media helps breed social disconnection and isolation:

• On social media apps like Instagram, many fall into the trap of comparing themselves with others and feeling that they are lagging behind their peers.
• Text messaging, by far the most popular form of digital communication, could be creating a barrier to authentic connection.

• And, perhaps unsurprisingly, some people who felt lonely also exhibited addictive personalities – in this case, to streaming videos – that kept them indoors.[46]

This reinforces our earlier analysis of how social media fosters a competitive and narcissistic "pursuit of attention" online, a devastating technological contribution to the larger sociocidal and policidal forces helping Trumpism gain deeper control of the nation in his second term. Social media is not, however, the prime force behind social disconnection and looming American sociocide. Rather, it is both a cause and a reflection of the larger economic and cultural forces turning social relationships into a brewing cauldron of "look-at-me" relations modeled on neoliberal markets and a hyper-individualistic American Dream. But while both the economic and cultural sociocidal threats are dire, counter-trends toward community and democracy persist in strands of the culture, economy, and politics.

* * *

Weakening of traditional forms of marriage and other social relations may reflect not just sociocidal destruction but changes aimed at creating more equal and, indeed, more liberating social relations and lives. This includes a recognition that many people, including women – including many career-women with the financial means to support themselves – are choosing to live on their own rather than endure unhappy patriarchal marriages. Many young women and men, in particular, are freely choosing not to enter into traditional marriages or families. Many young people, who are marrying at a far lower rate than earlier generations, may be choosing "parallel lives," as my students call it. This means that they seek close relations outside of traditional ties, which are seen as sexist, limiting of intimacy, or, alternatively, economically unaffordable.

This is an important caveat throughout the book. Weakening traditional ties does not necessarily involve sociocide if people are consciously choosing to live or work in new forms of social relations or alternative ways reflecting new values. I shall argue that a great deal of work, family, and political erosion is sociocidal, but show that the persistence and rise of democratic and sociophiliac forces may help restore sustainable relations and create different models of intimacy and connection than traditional forms. As shown in the last chapter, these arise from social instincts, democratic civic associations, and social and political movements that have flourished historically in the US and survive as powerful antidotes to sociocide. They are sometimes sources of solidarity arising contradictorily from sociocidal forces themselves, including forces lying latent and already surfacing in the new world of social media itself.

The critical importance of social media in the 2024 Harris and Trump campaigns remains powerful evidence of the strength of the contradictory forces – the extreme tension between social disconnection and social connection, between democracy and authoritarianism – both in social media and in the general culture in an increasingly online society. As discussed at the end of the last chapter, the Harris campaign initially came to electric life online, rocketing out of nowhere because of the power of social media to connect people socially and politically, in a deeply visceral way. Harris seemed initially in many ways the most important social media candidate in American history, a woman whose personality, age, and politics enabled her to reach many alienated and marginalized groups – and especially young people in the general population – to model a culture and politics based on connection with others, caring, and democracy, of social media and the new communication and political power of the online world that has, contradictorily, also helped fuel disconnection, egoism and Trumpist neo-fascism. As discussed in the last chapter, Trump ultimately leaned into the online world with more success than Harris, diving deep into the manoverse and reaching the millions of online young and middle-aged male and working-class voters who carried him to victory.

The cultural and online contradictions of sociocide surfaced in many different ways in the 2024 campaign. Harris' personality stood in stark contrast to Trump as the authoritarian and narcissistic bully, thinking only of himself and psychologically driven by grievance and rage. Harris was quickly seen as – and widely reported to be – a caring person, whose concern for others helped catalyze the support for her that emerged immediately after she declared her candidacy for president. This reflected a key cultural contradiction of a society threatened by the sociocide of hyper-individualism, competition, and increased isolation. While sociocidal culture galvanized people attracted to the anger and narcissistic egoism of Trump, it also bred a deep hunger in the population for values of caring and giving. It attracted people who reflected what millions felt was missing in their lives or in US society: the desire to bridge differences with others and to connect with them in a caring way.

Harris put at the center of her message that her race was not about herself; it was all about the American people, regardless of race, ethnicity, religion, gender, or age. Her campaign was to bring everyone together, in the same way that so many different racial, ethnic, and economic identities were bridged in herself and her own biography. These elements of Harris's personality and politics – the exact opposite of Trump's, as well as in direct opposition to the dominant culture of extreme individualism, egoism, and angry division – show how sociocide and policide can fuel a public hunger to reconstruct the civil society, love, and democracy they are undermining. The power of social media, while it ultimately helped power Trump to re-election, also initially helped Harris's messages of bringing everyone together in a "movement" to rebuild community and democracy feel real and magnetic through the cultural power –the videos, the memes, the emotional outbursts – of social media itself. Her campaign, in its few weeks, sparked a fire not seen in young voters since Obama.

In the first couple of weeks of her campaign, headlines blared "Gen-Z voters spread the 'Kamalove.'"[47] Gen Z immediately launched its own campaign for Harris, with thousands of young people attending a virtual and in-person summit led by Voters of Tomorrow.[48] Calls for young people to "break Zoom" in the same spirit and numbers as Black women and Black men, white women, and "white dudes" radiated across TikTok, Instagram, and LinkedIn. "Do you feel it too?" Brian Baez posted to almost 100,000 viewers on TikTok – and polls suggested they did, with Harris a few days after announcing her candidacy running up a 60–40 lead over Trump among young people compared to a 53–47 Biden edge.[49] Like Trump fans, Harris fans were now reveling in the joy of being part of an exhilarated political community, with many feeling the same sort of deep pleasure in being in the company of others after feeling isolated and despairing.

None of this early and brief cultural online-driven response was powerful enough, in light of her other fatal failures, to challenge the corporate Robber Baron oligarchy and the deep legitimate economic grievances of the Trump working-class base – to avoid the defeat she suffered at Trump's hands. Nonetheless, it was a powerful demonstration of the contradictions of both sociocide and social media. The despair, cynicism, loneliness, fear, and rage evoked by the sociocidal breakdown of social relationships also sparked an enormous hunger for joy and other positive feelings. Moreover, despite social media's own breeding of distrust and fear, it also amplified the positive feelings spilling over when Harris announced her candidacy. Gen Z may be the demographic most harmed by sociocidal forces and social media, but it may also be the group most mobilized and empowered by social media, as in the immediate wildfire response to the Harris campaign, to rally together online, create new youth communities, and add enormous new force to the pro-democracy movement. In a new candidate representing a Democratic Party with a progressive populist agenda seeking to counter Far-Right authoritarianism – a party and a candidate with a Left populism that could end corporate oligarchy and promote both economic and political democracy – the online world might help boost such a party and candidate to victory in 2028 or beyond.

Notes

1 Charles Derber, *The Wilding of America*. NY: Worth, 2014. Charles Derber, *Sociopathic Society*. NY: Routledge, 2013.
2 Emile Durkheim, *The Division of Labor*. Digipress Annotated Edition, 2002. Emile Durkheim, *Suicide*. 2nd edition. NY: Harper and Row, 2013. Steven Lukes, *Emile Durkheim*. Harmondsworth: Penguin, 1973.
3 Emile Durkheim, *Suicide*. 2nd edition. NY: Harper and Row, 2013; Steven Lukes, *Emile Durkheim*. Harmondsworth: Penguin, 1973.
4 Colin Turnbull, *The Mountain People*. NY: Touchstone, 1987.
5 Charles Derber, *The Wilding of America*. NY: Worth, 2014.
6 Charles Derber, *The Wilding of America*. NY: Worth, 2014.
7 Ipsos, "Over Half of Americans Report Feeling Like No One Knows Them Well." May 1, 2018, ipsos.com
8 Steven Zauderer, "49 Loneliness Statistics: July 23, 2023." crossrivertherapy.com. See also "Loneliness in the United States." RootsOfLoneliness.com
9 Steven Zauderer, "49 Loneliness Statistics: July 23, 2023." crossrivertherapy.com. See also "Loneliness in the United States." RootsOfLoneliness.com
10 For another analysis reporting different findings, see Claude Fischer, *Still Connected*. NY: Russell Sage Foundation, January 1, 2011.
11 Durkheim, *Division of Labor*; Emile Durkheim, *Suicide*. 2nd edition. NY: Harper and Row, 2013; Lukes, *Durkheim*.
12 Pew Research Center, "Analysis of 1900–2000 Decennial Census and 2010 and 2021 American Community Survey." *Pew Research Center*, 2021, pewresearch.org
13 Pew Research Center, "Striking Findings from 2023." December 8, 2023, pewresearch.org
14 Census Bureau, "Census Bureau Releases New Estimates on America's Family and Living Arrangements." November 17, 2022, census.gov
15 Jannae Bowens, "Rising Trend of Living Solo." *CBS Austin*, July 10, 2023, cbsaustin.com. See also Bella DePaulo, *Single at Heart*. NY: Apollo Publishers, 2023.
16 Charles Derber, *The Wilding of America*. NY: Worth, 2014.
17 Vivek Murthy, *Our Epidemic of Loneliness and Isolation*. US Surgeon General's Advisory. Department of Health and Human Services, 2023, hhs.gov
18 Sherry Turkle, *Alone Together*. NY: Basic Books, 2017.
19 Vivek Murthy, *Our Epidemic of Loneliness and Isolation*. US Surgeon General's Advisory. Department of Health and Human Services, 2023, hhs.gov
20 Vivek Murthy, *Our Epidemic of Loneliness and Isolation*. US Surgeon General's Advisory. Department of Health and Human Services, 2023, hhs.gov
21 Vivek Murthy, *Our Epidemic of Loneliness and Isolation*. US Surgeon General's Advisory. Department of Health and Human Services, 2023, hhs.gov
22 Vivek Murthy, *Our Epidemic of Loneliness and Isolation*. US Surgeon General's Advisory. Department of Health and Human Services, 2023, hhs.gov
23 Vivek Murthy, *Our Epidemic of Loneliness and Isolation*. US Surgeon General's Advisory. Department of Health and Human Services, 2023, hhs.gov
24 Vivek Murthy, *Our Epidemic of Loneliness and Isolation*. US Surgeon General's Advisory. Department of Health and Human Services, 2023, hhs.gov

25 Vivek Murthy, *Our Epidemic of Loneliness and Isolation*. US Surgeon General's Advisory. Department of Health and Human Services, 2023, hhs.gov

26 Daniel A. Cox and Sam Pressler, "Disconnected: The Growing Class Divide in American Civic Life: Findings from the 2024 American Social Capital Survey." *AEI, Survey Center on American Life*, August 22, 2024, Americansurveycenter.org

27 Daniel A. Cox and Sam Pressler, "Disconnected: The Growing Class Divide in American Civic Life: Findings from the 2024 American Social Capital Survey." *AEI, Survey Center on American Life*, August 22, 2024, Americansurveycenter.org

28 Daniel A. Cox and Sam Pressler, "Disconnected: The Growing Class Divide in American Civic Life: Findings from the 2024 American Social Capital Survey." *AEI, Survey Center on American Life*, August 22, 2024, Americansurveycenter.org

29 Daniel A. Cox and Sam Pressler, "Disconnected: The Growing Class Divide in American Civic Life: Findings from the 2024 American Social Capital Survey." *AEI, Survey Center on American Life*, August 22, 2024, Americansurveycenter.org

30 David French, "The Loneliness Epidemic Has a Cure." *NY Times*, September 1, 2024, nytimes.com

31 David Smith, "Inside the MAGA Mind: Trump's Most Dedicated Fans Explain Their Fervor." *The Guardian*, August 3, 2024, theguardian.com

32 David Smith, "Inside the MAGA Mind: Trump's Most Dedicated Fans Explain Their Fervor." *The Guardian*, August 3, 2024, theguardian.com

33 Michael Bender, "To Trump's Hard-core Supporters, His Rallies Weren't Politics. They Were Life." *Washington Post*, July 16, 2021. washingtonpost.com. See also David French, "The Loneliness Epidemic Has a Cure." *New York Times*, September 1, 2024.

34 Steven Hassan, *The Cult of Trump*. NY: Simon and Schuster, 2024.

35 Emile Durkheim, *Suicide*. 2nd edition. NY: Harper and Row, 2013; Lukes, *Emile Durkheim*. Harmondsworth: Penguin, 1973.

36 Emile Durkheim, *Suicide*. 2nd edition. NY: Harper and Row, 2013.

37 Emile Durkheim, *Suicide*. 2nd edition. NY: Harper and Row, 2013.

38 Vivek Murthy, *Our Epidemic of Loneliness and Isolation*. US Surgeon General's Advisory. Department of Health and Human Services, 2023, hhs.gov

39 Charles Derber, *The Pursuit of Attention*. 2nd edition. NY: Oxford University Press, 2000.

40 Christopher Lasch, *The Culture of Narcissism*. NY: W.W. Norton rev. edition, 1991. Philip Slater, *The Pursuit of Loneliness*.

41 Sherry Turkle, *Alone Together*. NY: Basic Books, 2017.

42 Vivek Murthy, *Our Epidemic of Loneliness and Isolation*. US Surgeon General's Advisory. Department of Health and Human Services, 2023, hhs.gov

43 Vivek Murthy, *Our Epidemic of Loneliness and Isolation*. US Surgeon General's Advisory. Department of Health and Human Services, 2023, hhs.gov

44 Steven Zauderer, "49 Loneliness Statistics: July 23, 2023." crossrivertherapy.com. See also "Loneliness in the United States." RootsOfLoneliness.com

45 Brian X. Chen, "How Tech Created a 'Recipe for Loneliness.'" *New York Times*, November 10, 2024, nytimes.org

46 Brian X. Chen, "How Tech Created a 'Recipe for Loneliness.'" *New York Times*, November 10, 2024, nytimes.org

47 Lauren Gambine, "Gen-Z Voters Spread the 'Kamalove' as Harris's Popularity Earns Youth Support." *The Guardian*, July 27, 2024.

48 Lauren Gambine, "Gen-Z Voters Spread the 'Kamalove' as Harris's Popularity Earns Youth Support." *The Guardian*, July 27, 2024.

49 Brian Baez, posted on TikTok, July 28, 2024. Erica Pandey, "Exclusive Poll: Harris Opens Up Early Edge with Young Voters." *Axios*, July 29, 2024, axios.com

5 The bonfire of environmental devastation

Climate change, COVID-19, and the sociocidal shock doctrine

Environmentalists are familiar with the concept of "ecocide," the destruction of the environment. But they should be just as familiar with the idea of "sociocide" because climate change and other manifestations of environmental death are systemically and tightly intertwined with the breakdown of social relations and society. Climate change is the most widely recognized existential threat to all social life, and the analysis of climate change as a series of escalating and potentially irreversible tipping points toward ecocide helps vividly illustrate how the peril of sociocide unfolds. Moreover, climate change, while fueled by our corporate system and reflecting the sociocide created by overproduction for the private market and the hyper-individualism of the market itself, is also one of the greatest forces fueling sociocide, and perhaps the most catastrophic, since it endangers the existence not just of social connections and relations in the US but of all societies. As people compete for land and resources to survive, they enter a new, increasingly desperate sociocidal competition as floods, drought, extreme heat, and other manifestations of climate change make all resources increasingly scarce. This turns more and more of the world toward a globalizing "loveless" culture of the IK, where the overwhelming quest for survival overcomes the desire and ability to care for others.

The US and other wealthy nations created climate change through their intense fossil-fuel-based development driven by profit at the expense of the environment. In the US, the neoliberal regime beginning in the Reagan era incentivized unlimited production for profit and unsustainable mass consumption, leading America to create more per capita carbon emissions than any other country. The US is now seeing its own environmental crisis of unsustainable production and mass consumption come scarily home. One need only think of the fires, floods, droughts, and extreme heat devastating much of California in the early 2020s, forcing Americans to realize that their homes and livelihoods are already at risk from environmental destruction. Many people all across the US are now forced to leave overheated, flooded, or burned-down communities and become climate migrants themselves, competing with other at-risk Americans for a place elsewhere. Floridians, New Yorkers, Louisianans, and even inland Kentuckians can't get insurance for their homes, which insurance companies see as too risky to cover.[1] Texans and Arizonans can't easily survive the extreme heat in summer and brutal cold in winter. Sociocidal climate disasters fed by unsustainable production and mass consumption cause newly scarce inhabitable land, and shortages of water and food. Family, friendship, and community relations are stressed, sometimes to the breaking point, related to the limits and cost of inhabitable land, food, and social support.

Pandemics are also fueled by globalizing neoliberal capitalism, in large part through the expansion of Big Agriculture, mining, and logging companies into more and more

DOI: 10.4324/9781003491798-6

wilderness and other public and private land. This brings humans into contact with animals and plants that thrive in wilderness and harbor viruses that can easily spread to invading humans. Industrial capitalism fueled pandemics like typhoid, tuberculosis, and cholera and is now fueling avian and bird flu, Zika, and COVID-19. COVID-19 made Americans viscerally aware of capitalist and climate-fueled pandemics, as people isolated themselves from 2019 to 2023 while COVID-19 raged, and workplaces, schools, and other public centers closed. This intensified a longer-term trend for students to attend school less frequently and for workplaces to go remote. The general lack of public spaces in a market-centered American society intersected with COVID-19 and other pandemics to drive people away from limited public space toward more and more privatized space. In Trump's second term, the individualistic culture of the corporate oligarchy will intensify the decline of public goods and public space essential to a healthy environment, reflected in recent decades in the acceleration of mass consumerism and an unsustainable suburban and car-based lifestyle that seeks to emulate the opulent lifestyle and expensive private space of the ultra-rich. Both the climate and public health threats are now escalating to extreme levels in the second Trump term, reflecting Trumpist sociocide and policide that spell more neoliberal deregulated fossil-fuel-driven production and mass consumerism, accelerating environmental and public health death for millions of Americans and people around the world.

* * *

Climate change fuels and reflects many of the sociocidal economic and cultural forces that we have discussed in earlier chapters. Both can be seen as the fruit of 21st-century American neoliberal capitalism and its hyper-individualistic culture. Climate threats are amplified by the resurgent anti-government and anti-science politics of the Far-Right, and have now risen to an extreme emergency under Trump and our empowered corporate oligarchy in his second term.

The shift from a sociopathic industrial system spewing vast but manageable pollution into a sociocidal economic regime grew out of the centuries-long movement from early industrial capitalism to the 21st-century global neoliberal system. Climate researchers, most notably those associated with the Intergovernmental Panel on Climate Change (IPCC), have been tracking climate change levels and risks since at least the mid-20th century. They have established that the rise of Western industrial capitalism was a critical tipping point. Since 1750, just prior to the Industrial Revolution and the beginning of industrial capitalism, CO_2 has risen 20,000 times higher because of human activity. In the almost 300 years since 1750, when CO_2 ppm was under 280 ppm, the level rose almost 50% beyond the earlier feared threshold of 350 ppm to 414 ppm, the highest in 14 million years. A critical turning point was 1980, with half of that increase happening since 1980 and a fourth since 2000. A torrent of extreme weather events since 2020 suggests we are in the middle of another extremely perilous tipping point. 2023 was the world's hottest year by far, and 2024 was even hotter. The ten hottest years since 1850 have all happened in the last decade.[2] In May 2024, hundreds of IPCC scientists issued their most dire warning, with 80% surveyed expecting temperature rises blasting past IPCC targets to 4.5°F degrees above preindustrial levels this century leading to:

> a "semi-dystopian" future, with famines, conflicts and mass migration, driven by heatwaves, wildfires, floods and storms of an intensity and frequency far beyond those that have already struck.

Numerous experts said they had been left feeling hopeless, infuriated and scared by the failure of governments to act despite the clear scientific evidence provided.[3]

Climate scientists were clear before 1980 that an existential climate threat loomed, but it appeared to be associated with sociopathic forces that could be curbed well before societal extinction. Since 1980, and most notably in the 21st century, the scientific community has been reporting extreme climate data that are sociocidal because the level, scale, and frequency of climate tipping points and disasters appear to be reaching a level of irreversibility, involving either significant decline in life possibilities or full-scale sociocide, in which competition for personal survival destroys social solidarity, creating dangerously atomized communities and polarized nations.

In 1981, the Reagan Revolution unleashed deeply sociopathic and ecocidal forms of neoliberal capitalism, including privatization, corporate deregulation, and subsidized corporate expansion into the Global South in environmentally unprotected, pollution-friendly zones. In the last decade of the 20th century, President Clinton explicitly announced that the Democratic Party was abandoning the New Deal's "big government" and embracing its own version of neoliberalism.

As neoliberalism became bipartisan, early 21st-century US neoliberalism triggered new climate tipping points. It fueled a new sociocidal generation of Big Ag land grabs to expand into wilderness and deplete animal species, as well as intensify mono-crop soil depletion and spray more chemicals to increase profits. Big Oil and Big Gas – firms such as Exxon, Chevron, and ConocoPhillips – increased oil drilling and methane-intense gas fracking to ensure windfall profits before climate regulation could curb their wealth buried in the fossil-fuel energy infrastructure on which US capitalism was built.

By the early 2000s, when I was living in the small suburban Boston town of Dedham, Massachusetts, large pipeline companies were building gas pipelines through the town, putting junctures where gas was most likely to leak next to town stone quarries surrounded by homes, schools, and senior housing. Dedham residents began protesting by climbing into and laying down inside the new pipeline trenches being dug near the quarries, recognizing that leaking methane could trigger larger dynamite explosions in the quarries, killing many people nearby in schools and homes. Dedhamites were waking up to the reality of the American climate-fueled emergency. By 2025, total US carbon emissions are projected to be 1.972 billion metric tons of CO_2, of which 1.180 billion tons would be produced by gas, as reported by the Union of Concerned Scientists.[4]

All of this reflects the lobbying and political power of the big fossil-fuel companies that I call the Carbon-Industrial Complex (CIC). Huge CIC firms like Koch Industries have successfully lobbied to increase the enormous government subsidies to Big Oil and Gas, now far exceeding $20 billion annually and a central driver of climate change. In discussing his recent book, *Kochland*, Christopher Leonard shows how Koch is creating a "kochamamie" democracy, in which massive Big Oil donations have levels of influence "that they haven't had in 100 years."[5]

While Big Oil and Gas have aggressively promoted the idea of their transition to green energy, recent legal suits have demonstrated that the CIC companies make clear they have too much profit invested in the fossil-fuel infrastructure to forgo it. On October 22, 2019, the New York Attorney General filed a lawsuit against Exxon, charging them with lying to shareholders about the true environmental cost of their business strategy, while also lying to the public about the health and climate effects of their policies. By 2024, Exxon and other Big Oil and Gas firms were facing dozens of lawsuits from both shareholders and public citizens, accusing them of the same lies. In response, Exxon filed a January 2024 legal suit against its own shareholders and investors as "activist" disrupters.[6]

The rest of corporate America is watching closely; as one observer notes, few firms "have shown credible plans to achieve their (climate) targets."[7] Such sociopathic corporate greed bodes poorly for limiting climate change and preventing ecocide – and it will not be new or surprising to many readers. However, what may surprise many are the intimate connections between climate change, ecocide, and sociocide. Climate change reflects and fuels major sociocidal forces that are breaking social relations apart and creating a more isolated, fearful, and angry population.

Sociocidal environmental climate catastrophe grows out of the neoliberal crusade to maximize profit without letting environmental or social "externalities" stop the profit juggernaut. The sociocide is also cultural, embodied in the new extreme American Dream of hyper-individualism and mass consumption bred by neoliberalism and now sweeping through the population.

Remember that neoliberalism is the deification of the market and the systemic imperative to sell and buy as much as possible in the market. The neoliberal culture of "everything for sale" takes the form of a new and extreme American Dream that goes beyond traditional individualism to hyper-egoistic behavior in all spheres of life, a force incompatible with reciprocal and humanizing social relations. Since the mid-20th century, this has taken the form of an automobile and suburban lifestyle in which maximizing one's own private land and space for comfort and status replaces the collective security of public space and public goods, including sustainable urban housing and public transit. In neoliberal 21st-century America, "living big" in private suburban or exurban houses with big lots and large commutes is accelerated, creating a lifestyle organized around separating oneself from others rather than living close together in dense, urban, and publicly subsidized communities. This sociocidal lifestyle rooted in neoliberal values of competition and greed is now fueling new levels of overproduction and mass consumerism that are accelerating climate change, with the threat of irreversible climate change looming over us in the next few decades.

The key to the sociocidal threat here is that as climate change gets worse, the competition to make more money and win the consumer race to "live big" becomes more difficult and poisonous. As climate change makes inhabitable land, food, and safe homes scarcer and more expensive, people have to fight harder to "make it" and win big, satisfying their bigger egos and need for more validation. This requires a willingness to engage in fiercer and more aggressive behavior to defeat competitors in the workplace and the market. It is something that I have seen my students struggle with as they seek to sustain moral values in a cut-throat corporate and market environment. More than one-quarter of the undergraduates in my university are becoming finance, business, and economic majors, looking for the big money and the high life on Wall Street. The egoism required to "win" and gain the great wealth and status always valued in American society now becomes more anti-social, increasingly limiting the ability of competitors to empathize with and care for each other, even when they need and want to do so.

As corporate elites and working people reshape themselves to make as much money as possible and consume more, they unwittingly intensify the climate crisis. Modeling themselves on the extreme self-interest displayed by Big Oil and Gas, they don't feel it is their responsibility to limit their own income or consumption to help prevent climate change. The cultural quest for more consumption and living big translates into increasingly unsustainable pressure on the environment, with companies happy to serve unlimited consumer demand by producing as much as possible from ever scarcer resources. The growing environmental stress and scarcity in turn fuel more brutal and anti-social behavior by companies and consumers, both unable to turn down the heat on their own egoistic and competitive behavior, leading to living bigger in bigger private houses with bigger lawns and bigger cars, which build more separation among people, add more competitive stress in social relations, and heat up the bonfire of climate change yet further.

Trumpism has added a massive political force to the corporate oligarchy's profit-seeking, thereby weakening and worsening US climate policies. We saw disastrous effects in Trump's first term as he vehemently denied the very existence of man-made climate change. Trump made climate change one of the symbols of dangerous and misguided liberal government crusades. He not only rejected the IPCC international scientific conventions on climate disaster but also claimed their critiques of US and global fossil-fuel carbon emissions would destroy our economy. In his first term, he required that all government scientists and agencies scrub any mention of the words "climate change" from their scientific reports and official documents. Moreover, while running for re-election, he said that on "day one" of his second term, he would become "a dictator on Day One" and immediately command: "Drill, baby, Drill!!" In his campaign, he asked CEOs from Big Oil and Big Gas to donate a billion dollars to his campaign, promising in return to end the regulations they hated on drilling, fracking, and mining. Trump's campaign for re-election made clear his second term would focus on destroying the liberal government crusade to end the "hoax" of climate change:

> When Donald Trump embarked upon a lengthy complaint at a recent rally about how long it takes to wash his "beautiful luxuriant hair" due to his shower's low water pressure, he highlighted the expanding assault he and Republicans are launching against even the most obscure environmental policies – a push that's starting to influence voters.
>
> In his bid to return to the White House, Trump has branded Joe Biden's attempt to advance electric cars in the US "lunacy," claiming such vehicles do not work in the cold and that their supporters should "rot in hell." He's called offshore wind turbines "horrible," falsely linking them to the death of whales, while promising to scrap incentives for both wind and electric cars.[8]

Even before the 2024 election, MAGA Congressional Republicans were legislating against energy efficiency and environmental laws, making it clear that they saw wiping out climate change as part of their culture war, foreshadowing the end of climate regulation whenever MAGA gains decisive power:

> But Republicans in Congress are now following Trump's lead, introducing a flurry of recent bills in the House of Representatives targeting energy efficiency standards for home appliances. The bills – with names such as the "Liberty in Laundry Act," "Refrigerator Freedom Act" and the "Clothes Dryers Reliability Act" – follow a conservative furore over a confected, baseless claim the Biden administration was banning gas stoves, which prompted further GOP legislation.[9]

While still running for re-election in 2024, Trump promised to deliver on his fossil-fuel agenda. He announced that he would pull out of the global Paris climate convention, which is the framework underpinning all United Nations' global climate negotiations.[10] He pledged to ignore global climate agreements negotiated to cut American carbon emissions and fund urgent climate mitigation in the Global South. He would take immediate executive actions to open up the Arctic and large amounts of public lands for drilling for oil and gas. He claimed that economic growth would spike upwards as he opened the door to the Carbon-Industrial Complex's – Exxon, Chevron, and Koch Industries – greatest dreams of expansion and profit as he defunded the EPA and other environmental agencies.

After his re-election, Trump followed through on his promises, withdrawing from the United Nations' global climate negotiations, opening new lands and shorelines for drilling, and ending government environmental regulations with executive orders. He began to fire thousands of civil servants in the EPA, who were reported as democratized and even terrorized, with a large number preparing to step down and retire early, feeling they could no longer carry out their mission. Moreover, even as Trump seeks to cut more Biden-era climate infrastructure and investment funding, his tariffs increase the cost of building sustainable infrastructure not only federally but in US states and localities. Trump tariffs will hike the price of imports required for building new solar and wind energy infrastructure and significantly increase the price of the supply chain goods essential for constructing a new green infrastructure.

Trump's anti-climate policies made clear his close ties to neoliberal US and global corporate forces that he railed against. Moreover, the 2024 disastrous Chevron decision by the Trumpist Supreme Court swept away the ability of much of the government to regulate the environment through the Environmental Protection Agency and other agencies. The Chevron decision, one of the most monumental court decisions in US history, gave a constitutional stamp to both neoliberal and Trumpist rejection of government and public regulation of corporate climate criminals. Chevron ensured that essential environmental regulation would be extremely difficult under both Democratic and GOP administrations, one of the most poisonous legacies of the Roberts court. Meanwhile, Trump's embrace of Project 2025, which rejected the reality of man-made climate change and called for ending EPA climate regulations, led him to make climate change de-funding a top priority.

Less than a week after winning the election, Trump named his new head of the EPA, Lee Zeldin. Zeldin is a Republican Congressman whose quick appointment symbolized Trump's commitment to deregulating fossil fuels and creating more rapid oil and gas development in the name of "energy independence." While Trump and Zeldin use rhetoric of clean water and air, the reality is a "thorough shakeup" of the regulatory body, as Politico reported:

> At EPA, Zeldin will carry out Trump's energy and environmental agenda, which includes pulling back Biden-era rules on climate and air pollution and potentially rescinding millions of dollars in funding for clean energy under the Inflation Reduction Act. And the administration is expected to take a more aggressive stance in challenging California's autonomy in enforcing environmental standards that are more stringent than those set by the federal government – many of which picked up as models for more than a dozen other blue states.[11]

The spiral between ecocide and sociocide will only intensify as hyper-individualist consumption and climate change accelerate, fueled by the power of Big Oil and Gas and Trumpist, Far-Right politics. Mass consumption depletes more land and resources. This growing material scarcity intensifies the competition to make and consume more, breeding more egoism and less concern for others in the race. Social relations continue to become acutely overstressed, and sustainable connections and the social infrastructure are depleted as the earth's infrastructure also is breaking down. All of this can help expand a desperate Trumpist base, with many believing that Trump, inspired by God, is the only leader who can save them, even as he doubles down on the anti-science, anti-government, and anti-public-health legislation that he has long promised. The intensifying spiral between ecocide and sociocide does not self-correct.

* * *

The second major environmentally driven sociocidal force – intertwined with climate change and neoliberalism – is the escalating threat of pandemics. Pandemics are obviously a death threat to social relationships, since pandemics turn each of us into a potential carrier of lethal illness to anyone we interact with face-to-face. COVID-19 was just the most recent example of a new era of pandemics, including SARS, MERS, Ebola, and avian flu, all bred in the era of neoliberalism and climate change. In the spring of 2024, after the worst of COVID-19 was over, the rise of a new strain of bird flu led scientists to warn of yet another pandemic. Pandemics are in many ways the most obvious sociocidal force in the world today. But their relation to neoliberalism, the breakdown of environmental and social relations, as well as to political authoritarian movements such as Trumpism, are not widely understood.

The sociocidal dimension of pandemics, however, is not hard to see. Pandemics make social relationships dangerous. Social contact of any form is potentially harmful to your health, since exposure to anybody with the virus can make you sick. When people are not responsible or concerned about others, they can easily become deadly to you. We all got a taste of that in COVID-19 in America, where more than a million people died of the disease, and a new culture of social distrust, fear, and isolation became a larger part of our culture.

Endless market expansion and the relentless search for more resources – unfettered by government – have created a new era defined by an extremely high risk of deadly pandemics like COVID-19. Before COVID-19 broke out, corporations dominating Big Ag, such as Cargill were rushing to cut down as much as they could of the Brazilian Amazon, spurred by the rising demand to clear forests for expanding cattle herding to meet the growing demand for meat from big retail and food companies such as Wal-Mart, McDonald's, and Stop and Shop. From 1993 to 2013, cattle herding based on deforestation expanded in the Amazon by 200%, reaching 60 million head of cattle.[12] Meanwhile, companies mining for coal and other minerals, including lithium and other rare minerals essential for electronic car batteries and superconductors, intensified their own exploits to enter or dominate the new high-tech economy gobbling up rare minerals.

Neoliberalism has unleashed a human invasion of wilderness and the sanctuaries where wild animals could roam free from fear of poaching, slaughter, or "human development." By 2019, experts estimated that just 23% of the world's surface could be classified as wilderness, a 10% decline since 1999. As early as 2017, two years before COVID-19 broke out, policy analysts, scientists, and political economists were already predicting that the human invasion of nature could create a fertile breeding ground for new pandemics. At the 2017 Aspen Ideas Festival in Colorado, policy analyst Nancy Sullivan, speaking alongside Ron Klain, destined to be President Biden's first Chief of Staff, warned that pandemics

> seem to be happening with increasing frequency, and it may have something to do with the increasing frequency with which humans are interacting with nature, and pushing into areas where these viruses are harbored in other animal species. And so we have what's called a zoonotic crossover … more than 70% of these viruses that occur in humans come from animals.[13]

In November 2020, after COVID-19 had broken out, a UN group of scientists fleshed out the same theme, warning that:

> Rampant deforestation, uncontrolled expansion of farming and the building of mines in remote regions – as well as the exploitation of wild animals as sources of food, traditional medicines and exotic pets – are creating a "perfect storm" for the spillover of diseases from wildlife to people. Almost a third of all emerging diseases have originated through the process of land use change, it is claimed. As a result, five or six new epidemics a year could soon affect Earth's population.[14]

The political economist John Bellamy Foster and his colleagues explicitly flesh out the connection between neoliberalism and pandemics, writing that COVID-19's rise is directly related to:

> a complex set of factors including 1) the development of global agribusiness with its expanding genetic monocultures that increase susceptibility to the contraction of zoonotic diseases from wild to domestic animals to humans: 2) destruction of wild habitats and disruption of the activists of wild species and 3) human beings living in closer proximity … global commodity chains … have become vectors for the rapid transmission of disease, throwing this whole globally exploitative pattern of development into question.[15]

The extremity of the social disconnections and death rates of pandemics has been uniquely high in the US. This is driven by American neoliberal economics and culture, heightened at this writing by the Far-Right Trumpist extreme political attacks on science and government. Trump built on traditional American hatred of government, defining public health masks, vaccines, and other public health measures as radical threats to freedom.

The sociocidal threats of pandemics – much intensified by free-market neoliberalism and Trumpism – were obvious to Americans who lived through COVID-19. Schools were shut down and millions of kids were isolated at home. Workplaces were shut down and millions of workers were out of work and out of touch. Sports events, concerts, and most other public events were shut down, leaving community residents to fend for themselves. Even hospitals became dangerous places to go, as doctors and nurses themselves became sick as they were overwhelmed with sick and dying patients. The Surgeon General, Vivek Murthy, documented the radical social disconnection caused by COVID-19 in his report on the Epidemic of Isolation and Loneliness, providing data reviewed in the last chapter of how social connections of virtually every type – family, friends, and community relations – drastically declined in the peak COVID-19 years between 2019 and 2022.[16] Meanwhile, more than 1.3 million Americans died from COVID-19, reflecting not only the inherent dangers of pandemics but the politicizing of pandemics and public health. Despite his initial work to help vaccinate Americans, Trump refused a few months into the pandemic to promote the vaccines, masks and other health steps that would have prevented hundreds of thousands of Americans from dying.

Pandemics are sociocidal because they introduce and heighten the very real dangers of connecting with people in one's social network, while also introducing many questions, doubts, and suspicions about whether others are simply out to protect themselves or are also committed to protecting you. In American culture, where the focus on the self is already normalized in the American Dream, trust is already a problem. Pandemics in such a society radically increase the likelihood of other people being less responsible and infecting family, friends, or workmates. And it is now rational for people to distrust or at least be cautious in social interactions, aware that the pandemic means that people may be more likely to act in ways that protect themselves but not adequately protect you. Is the person feeling some chills that they haven't told you about? Have they recently met with a friend who has COVID-19 or avian flu? Have they been tested and not told you the truth because they have other personal needs to see you? These are all reasonable questions in a society whose dominant egoistic norms are now reasonable grounds to enter any interaction during a pandemic with distrust or caution.

Where face-to-face relations have to be maintained during COVID-19, in the family, for example, the stresses can be just as powerful, much as they were in the sociocidal IK, where spouses did not help sick spouses and went scavenging to get food just for themselves. If an American husband got possible new symptoms of COVID-19, would he tell his wife about it if she was in the TV room watching a show he wanted to see? Would he be careful to not eat from the same bowl in the fridge as his spouse or kids if he was hungry? All the distrust built into social relations in an individualistic, egoistic culture is immediately magnified in a pandemic, explaining why COVID-19 in the US created far more per capita deaths, illness, and social disconnection than in European or other developed nations.

In COVID-19, these issues of trust and danger in relationships became more heightened in the US than in many European countries. In Europe, neoliberalism is less strong, government is more valued, and social networks and the collective good are more prioritized over egoism and self-aggrandizement. Trump's first term revealed how powerfully neoliberal and Far-Right American politics would intensify the danger of US pandemics. The unique sociocidal peril in the US became most visible in issues related to vaccines and masks. They became central political Far-Right symbols of government overreach and intrusion on personal freedom, intersecting powerfully with the hyper-individualism bred by neoliberalism.

The rejection of vaccines and masks grew rapidly in the US as COVID-19 got worse and lingered on, with rage against all public health measures stoked by Trump and the Far-Right in his first term. It is hardly surprising that millions of people would resonate with such Trumpist politics. The Far-Right's anti-public-health crusade melded powerfully with a long American history of hatred of government and corporate neoliberals' hyper-individualistic market philosophy. Both led Americans to think mainly about their own health and well-being rather than the health or safety of others, rejecting the obligations normalized in relations of more solidaristic societies and laying the ground for yet more sociocide.

After all, the American Dream is telling them that if they focus on their self-interest, the good of everyone will be maximized. To curb their ability to focus on themselves is an attack on their liberty. Such calculations, super-charged by Trump and the Far-Right, have led millions of Americans in the Covid era to claim the right to send their kids to school without getting vaccines, not only against COVID-19 but also against measles, yellow fever, or small pox. Such decisions turn parents against each other as they fear for the health of their kids, weakening social cohesion in schools, neighborhoods, and society at large.

The culture of individualism led millions of Americans during the COVID-19 era to see the demand to get a vaccine or wear masks as a violation of their basic rights. Even if they were sick and knew they might spread the virus to others, they believed that the right to focus on themselves – the self-interest basic to a free-market society – was central to their identity as Americans.

This self-interested interpretation of freedom has been explosively heightened by religious and political currents in America – particularly the rise of Far-Right politics as it played out in Trump's first term and in his race toward and into his second term. Protestant Evangelicals mobilizing inside the MAGA Republican Party led resistance to both masks and vaccines. Public health leaders such as Dr. Anthony Fauci, the top US infectious disease official under Trump and Biden during COVID-19, were targeted for death by white Christian nationalists as the embodiment of Satan; Trump himself threatened to jail Fauci when his second term began.

The toxic melding of Far-Right politics and religion plays out in the story of Karen Alea, a former Evangelical Christian, who later came to embrace science and public health. She said she had learned from her Church to see COVID-19 as "a message from God" and that she had to spread the Word without masks. You could either listen to God and connect with Him through your own free will or submit to government and public health orders that limited your freedom. To use vaccines or masks, she had learned, was violating her sacred religious freedom to obey only God and show that "God is more powerful than COVID-19." Vaccines and mask-wearing were forms of a cowardly lack of belief, suggesting that "God isn't powerful enough" to keep you safe.[17] These were all themes central to Trumpism and the MAGA use of religion to demonize liberals, Democrats, and government; they not only helped Trump build the MAGA GOP as not only the party of freedom but to also rally his MAGA movement as a spiritual crusade to create a great born-again nation.

These economic, cultural, and religious themes go a long way in explaining higher rates of death, illness and social disconnection in American COVID-19 experience compared to most European and Asian societies. Both European and Asian nations are less neoliberal and individualistic than the US. Americans who go to Seoul or Tokyo, for example, see ordinary people freely wearing masks just to protect themselves and others against germs and air pollution, even in eras when pandemics are not present, reflecting the great value placed on respect for others, government, and the common good. Especially in the Trump era, the US has become the world's laboratory for political rule based on hostility to public health and ideas of freedom politically defined as the sociocidal right to reject vaccines, masks and other protections for the community.

This sociocidal Americanism is becoming more intense in Trump's second term. Just when the country needs to modify this vision and increase public health investment, the Trumpist Republican Party has pushed the ideological needle so far the other way, it now points toward virtually all government and public health obligations as big government tyranny. As Trump's new Secretary of Health and Human Services, Robert F. Kennedy Jr., while he may lead some fights for healthier food and drugs against Big Pharma, will champion the Far-Right attack against vaccines as a threat to human health. Despite reversing himself supporting the right to a measles vaccine after a measles outbreak in Texas, early in Trump's second term, Kennedy is stoking the anti-vax movement of the first Trump term into something like a spiritual crusade, a major part of the extreme danger to the environment and public health. This is inherent in Trump's climate denialism, his marriage to the Carbon-Industrial Complex and the larger corporate oligarchy, and his hatred of government and public goods. This puts the US as a nation at overwhelming risk for future climate and pandemic disasters, both reflecting and fueling more sociocide and policide.

* * *

Social critic Naomi Klein, describes a "Shock Doctrine," pointing to the vulnerabilities of people in the US to new, more intense neoliberal deregulated and environmentally destructive initiatives in the name of "relief efforts."[18] As neoliberalism and Far-Right politics give rise to more poverty as well as fiercer floods, droughts, heat, hurricanes, and wildfires, the US and major American corporations offer more deregulated major investment and "rebuilding" programs which add yet more fire and heat to the areas receiving "relief." A population in shock lacks the resources or emotional and political mobilization to resist the "Disaster Capitalism" being delivered as a solution. This, in turn, gives rise to new floods, fires, cyclones, and heat which kick off yet another round of shock-facilitated neoliberal responses in a 21st-century sociocidal spiral of accelerated climate and socio-economic tipping points.

The Shock Doctrine helps explain why counteracting and healing forces to the horrific crises described here have not kicked in. The Shock Doctrine makes each environmental or pandemic disaster a recipe for more neoliberalism and more Far-Right bromides. Big corporations and Trumpists fire up more rejection of government and social obligations, leading to more extreme climate change and worsening public health, as vulnerabilities to pandemics increase under the Shock Doctrine.

As the Shock Doctrine continues to help fuel sociocidal spirals of neoliberal policy and climate disaster, the competition for making it and winning what was traditionally seen as God's blessing of wealth evolves toward a competition for survival itself. The very American individualistic competition for wealth and status is repeatedly intensified by new environmental disasters and social breakdowns, with repeated applications of the Shock Doctrine unleashing recurrent new spirals of consumption, neoliberal production, climate disaster, public health crises, and social breakdowns. The repeated hammer of the Shock Doctrine turns the market-based competition for God's blessing and moral worth into an "all-consuming" sociocidal competition to survive.

Politics is classically the arena where societal crises of this magnitude can be addressed. Historically, in the mid-20th century in the US, certain political forces made countervailing power possible to limit both economic exploitation and environmental destruction. On the one hand, the Democratic Party during the Great Depression organized around FDR's New Deal, which sought to curb the excesses of corporate capitalist power and exploitation. It promoted government investment and regulation, public goods in sustainable employment and energy such as the CCC and TVA, and legislated rights to unionize and build social relations of cooperation and solidarity that could support a less exploitative capitalism. While large sectors of the Republican Party opposed the New Deal, calling FDR a "traitor to his class," the corporate policies Republicans promoted were more sociopathic than sociocidal, with neoliberalism not yet on the horizon.

Today, the shift to neoliberalism that began in the Reagan era, the Democratic Party's abandonment of the New Deal, and the evolution of the Reagan Revolution and the Christian Right, has now culminated in the first and second Trumpist regimes and the MAGA Republican Party having dramatically changed the political game. It has made politics itself a major sociocidal force. In the era of climate change, the Republican Party has defined itself as a full-throated agent of sociocide by fully embracing climate denialism, promoting all-out fossil energy production, and rejecting the Democratic associations and solidarity that could help build a new Green New Deal and other emergency measures to save life. The second Trump term is a huge blow not just to the Democratic Party but to the voice and power of the American majority who want to save the environment and the lives of their children and grandchildren.

Contradictory sociophiliac forces, though, are still present and can rise to challenge both ecocide and sociocide. The Biden years and climate initiatives such as his infrastructure and inflation-reduction policies were the most important climate legislation in US history. They may presage more ambitious anti-climate Democratic and left-leaning social movements. In Trump's second term many of these will focus on new environmental laws and regulations at the state and local levels rather than the national level. In New York State, for example, a progressive coalition helped pass a strong 2019 climate justice mitigation bill in resistance to the first Trump term. After Trump's 2024 re-election, Trump's win appeared to bring together and mobilize far more state and local climate advocates, including both state government and local officials, as well as community and social movement activists in New York, California, Washington, and many other states. They started almost immediately after Trump's re-election to build a stronger climate community in cities and the state to implement as much of Biden's climate agenda as possible.

Along with his ambitious climate legislation that had been a training ground for many climate activists, Biden had contradictorily promoted the bipartisan militarized foreign policy that continues to fuel climate change disaster and sociocide. Despite his anti-war rhetoric, Trump is likely to continue the expensive build-up of nuclear weapons he started in his first term, as well as militaristic policies targeting Iran and China that could lead to more wars catalyzing more climate change and public health disasters.

In her short race for president in 2024, Kamala Harris discussed climate change as an existential threat; she said that she would move beyond the already strong climate investments of the Biden–Harris Administration. One of the great failures of her campaign was her inability to make center stage a challenge to both the neoliberal economics and the public health threats that climate change and pandemics represent. She could have run a campaign heavily focused on a 21st-century Green New Deal that would address working people's economic fears by targeting both the Carbon-Industrial Complex and the Military-Industrial Complex, both parts of the new Trump corporate oligarchy siphoning public investment from working people to corporate coffers. She could have headlined how she could create good new jobs, affordable housing, and healthy food by frontally attacking the oligarchy of the new Robber Barons and pouring public investment into green infrastructure, sustainable energy, and an environmentally friendly public space and transit.

During the second Trump term, the nearly 70 million Americans who see climate change as an existential and defining issue of the 21st century will need to organize militant environmental and public health movements, both locally and at the state level, while pushing Democratic office-holders and climate champions in Congress to double down on resistance to Trumpist climate denialism and defunding of public health. This must be at the center of a massive and long-term emergency pro-democracy political coalition uniting the Democratic Party and the climate movements powered now by young people, labor unions, service workers, environmentalists, and progressives inside and outside the Democratic Party at the local, state, and global levels. Hope not only for democracy but for survival depends on the success of these new movements that we profile in later chapters.

Notes

1 Aimee Picchi, "Homes in Parts of the US Are 'Essentially Uninsurable' Due to Rising Climate Change." *CBS News*, September 20, 2023, cbsnews.com.
2 NOAA, "2023 Was the World's Warmest Year On Record by Far." January 12, 2024, noaa.gov
3 Damen Carrington, "World's Top Climate Scientists Expect Global Heating to Blast Past 1.5C Target." *The Guardian*, May 8, 2024, guardian.com
4 Charles Derber and Suren Moodliar, *Dying for Capitalism: How Big Money Fuels Extinction and What We Can about It*. London: Routledge, 2023, p. 112.
5 Christopher Leonard, *Kochland*, cited in Charles Derber and Suren Moodliar, *Dying for Capitalism: How Big Money Fuels Extinction and What We Can about It*. London: Routledge, 2023, p. 113.
6 Molly Loe, "Oil and Gas Company Says Suing Climate Activists Isn't Political," March 1, 2024, techhq.com
7 Molly Loe, "Oil and Gas Company Says Suing Climate Activists Isn't Political," March 1, 2024, techhq.com
8 Oliver Milman, "'It's Nonsensical': How Trump Is Making Climate the Latest Culture War." *The Guardian*, July 2, 2024, theguardian.com.
9 Oliver Milman, "'It's Nonsensical': How Trump Is Making Climate the Latest Culture War." *The Guardian*, July 2, 2024, theguardian.com.
10 Ben Lefebvre and Zack Colman, "Trump Would Withdraw US from Paris Climate Treaty Again, Campaign Says." *Politico*, June 28, 2024, politico.com
11 Josh Siegel and Alex Guellen, "Trump Picks Lee Zeldin to Lead EPA." *Politico*, November 11, 2024, politico.com
12 "Companies Behind the Burning of the Amazon," mightyearth.org
13 Charles Derber and Suren Moodliar, *Dying for Capitalism: How Big Money Fuels Extinction and What We Can about It*. London: Routledge, 2023, p. 64.
14 Cited in Charles Derber and Suren Moodliar, *Dying for Capitalism: How Big Money Fuels Extinction and What We Can about It*. London: Routledge, 2023, p. 65.
15 Cited in Charles Derber and Suren Moodliar, *Dying for Capitalism: How Big Money Fuels Extinction and What We Can about It*. London: Routledge, 2023, p. 67
16 Vivek Murtha, *The Epidemic of Loneliness and Isolation*. US Surgeon General's Advisory. Department of Health and Human Services, 2023: Chapter 4, Chart, National Trends for Social Connection.
17 Cited in Charles Derber and Suren Moodliar, *Dying for Capitalism: How Big Money Fuels Extinction and What We Can about It*. London: Routledge, 2023, p. 132.
18 Cited in Charles Derber and Suren Moodliar, *Dying for Capitalism: How Big Money Fuels Extinction and What We Can about It*. London: Routledge, 2023.

6   The bonfire of the armed society

Packing heat, militarized America, and the new war system at home

The US has a long, unique history of guns, culminating today in the US suffering by far the highest level of private gun ownership and personal gun violence compared to all other developed nations. The Second Amendment of the Constitution made explicit that all American adult citizens had a Constitutional right to bear arms as part of a "well-regulated militia to ensure the security of a free State." The Second Amendment was explicit: the "right of the people to keep and bear Arms shall not be infringed."[1]

That Constitutional right today is viewed as sacred, but the history of gun ownership and violence is complex. The current unprecedented scale of private gun ownership and violence is relatively recent, an evolution with tipping points leading from a 20th-century sociopathic gun culture to a 21st-century sociocidal catastrophe. Nonetheless, private gun ownership and gun violence have always been unique in America, reflecting our distinctive Constitutional and deeply politicized culture of gun ownership. The Second Amendment made clear that gun ownership was always a core political right in America, central to protecting freedom. Defeating the threat of tyrannical government was Constitutionally viewed as requiring armed militias or private individuals who could curb authoritarian threats with their own weapons.

Ironically, this American recipe for preventing dictators and government tyranny became the foundation of a politics of guns and violence that now threatens to bring the very political authoritarian disaster it was created to prevent. We are witnessing the dramatic rise of an armed population. Many economic, cultural, and political forces both cause and reflect sociocidal trends, giving rise to explosive growth in many different categories of gun owners. These include a growing number of Americans across the political spectrum who say it may be necessary to use violence to gain their political ends.[2]

By the end of 2023, there were at least 400 million privately owned guns in America, more than the 330 million population.[3] Only 6 million of these guns are registered; 82.8 million Americans owned at least one firearm in 2023, and 43% of American households have at least one firearm. The rate of gun ownership increased by 28% between 1994 and 2023. In 2023, 73% of Americans said they owned guns for protection or safety; only 32% said for hunting or sport.[4]

This arms race at home needs to be interpreted in relation to several data points guiding this chapter. They all hint at a level of American sociocide akin to the Ik, where people feel that other people are threats to their survival, much like enemy combatants in war. The fact that individuals in almost half of American households feel they need to have a gun to feel safe makes clear that Americans view either strangers or people they know as dangerous.

DOI: 10.4324/9781003491798-7

The types of guns being bought today help confirm this view. In 1970, long guns like rifles and shotguns made up 64% of new US firearms; these are guns used for recreation and hunting. But by 2020, handguns, used mainly for personal protection, had skyrocketed to 58% of new guns purchased, confirming a cultural shift of people now mainly "buying guns for self-defense."[5]

The profiles of shooters at the Columbine, Newtown, or Parkland school shootings, as well as in grocery stores, theaters, or sports events, hint that growing social isolation – linked to rising distrust, bullying, and easy availability of guns – is a major underpinning of gun ownership and violence. The Columbine shooters, Eric Harris and Dylan Klebold, dubbed "dorks, loners, and outcasts," were young men who had few friends in school and were often bullied.[6] This profile of mass shooters as young males who are loners or are "failed joiners," as journalist David Brooks puts it, emerges repeatedly in accounts of mass shooters at Newtown and Uvalde, who are poorly integrated into social groups.[7] Yet most shooters are not mentally ill and are reported to be "normal." Indeed, they are hard to distinguish from the general population:

> If you're wondering who else in the United States might fit a "profile" of becoming a mass killer, just look around: They are everywhere, and they're most likely harmless.
> … Experts say that risk factors, such as social isolation and rejection, are found in many people across the United States …
> The truth is that there are many people who have all the symptoms and don't get the disease … They may be loners, and strange and angry and have access to firearms.[8]

The great sociologist, Emile Durkheim, would recognize the profile of the loner, as well as the difficulty in distinguishing mass shooters from the rest of the population. As noted in earlier chapters, Durkheim famously argued that a lack of social integration created egoism, anomie, and anger – and leads to violence and suicide. If large sectors of the public, as documented by the Surgeon General's report on "Our Epidemic of Loneliness and Isolation" and throughout this book, face sociocidal threats of eroding work, family, and community relationships, millions of Americans have the "risk factors" noted among mass shooters. As more and more Americans experience the lack of social integration and anomie that Durkheim describes, the US will become an increasingly fertile breeding ground not only for the mass arming of the public but also for increased gun violence against others and oneself.[9] This is especially true in a culture noted for anger, bullying and militarism, with guns readily available on Walmart and store shelves everywhere.

Hints of growing fear of friends or family among Americans buying guns also point to sociocidal factors playing a major role in the arming of America. For example, women are the fastest-growing gun-ownership group in the US, with gun ownership by women increasing by 179% between 1972 and 2023.[10] This suggests that fear of violence from spouses or neighbors is a major factor, especially given high levels of domestic and family violence. Not only are people avoiding public spaces they might now deem as sites of gun violence, but appear increasingly afraid of family, friends, or neighbors. They have read the headlines or true crime books about people like Charles Stuart. This both reflects and fuels a sociocidal fear of others, breeding a focus on oneself and avoidance of social life just to survive.

Statistics indicate that 1 out of 20 Americans bought a gun for the first time during COVID-19. In 2020, the pandemic spurred a record demand for new guns in America;

between 2019 and 2020, COVID-19 resulted in an "unprecedented 40 million guns flying off the shelves," the biggest year-over-year jump on record.[11] While pandemics in every country make social relations more dangerous, other forces in America made the pandemic as a spur of gun-buying worse in the US. Pre-existing individualism, income inequality, and racial division all helped drive the sale of more guns in America during COVID-19 and increased deaths – more than a million in the US – and social isolation more than in other developed nations.[12]

The rise in the number of gun owners starting in the early 1990s links the gun epidemic with neoliberal economics and with rising white Christian nationalist and Far-Right forces, as highlighted in earlier chapters. Neoliberalism and the Christian nationalist movement radically spiked in the 1980s under President Reagan, and gun manufacturers began increasing their promotion and sales, while neoliberal politicians sought to ensure that guns were seen and treated just like any other commodity for sale on the market. Government regulation of guns was deemed as inefficient and dangerous to freedom as government intervention and regulation in any other sector of the economy. Under neoliberalism and Far-Right Christian nationalist movements, rising under Reagan and intensifying under Trump, gun manufacturers and Trumpists framed gun control as anti-patriotic and government overreach. It was tantamount to public health control during the pandemic, framed especially by the MAGA Republican Party and its base as an attack on liberty, just like government mandates to wear masks and require vaccines.

The political forces tied to the gun crisis here lead, not surprisingly, to race and racism, always a potent force in the history of US gun violence. A dominant conservative and Trumpist Far-Right narrative today is that Blacks are now "replacing" whites and are arming far more quickly to get control. The data do not support this story. The rate of gun ownership among Blacks did rise from about 17% in 1994 to 24% in 2023. But the rate of gun ownership among whites increased from 26% in 1994 to 38% in 2023[13] Thus both Blacks and whites – and also Hispanics – increased gun ownership significantly in this period, but the percentage of whites with guns was and remains substantially higher; less than one-fourth of Blacks own guns today compared to more than two-fifths of whites.[14]

Racism, politically mobilized by Trumpism, has falsely inflated gun ownership and violence by Blacks. The rise in guns should be considered in the context of resurgent white nationalist politics – and rising police and political violence directed against Blacks, Brown people, and immigrants. The frenzied arming of the population is a central part, as noted earlier, of Trump's Far-Right politics and authoritarian agenda. It is breeding an army of MAGA-armed partisans committed to violence to ensure their political victory. This, in turn, is part of an emerging war at home – leading to continued political violence during Trump's second term and his politics of "retribution" against all enemies of MAGA. The acceleration of gun ownership and gun violence, as well as the rejection of all gun control by Trump, the Far-Right, and the Roberts Supreme Court, breeds a new highly politicized arming of America, with arsenals of private gun ownership accumulating especially among Trump's base.

* * *

The history of US private gun ownership cuts against some existing stereotypes. The Second Amendment was always viewed by American federal and state governments as central to state security and freedom, and private ownership of guns was always more protected in the US than in most European societies. But this did not translate until relatively recently into today's distinctive levels of urban gun violence or daily reports of mass shootings. While data suggest that between 40% and 70% of Americans owned guns in the 18th century and much of the 19th century, the movie version of a "Wild West" where most Americans were armed and routinely shot each other on town streets is exaggerated and mythical.[15]

The gun culture that existed in the US before the Civil War was different than the one reigning today; the transformation helps explain how private ownership of guns and gun violence has become sociocidal only in recent times. Before the Civil War, Americans who owned guns used them largely for hunting and protection against agricultural pests and wild animals in rural and farming areas, as well as defense against indigenous populations resisting American expansion.[16] There was no significant gun manufacturing before the Civil War, though Colt became the first US gun manufacturer in 1836, helping produce guns for the Mexican wars of the 1840s and eventually the Civil War. The rates of gun production began to rise in the run-up to the Civil War, when Colt opened a larger new company in 1856. The war trained more Americans in the use of guns and began to change views about the relation between personal guns and personal security. The Civil War increased the perception that an American might need a gun to protect himself from other Americans. Meanwhile, the Civil War had helped stimulate an American gun manufacturing industry that joined with government to promote the importance of gun ownership. The NRA was founded in 1871 to organize arms manufacturing companies and promote ownership and use of guns for sport, hunting, and safety.

After the Civil War, gun culture evolved ominously in the South, where former slave owners began to see gun ownership as a way to keep order in a turbulent new era. After the Civil War, former slave owners in the South began to see gun ownership as central to their new identity in a transformed region.[17] Racial violence to reverse multi-racial democratic Reconstruction and to enforce the Jim Crow regime helped reshape the new gun culture and evolving Southern identity, as it became intertwined with initiatives by white supremacists to keep newly freed Blacks and other minorities in their place.[18]

Jim Crow established guns as a major sociopathic force in the late 19th and early 20th centuries. American politics had long included extremist groups advocating not just segregation but removing or exterminating Blacks.[19] Far-Right armed white supremacist groups like the Ku Klux Klan dramatically increased in the 1920s, followed by neo-Nazi groups and American Firsters in the 1930s. By the 1980s, in association with the rise of neoliberal capitalism across the entire nation, another white supremacist surge developed under Reagan and the Republican "Southern strategy," an important foundation of the transition from sociopathic to sociocidal gun culture.[20] Most recently, the rise of Far-Right MAGA Republican Party politics, leading to Trump's election as president in 2016 and his 2024 re-election, crystallized a new surge of politically driven white Christian nationalism. This was associated not only with rising white gun ownership and attacks on Blacks; it fueled the growth of armed Trumpist partisan militias that helped lead the January 6 attempted violent coup at the Capitol and helped arm millions of other Trump followers, as detailed later in this chapter, with many embracing violence to win and keep political power.

The long 20th-century rise of sociopathic gun culture developed not just in the South or on the frontier, but in industrial cities all over America, fueled by growing inequality and poverty. Urban populations marked by new grievances and fear became the target of not just crime but vast new marketing efforts of the rising gun industry and the increasingly powerful NRA. By the 1980s, the final dismantling of the New Deal and enshrinement of neoliberalism by President Reagan vastly intensified the economic and social divisions that tipped gun culture and the larger society from sociopathy to sociocide.

The mid to late 20th century saw the US emerge as the nation with by far the highest rate of gun ownership and gun violence, an early marker of the shift toward sociocidal gun culture.[21] By the late 1990s, gun ownership and violence especially among young people, became a distinctively American pathology.[22] It grew most rapidly in cities; while associated with drugs and gangs, it was also becoming a broader problem among children and teenagers in schools. While mass shootings remained relatively rare in this period, they began to escalate in the early 1990s with mass shootings in El Paso and Dayton, Ohio, still shocking enough then that they triggered public outrage and new calls for gun control. In 1994, President Clinton signed a ban on assault weapons which George W. Bush allowed to lapse in 2004.

* * *

As we moved into the very late 20th and early 21st centuries, decisive tipping points of multiple mass shootings and huge new gun sales led to the current catastrophe of gun sociocide reaching full bloom in the early 2020s. Horrific stories of gun ownership and violence spill daily into the headlines. In 2021, 2022, and 2023, there were more than 630 mass shootings each year, averaging almost two mass shootings a day.[23] *New York Times* reporter Nicholas Kristof estimates that in April 23, 2023, there were 450 million guns in the US – and growing because of a spiral in which more guns create more violence, which creates more fears, which creates more guns.[24] By 2020, the US had 4% of the global population and 40% of privately owned guns globally.[25]

Kristof, who is best known for his reporting on war zones, is more sensitized than other journalists to see hints of a war zone in America's gun-saturated civilian society. In both cases, high levels of social fear and anger increase the numbers of guns and gun violence, leading to more fear and anger, leading to more shootings of innocents. Americans engaging in perfectly normal social life are now fair game because of innocent mistakes or just being in the wrong place at the wrong time. Among Kristof's examples:

–   In Kansas City, Mo., a Black 16-year-old was shot twice, in the forehead and an arm, when he went to the wrong house to pick up his younger brothers; he is recovering from a traumatic brain injury. The 84-year-old white man who, according to the prosecutor, shot him through a glass front door has been charged with first-degree assault; the man said he thought the boy was breaking into his home.
–   In upstate New York, a 20-year-old woman was killed when she and several friends drove to the wrong address. As their car was turning around to leave, the homeowner allegedly fired his gun and struck her.
–   In Texas, two cheerleaders were shot after one of them mistakenly got into the wrong car in a parking lot. One of the girls, age 18, was hit in the back and a leg and taken by helicopter to a hospital; she was initially reported to be in critical condition.[26]

These now commonplace examples suggest that the line between "normal" social life in America and a war zone has been rapidly blurring. Kristof notes that this is utterly bewildering to people in other developed countries. He writes about a 16-year-old Japanese exchange student who was shot dead after knocking on the wrong door in Louisiana, with the homeowner saying he thought the student was a burglar. Japan has fewer people murdered by guns in a whole year than in a single mass shooting in the US. The Japanese government has prepared a booklet for Japanese tourists to help them survive in the US, teaching English phrases to understand like "freeze" and "hands in the air."[27] The teenage sons of a British journalist friend of mine told me they were afraid to travel around the US, since they might get shot. Visiting the US increasingly feels like coming to a war zone if you are from a European or Asian country where gun violence is rare.

More and more Americans are seeing their own country as a war zone. In the last few decades, we have seen an explosion of survivalists and preppers arming up for doomsday, religious cults collecting guns for self-defense as in Waco, Texas, and a huge array of groups of mostly young men, who are preparing for civilian violence by buying more guns, joining shooting clubs, training at gun ranges, and learning how to "take out" any potential threat. Forbes reported in January 2024, that one out of three Americans say they are "preppers" who believe we are living in end times; the demographic with the highest percentage of preppers are Gen Z youth, hardly surprising as they are growing up to expect that their own life can end at any time because of a school shooter.[28] The majority of kids who are not preppers still have to prepare to deal with a civil life where their teachers and parents teach them that doors have to be locked, that they have to take safety precautions against possible shooters in playgrounds, parks, and on the streets, and that they have to be on the alert for menacing strangers or familiar bullies in the schoolyard who are likely armed. The entire younger generation is being socialized into a culture in which anybody and everybody has to be seen as dangerous and a potential shooter; all of Gen Z are essentially learning the culture of sociocide.

The skyrocketing numbers of guns and incidences of gun violence are associated with spectacular rises in both the ascendancy of a culture of bullying in schools and workplaces, as well as threats of violence and use of guns in all types of public spaces. Again, young people are most at risk. The dramatic increase in mass shootings in schools – from kindergartens and grammar schools such as Newtown, Sandy Hook, and Parkland to colleges and universities such as the University of Virginia, UNLV, and Michigan State – has made fear of being shot at school a central issue for Gen Z. By 2021, guns were the number one killer of kids in America, a tragedy not experienced by any other developed nation.[29]

Meanwhile, gun manufacturers are producing more and more assault weapons, like the AR-15, for personal use by adults and kids alike. The issue of gun violence has sparked an existential movement among the young, who now see guns as a central threat to their survival, an indicator of the shift toward sociocide. The danger is breeding a new social movement against guns – and the larger sociocidal perils – concentrated among Gen Z itself. The vibrancy of this new movement – led by Gen Z 20-somethings like Parkland mass shooter survivor David Hogg, selected in 2025 as vice-chair of the Democratic National Committee – is another illustration of the contradictory forces brewing in sociocidal America, which can breed sociophiliac life-affirming movements among those most endangered.

But mass fear of being shot in public is now rising among adults along with kids. A torrent of public shootings in stores, malls, and city centers has erupted in the last decade. In 2022 and 2023, mass shootings in public spaces – from grocery stores to big box stores to the post office to office buildings to city and suburban streets and parks – occur every week and sometimes every day.[30] Stand your ground laws introduced in Florida have normalized the view that people are entitled to shoot first when they see strangers in their neighborhood or even knocking on their front door, especially when racial differences are taken into account. Police violence, such as the murder of George Floyd, makes it clear that race is a key trigger. But it is only the most important of a wide variety of political, economic, and cultural forces intersecting to create a sociocidal gun crisis. The worry about simply surviving in public is a strong hint of the rise of the new gun sociocide that increasingly haunts the consciousness of all Americans.

* * *

Three recent Supreme Court cases are Constitutional tipping points, helping fuel this transition to sociocide across the entire population. For two centuries, the Supreme Court had left key issues about the Second Amendment unclear and open to state government interpretations. In the 2008 Heller decision, the Court, for the first time, made explicit that gun ownership by individuals unconnected to militias was Constitutionally federally protected. In the 2010 *McDonald v Chicago* case, the Court, again for the first time, ruled that personal rights to bear arms were "fundamental," superseding state laws. In the 2022 Bruen case, the Court decided that the right to carry arms without a permit in public was also Constitutionally protected.[31] These three cases both affirmed and enabled the shift toward gun sociocide.

Economic, political, and cultural changes are now intersecting to sweep the sociocidal transition through the doors opened by the Supreme Court. Economically, the gun industry, along with related industries such as home security, has become a major corporate force, using its trade association, the NRA, to promote profits through maximum gun sales and promoting personal gun rights for security at an unprecedented scale. Three major companies dominate the gun manufacturing industry, led by Smith and Wesson.[32] The gun industry more than quadrupled its number of new firearms manufactured from an already eye-popping 3 million in 2004 – the norm at the turn of the century – to an unprecedented 13.8 million in 2021, a figure reflecting a steep spike upward annually since 2014.[33] The gun industry is now a $50 billion industry producing hundreds of thousands of pistols, rifles, and other guns annually, including AR-15 assault weapons, called by the NRA "America's rifle," with 1 in 20 Americans owning one and over 20 million AR-15s legally in circulation in 2023.[34]

The NRA has long been a uniquely powerful corporate trade organization.[35] Since 1991, the NRA has been led by Wayne LaPierre, famous for his phrase, "The only way to stop a bad guy with a gun is a good guy with a gun." This would become the NRA brand, encouraging not only arming teachers in elementary schools to carry guns to class but also arming virtually every public facility – and potentially every student, customer, patient, or pedestrian – with a gun. That image of an armed society, always prepped for conflict with the bad guy or "other" – whether that be an individual, group, or political enemy – in any public interaction, or at home as households build up private arsenals for home security, is the brand as well of a sociocidal society.

It is a blessing that by 2024, rampant NRA corruption and scandals weakened the organization, as detailed by the youthful anti-gun leader, David Hogg, in an email to his supporters:

> What once appeared to be an unstoppable force in American politics, the NRA has seen a mass exodus of over one million members, corruption charges, and millions of dollars in legal fees – meanwhile their overall revenue dropped 52% since 2016.

A former top NRA official told *The New York Times*: "The NRA is little more than a shell of itself."[36]

This does not mean that the NRA will not rise again, but it offers a temporary respite from the NRA's successful marketing of every possible kind of gun for profit, from assault weapons to stylish guns designed for women to "cute" small guns designed for toddlers as Christmas presents. As with climate change, there is simply too much profit in guns to imagine that their manufacture and sales will be curbed, even if the NRA is legally bankrupted or dismantled. Moreover, leading GOP figures like President Donald Trump made clear in his 2024 re-election campaign that he would be an unwavering ally of the NRA and accepted the NRA endorsement at its 2024 convention.[37]

Intersecting with the economic forces fueling gun sociocide are critical cultural and social forces discussed in earlier chapters. As people become more insecure in jobs, marriages, and other key social institutions, fear and distrust of others markedly increase. A sociocidal tipping point spiral emerges as more isolated and fearful people come into contact with armed people, particularly when encounters are aggressive or argumentative. Such interactions could happen in parks, in schools or while driving.

Road rage incidents involving shootings rose every year after 2018, doubling between 2018 and 2022, and have continued to spike. In 2022, 550 people were injured or killed in road rage shootings, meaning an American was shot in a road rage shooting every 16 hours on average.[38] The stories are striking in how ordinary the people and road encounters seem:

> Fifty-year-old Ronald Butler was driving his four children to a birthday party in Milwaukee when he leaned out the window to tell another driver to slow down and was fatally shot, according to his older sister, Romonia Butler-Foster.

> Beloved youth baseball coach Jay Boughton, 56, was driving home from a game with his son in Minnesota in July 2021 when an exchange with a man in another vehicle escalated and the man shot Boughton to death.[39]

When drivers are routinely armed, negotiating traffic becomes its own kind of warfare. In today's culture, people quickly get angry if others are seen as holding them up in traffic or otherwise inconveniencing or insulting them. Annoyance can easily spiral into rage and violence if drivers are packing heat and bringing to their driving the sociocidal posture that might say "the streets belong to *me*, and get out of my way." Safe driving requires a "we" mentality that treats other drivers with the same rights and courtesy one wants for oneself. Sociocidal impulses can be particularly strong in one's car, where one is separated physically from other drivers, and the feeling that "I own this space and owe nothing to you" is a mindset that festers easily inside one's car.

Such face-to-face violent physical contacts with other drivers or pedestrians are multiplied by online interactions, where threats of bullying and violence can be massively amplified. Indeed, the technological communication shifts toward online interaction constitute another major technological and cultural tipping point that increases violent threats and fears. Tipping points in the number of physical or online threatening communications, with at least one person making it clear they have guns and might use them, scale up the volume of dangerous interactional spirals. Those not owning or carrying guns – and many lacking the strong social relationships that help them feel safe – will feel more afraid and have a greater need to pack heat themselves. This, in turn, will lead to more face-to-face or online interactions between armed and unarmed people, spiraling into another round of more people buying and carrying guns. Such spirals also increase the tendency to build larger arsenals at home, as almost half of all Americans live in households with guns, and at least 7 million own more than ten guns. Gun ownership is concentrated especially among white male adults, with about 48% owning guns. As noted at the beginning of this chapter, white males who are at high risk of lower social integration and are prone to the status of loners are those most likely to become shooters, as in Columbine and so many other school shootings.

This is all aggravated by the culture of bullying that has intensified in recent years, as discussed in my book with Yale Magrass, *Bully Nation*.[40] Bullying grows along with fear and anger in a society of people increasingly isolated and plagued by mental health crises and drugs. Bullying is also intensified in a highly militarized society, where large numbers of people, especially men, are trained in a culture of violence and identify with the power that comes from military command structures and domination through war or policing borders or poor communities. The armed society is a natural outcome of a militarized, sociocidal culture of disconnection, distrust, and bullying. This spills into politics, where autocratic and neo-fascist politicians appeal to raw power and violence in an angry, divided, and armed society.

Since the founding, gun ownership has been defined as a Constitutional right essential to defending democracy. The political dimension of gun ownership and violence has always been a defining part of the gun problem in the US. The irony is that the political view that equated citizen gun ownership with the protection of democracy is now a looming threat to democracy itself, helping fuel the armed Far-Right Trumpist GOP politics leading America toward extreme political polarization, possible civil war, and American fascism.

In the next chapter, we detail the growing role of political violence in Trump's race to be re-elected for a second term. After his failed, violent January 6 coup, Trump repeatedly incited violence among his base to prevent another "steal" of his rightful Presidency. This was all presaged in his first Presidential term by the rage, bullying, and aggression that Trump modeled in his own personality, as well as in his political speeches encouraging more gun ownership among his base as ownership and mass gun violence were escalating in the nation.

In his first term, Trump repeatedly called for violence long before inciting the insurrectionists on January 6, whom he knew were armed as they walked through metal detectors toward the Capitol. Shortly after his election, Trump described some "very fine people" among the gun-toting neo-fascists congregating against liberal protesters in the 2017 Charlottesville, Virginia, tragedy, including one Far-Right militant who drove his car into the protesters marching on the streets and killed one of them. During the 2020 street protests and demonstrations, most of which were peaceful, organized by Black Lives Matter activists after the police murder of George Floyd, Trump openly called for more police violence against the protesters. Trump also famously asked the US military to step in and shoot protesters, an order that was so blatantly unconstitutional that his own Defense Secretary, Mark Esper, refused to obey. The attempted assassination of Trump in 2024 reflected partly the normalization of political violence by Trump himself, with a growing number of Democrats prepared to use violence to stop Trump's election, joining the escalating number of all Americans –8% of the public – telling pollsters they were buying guns because they believed political violence might be justified in the next few years.[41] Another credible PBS/Marist poll in April 2024, found that 20% of the public believe "Americans may have to resort to violence to get their own country back on track."[42]

Trump's mobilization of political violence is associated with his fervent support of the NRA and rejection of any form of gun control. As gun violence and mass shootings escalated, a large majority of Americans supported common-sense background checks, denial of gun sales to criminals and domestic abusers, and getting AR-15s and other military-style assault weapons off the shelves of Wal-Mart and banned from sale at gun conventions. Trump opposed all forms of gun control, arguing with the NRA, which endorsed him in all three of his Presidential races, that the only way to stop mass gun shootings was to arm the entire population, including teachers, pastors, and managers and customers at stores, theaters, and groceries. Successfully running for re-election in 2024, Trump called himself "the best friend gun owners have ever had in the White House" and said that the Second Amendment is "very much on the ballot" and that if President Biden:

> gets four more years they are coming for your guns, 100% certain. Crooked Joe has a 40-year-record of trying to rip firearms out of the hands of law-abiding citizens.[43]

In 2023, Trump promised to sign legislation in his second term that would allow Americans living in "concealed carry" states to have the right to carry concealed guns. to keep that right whenever they travel out of their state:

> I will protect the right of self-defense everywhere it is under siege. And I will sign concealed carry reciprocity. Your second amendment does not end at the state line.[44]

Trump was universalizing the right to carry a concealed weapon everywhere in the US, including for members of states who don't need a permit to carry a hidden weapon. He was making it clear that in his second term, the existing limits on gun ownership and carrying guns into public spaces like supermarkets, churches, or streets would be decisively rolled back.

Trump's open embrace of militias like the Proud Boys and Oath Keepers was part of his broader political message to arm up and prepare for the political war to save the country. Gun ownership in the US had long been partisan; after World War II, the rise of the Far-Right Republican Southern base and white Christian nationalist strategy that came to power under Nixon and Reagan built a strong partisan divide, with almost double the percentage of Republicans than Democrats owning at least one gun or living in a household with at least one gun. This division continued and rose under Trump. By 2023, according to a comprehensive Pew Research Report, 45% of GOP and GOP-leaning Independents owned a gun compared to 20% of Democrats or Democratic-leaning Independents.[45] Moreover, the demographics of gun ownership overwhelmingly skewed toward Republican voters; 47% of people living in rural areas, who lean overwhelmingly Republican, own a gun compared to 30% who live in surburbs and 20% who live in urban areas, which are increasingly Democratic. Moreover, 38% of whites, who vote more Republican than other racial groups, own guns; while only 24% of Blacks, 20% of Hispanics and 10% of Asian-Americans, all the latter disproportionally Democratic. Moreover, the percentage of Americans who can imagine buying a gun in the future is higher among Republicans than Democrats; 61% of Republicans who didn't own a gun in 2023 said they would consider owning a gun in the future compared 40% of Democrats who report they might in the future own a gun.[46]

The surprise initial excitement about the emergence of Kamala Harris as the Democratic Party's 2024 Presidential candidate appeared like it might begin to change the political conversation on guns. Even more than Biden, Harris had long focused on gun violence as a major American crisis, as a prosecutor as well as politician. Harris had overseen the White House Office of Gun Violence Prevention and said at one of her first political rallies as a candidate in July 2024:

> We, who believe that every person should have the freedom to live safe from the terror of gun violence, will finally pass red flag laws, universal background checks and an assault weapons ban.[47]

She made the fight against gun violence part of her campaign and was immediately endorsed by major gun control and safety groups, including the Brady Campaign to Prevent Gun Violence, Everytown, the Community Justice Action Fund, the Newtown Action Alliance, and March for Our Lives. The NRA, MAGA, the Firearms Policy Coalition, and the Gun Owners of America viewed her as "radical" on guns. The Gun Owners of America called her a "gun-grabber," while others labeled her "authoritarian" on guns, taking away Americans' Constitutional freedoms.[48]

Gun control became one of Harris' more popular issues, reflecting once again the contradictions inherent in sociocide and the authoritarian policide that it helps breed. Because sociocide has brewed such an overwhelming spike in gun ownership and violence as discussed in this chapter, it has also given rise to a new movement against gun violence that is one of the strongest forces in the pro-democracy movements, especially among the young. A generation raised in locked schools, hiding under desks against mass shooters and fearful of being killed, will have to fight the impulse to get guns to protect themselves for the rest of their lives. But that same impulse – and the terror that underlies it – also gives rise to people banding together against the epidemic of gun violence that their generation has uniquely suffered. The freedom to feel safe and to stop gun terror is a sociophiliac force created by sociocide and policide; it makes the younger generation committed at a gut level to change.

Anti-gun movement leader and current Vice-Chair of the Democratic National Committee, David Hogg, speaks strikingly with anti-sociocidal messages such as "Whatever affects one directly, affects all indirectly" and "Life's most persistent and urgent question is, 'What are you doing for others?'"[49] He tells Gen Z about guns:

> Change will not come if we wait for some other person or some other time. We are the ones we've been waiting for. We are the change that we seek.[50]

Despite Gen Z's mobilization against gun violence, Trump's re-election and MAGA's dominance of all three branches of the federal government is a sign that the gun crisis is going to worsen through the 2020s. The arming of the base and leaders of the country's dominant political party – with Trump encouraging gun ownership and his threats of political violence against "the enemy within" – signals the looming authoritarian policide that sociocide breeds. As interpersonal, economic, racial, and other social forces become more violent among an armed population increasingly isolated, insecure, and angry, the social ties and associations of civil democratic society are undermined. This leads toward the authoritarian politics and the long-term US crisis of democracy that are the hallmark of Trump's second term and the subject of the next chapter.

Notes

1 "Constitution Annotated, Second Amendment." constitution.congress.gov
2 Alan Feuer, "Recent Poll Examined Support for Political Violence in US." *New York Times*, July 13, 2024, nytimes.com
3 Ammo Report Highlight, "How Many Gun Owners are in America." 2024, ammo.com
4 Ammo Report Highlight, "How Many Gun Owners are in America." 2024, ammo.com
5 Jennifer Mascia and Chip Brownlee, "How Many Guns Are Circulating in the US?" *The Trace*, March 6, 2023, thetrace.org
6 Deb Kiner "'The Dorks, the Loners, the Outcasts' That Killed 13 People at Columbine High School in 1999." *PennLive Patriot-News*, April 20, 2021, pennlive.com
7 David Brooks, "Why Mass Shooters Do the Evil They Do." *New York Times*, July 7, 2022 nytimes.com
8 Elizabeth Landau, "Rejection, Bullying Are Risk Factors Among Shooters." *CNN*, December 19, 2012, cnn.com
9 Emile Durkheim, *Suicide*. 2nd edition. NY: Harper and Row, 2013.
10 Jennifer Mascia and Chip Brownlee, "How Many Guns Are Circulating in the US?" *The Trace*, March 6, 2023, thetrace.org
11 Jennifer Mascia and Chip Brownlee, "How Many Guns Are Circulating in the US?" *The Trace*, March 6, 2023, thetrace.org
12 Charles Derber and Suren Moodliar, *Dying for Capitalism: How Big Money Fuels Extinction and What We Can about It*. London: Routledge, 2023.
13 Ammo Report Highlight, "How Many Gun Owners are in America." 2024, ammo.com
14 Ammo Report Highlight, "How Many Gun Owners are in America." 2024, ammo.com
15 Statista, "History of Guns in the US – Statistic and Facts." statista.com. See also James Lindgren, "Fall from Grace." *Northwestern Pritzker School of Law,* March 30, 2005, papers.ssrn.com.
16 Sara Novak, "How the Gun Became Integral to the Self-Identity of the Millions of Americans." *Scientific American,* March 29, 2023. scientificamerican.com
17 Nick Buttrick, cited in Sara Evans, "How the Gun Became Integral to the Self-Identity of Millions of Americans." Novak, "How the Gun Became Integral." See also Olivia Waxman, "The Inside History of How Guns are Marketed and Sold in America,." *Time Magazine*, August 19, 2022, time.com
18 Nick Buttrick, cited in Sara Evans, "How the Gun Became Integral to the Self-Identity of Millions of Americans." Novak, "How the Gun Became Integral." See also Olivia Waxman, "The Inside History of How Guns are Marketed and Sold in America,." *Time Magazine*, August 19, 2022, time.com.
19 Charles Derber and Yale Magrass, *Who Owns Democracy?* NY: Routledge, 2024.
20 Charles Derber and Yale Magrass, *Who Owns Democracy?* NY: Routledge, 2024.
21 Katherine Leach-Kemon, Rebecca Sirull, Scott Glenn, "On Gun Violence, the United States Is an Outlier." *IHME*, October 31, 2023, healthdata.org
22 Katherine Leach-Kemon, Rebecca Sirull, Scott Glenn, "On Gun Violence, the United States Is an Outlier." *IHME*, October 31, 2023, healthdata.org
23 Clarissa-Jan Lim, "US Hits a Gruesome Mass Killing Milestone." December 5, 2023, msbnc.com
24 Nick Kristoff, "It is a Delusion to Think Having a Gun in the Home Makes Us Safer." *New York Times*, April 23, 2023. nytimes.com
25 Nick Kristoff, "It is a Delusion to Think Having a Gun in the Home Makes Us Safer." *New York Times*, April 23, 2023. nytimes.com
26 Nick Kristoff, "It is a Delusion to Think Having a Gun in the Home Makes Us Safer." *New York Times*, April 23, 2023. nytimes.com
27 Nick Kristoff, "It is a Delusion to Think Having a Gun in the Home Makes Us Safer." *New York Times*, April 23, 2023. nytimes.com
28 Chris Dorsey, "When It Comes to End Times Survival, Viewers Can't Get Enough." *Forbes*, January 4, 2024, forbes.com
29 Matt McGough, Krutika Amin, Nirmita Panchai, Cynthia Cox, "Child and Teen Firearm Mortality in the US and Peer Countries." *KFF*, July 18, 2023, kff.org

30 Everytown, "Mass Shootings in the United States." *Everytown*, March 2023, everytownresearch .org

31 Justia, "Gun Rights Supreme Court Cases." *Justia US Supreme Court*, supreme.justia.com

32 CAP20, "The Gun Industry in America." August 6, 2020, americianprogres.org

33 Earl Rinand Margallo, "40 Firearms Sales Statistics." *Legal Jobs*, May 23, 2023 legaljobs.io. See also Jennifer Mascia and Chip Brownlee, "How Many Guns Are Circulating in the US?"

34 Emily Guskin, Aadit Tambe, and Jon Gerberg, "Why Do Americans Own AR-15s?" *Washington Post*, March 27, 2023, washingtonpost.com

35 BBC, "US Gun Control: What Is the NRA and Why Is It so Powerful?" *BBC*, April 13, 2013, bbc.com

36 David Hogg, email, April 16, 2024.

37 AP, "Trump Receives NRA Endorsement as He Vows to Protect Gun Rights," *AP*, May 18, 2024, usnews.com

38 Grace Hauck, "Road Rage Shootings are Increasing." *USA Today*, March 21, 2023, usatoday.c om

39 Grace Hauck, "Road Rage Shootings are Increasing." *USA Today*, March 21, 2023, usatoday.c om

40 Charles Derber and Yale Magrass. *Bully Nation*. Kansas City: University Press of Kansas, 2016.

41 Alan Feuer, "Recent Poll Examined Support for Political Violence in US." *New York Times*, July 13, 2024, nytimes.com

42 Laua Santhanam, "1 in 5 Americans Think Violence May Solve US Divisions, Poll Finds." *PBS*, April 3, 2024, pbs.org

43 AP, Trump Received NRA Endorsement as He Vows to Protect Gun Rights."

44 Alia Shoaib, "What Donald Trump's 'Concealed Carry Reciprocity' Means for Gun Rights." *Newsweek*, November 11, 2024, Newsweek.com

45 Kathrine Schaeffer, "Key Facts about Americans and Guns." Pew Research Center, September 13, 2023 pewresearch.org

46 Kathrine Schaeffer, "Key Facts about Americans and Guns." Pew Research Center, September 13, 2023 pewresearch.org

47 Chip Brownlee, "Kamala Harris' Record on Guns." *The Trace*, July 24, 2024, thetrace.org.

48 Chip Brownlee, "Kamala Harris' Record on Guns." *The Trace*, July 24, 2024, thetrace.org.

49 "30 Best David Hogg Quotes with Image," bookey.app

50 "30 Best David Hogg Quotes with Image," bookey.app

7   The bonfire of American fascists

Racial and class policide, the anti-Democratic Party, and ballots to bullets in the Trump era

In *Democracy in America*, French visitor and writer Alexis de Tocqueville was struck by the propensity of early Americans to build social relations and solidarity in civic associations, from neighborhood groups to religious organizations to political bodies. De Tocqueville saw this as the strength of the new nation. He said that the multiple social associations and networks which bonded Americans together as a society provided a basis for a robust American democracy, despite serious divisions related to race and class.[1]

De Tocqueville's analysis is critical to understanding the relation of politics and democracy to sociocide. As de Tocqueville hinted, Americans tend to think of politics as the sphere in which citizens can contest differences and still sustain social order and cohesion by agreeing to play by common rules – and that democracy rests on social relations and solidarity. De Tocqueville recognized that democracy requires a foundation of civil society in which people share enough caring connections, mutuality, and solidarity that norms of democracy and shared rules are accepted by citizens who differ strongly on political issues.

Another way of framing this is that democracy is always perilous, in the sense that it depends on the strength of social connections and relations in multiple spheres of life. When those connections are endangered, democracy itself is at severe risk. If people are disconnected and lack social ties that build solidarity at work, in the neighborhood and in broader civil society, the social threads underpinning democracy unravel. Without strong and sustainable social relations and solidarity, the only durable way to hold people together is with force. Coercion, typically through some form of authoritarian politics, is the only way to prevent socially disconnected people from breaking apart and moving toward chaos and civil war.

Sociocide is, then, a killer of democracy. It is also a threat to any form of civil political sphere. The noted public intellectual Michael Walzer and political scientist Steve Stern have each discussed the concept of "policide," which is the end of any free and consensual politics reflecting the will or interests of the people. Stern uses the term policide to describe the 1973 right-wing violent, anti-democratic coup and brutal dictatorship installed and ruled by General Augusto Pinochet in Chile.[2] In the sociocidal context discussed in the US, the absence of social cohesion and caring connections can help fuel a violent, tyrannical politics based on corporate power and police or military force rather than any social consensus or democratic consent. It is the replacement of civil politics and rule of law with looming American neo-fascism. Fueled by a lack of strong social relations, it also creates more social breakdown, leading to more sociocide and more political tyranny.

DOI: 10.4324/9781003491798-8

While the US has defined itself as a democracy since the founding of the nation, the reality is that American democracy has always been weakened by anti-democratic corporate and racist forces, making it vulnerable to policide. American capitalism and Jim Crow combined for almost two centuries to create a sociopathic politics.[3] The sociopathy became sociocidal and policidal in the American proto-fascism of the Confederate South, which used tyranny to unite rich and poor whites against Black slaves, leading to the 1860 breakdown of sustainable relations between North and South in the Civil War. After a short multi-racial democratic Reconstruction from 1865 to 1876, Jim Crow and Gilded Age modern industrial capitalism created more than a century of sociopathic society, in which a "shallow democracy" survived but remained fragile and vulnerable to civil war and extreme authoritarianism.[4] American neo-fascism based on racist codes and violence continued to rule in the Jim Crow Southern states; Hitler sent his scientists to study US Jim Crow racial laws because he found in them a basis for his own fascism based on Aryan racial supremacy.

In the late 20th century, American economic and social relations evolved from the sociopathic model toward a sociocidal one, which has now become an existential peril for US democracy. An increasingly authoritarian political system, embodied in Trumpism, is intertwined with our 21st-century capitalist order. Trumpism has become a critical driver of both policide and sociocide, offering a new neoliberal corporate oligarchy and nationalist neo-fascist politics to unite angry and disposable working people against non-white races and immigrants. Despite Trump's overt hostility to democratic norms, his re-election in 2024 and first months of his second term made it clear that our imperfect democracy is more at risk of destruction than at any period since the Civil War.

***

Two sociocidal political spirals are destroying the social relations and civil associations that de Tocqueville saw as the foundation of democracy. The first is the Neoliberal Spiral born in the Reagan years. This evolved with new anti-globalist and pro-worker rhetoric during the Trump years into an authoritarian agenda codified in Project 2025. This was Trump's roadmap for his second term, constitutionalized by major anti-democratic Supreme Court decisions that enshrined elements of political authoritarianism even before the 2024 Presidential election. They are a major concern of this chapter since they make clear the path that Trump, after his decisive Presidential victory in 2024, is moving the country toward policide and a possible new American fascism.

In the first few chapters, we documented the breakdown of work, community, and personal relations, as neoliberalism created a class of contingent workers losing secure jobs and social connections with other workers in the workplace or unions; 61% of workers in 2023 told pollsters they live "paycheck to paycheck."[5] This makes working people insecure and more isolated, helping fuel a larger cultural shift toward hyper-individualism as people focus on themselves simply to survive. As summarized in Chapter 4, they are now also less likely to be married, to have friends, or strong community relations. These sociocidal trends have major political consequences, undermining the social cohesion and connections supporting democracy.

In such dire circumstances, people need a New Deal-style government and populist labor movement – as well as strong associations in civil society and broader political movements - to bring them together and support them with secure jobs and job training, unions, affordable health care, and an expansive safety net. But the neoliberal economic revolution came in the 1980s wrapped in the opposite political agenda. Reagan ushered in his economic regime change with a political regime change, blowing up the New Deal. It was symbolized by Reagan's famous August 12, 1986, phrase, laced with wit and anti-government anger:

> The nine most terrifying words in the English language are "I'm from the govern-ment and I'm here to help."[6]

Reagan was not joking about cutting back on government, starting a bipartisan decades-long assault by both parties on government. In the 1990s, Bill Clinton joined Reagan, saying that the Democrats, too, were done with "big government." Both parties however, increased government spending on the military and helped corporations access cheap global labor and resources on friendly terms. Reagan was the first of a series of neoliberal Presidents who ran huge deficits by spending lavishly on corporations and the military while drastically cutting taxes on corporations and the rich. Attacking "big government" was the emerging policidal tool to attack and undermine the collective "we" and unleash the neoliberal market's "me."

Reagan's attack on government was the first and foundational pillar of neoliberal and future Trumpist policide, fueling and reflecting rising sociocide. He then signaled the second pillar when he fired 11,359 striking air-traffic controllers in October 1981 and destroyed their union, PATCO.[7] It was the first time the federal government ever decer-tified an existing union. Reagan began a full-scale political attack on unions, with the percentage of unionized workers collapsing from over 20% in the 1970s to under 10% at the end of the first Trump term in 2020.[8] The political attack on unions was integral to rising neoliberal sociocide and policide because it broke down the worker solidarity essential to democracy.

All forms of consensual politics and democratic government rest on a shared commit-ment to civic community and a collective good. Neoliberalism destroyed such a political "we" by turning the very idea of community into a market-driven collection of self-interested individuals, a key pillar of policide. Americans learned to see the "me" of the market as the basis of a good society. Such market-driven individualism was advanced by the cultural icon, Ayn Rand, in her best-selling book, *The Virtue of Selfishness*.[9] Rand popularized a crude view of Adam Smith's idea of the "invisible hand," which argued that protecting self-interest in the market is the best path toward the common good; she persuaded millions of Americans that selfishness is the highest moral virtue.[10]

Reagan politicized Rand's call for the "me," unleashing the neoliberal regime change that unfolded over several decades, moving toward its logical conclusion under Donald Trump. Trump was the inheritor of Reaganism but helped move it from the very imper-fect capitalist democracy of the late 20th century toward what might become a resurgent 21st-century American fascism, a looming US form of policide.

Policide, particularly in its current rising Far-Right form, did not arise spontaneously from neoliberal economics; it had to be midwifed politically. In the US, this required violently ramping up the domestic regime change Reagan began. Building on Reagan, Trumpism covertly coalesced with the global neoliberal elites that he attacked, bringing capitalism and American fascism closer together in the fertile soil of a fearful, socially disconnected precariat.

But the movement toward policide was bipartisan. Underlying all of it was polit-ical abandonment by both parties of an increasingly atomized working class deemed disposable.[11] Republicans and Democrats each engineered their own abandonment of working people. It is an essential story about how capitalist democracy becomes vulnerable under sociocidal conditions to neo-fascism.

* * *

While the Reagan Revolution inaugurated the neoliberal regime change, Presidents Clinton and Obama operated largely in the neoliberal spirit – and Biden's support for globalism and militarism sustained major neoliberal policies. A precariat working class continued to see the Democratic Party as an "Establishment" helping liberal East Coast cultural elites and racial minorities at the expense of hard-pressed white working people. White workers, feeling increasingly precarious economically and socially, continued to flee the Democratic Party into the waiting arms of the Republican Party, which offered them a sense of belonging and importance in a fight against enemies at home and abroad, leading to an increasingly authoritarian government based on the promise of restoring a pre-eminent white Christian nationalist community.[12]

The Democratic complicity in this catastrophe started with Bill Clinton, who cemented neoliberal regime change in his January 20, 1997, Inaugural Address:

> We know big government does not have all the answers. We know there's not a program for every problem. We have worked to give the American people a smaller, less bureaucratic government in Washington. And we have to give the American people one that lives within its means.
>
> The era of big government is over. But we cannot go back to the time when our citizens were left to fend for themselves … Self-reliance and teamwork are not opposing virtues; we must have both.[13]

This was Clinton's way of saying that the Democratic Party was abandoning the New Deal and joining in its own version of globalist neoliberal politics. While Clinton gave lip service to the idea of teamwork and working together to create more job security and better wages, workers were not fooled. Clinton accelerated their migration to the Republican Party, as working people realized that Clinton was abandoning FDR's politics of bringing workers together in unions and the New Deal, leading working people to suffer more wage stagnation and precariousness, both in their jobs and their social status and belonging.

This does not fully answer why workers flocked to choose the billionaire corporate party championed by Reagan over moderate Democrats – and why so many Trump fans supported him because they thought he was the true anti-Establishment candidate promising to "drain the swamp." The answer lies in the sociocidal Democratic shift from the class politics of the New Deal to the new identity politics brewing under Democrats. It would fragment the working class into competing racial groups; moreover, rather than leading workers in an anti-corporate class politics to secure their economic future, Democrats now appeared to attack white working people by using terms like "white privilege," blaming white workers for the problems of minorities and shifting Democratic focus from an attack on corporate Establishment power.

The Clinton Democrats created a splintered "we" based on race, ethnicity, gender, or other identities. This was a liberal identity politics, replacing the Democratic New Deal class politics. It fragmented the working population and turned them against each other as their economic struggles increased. Black workers would now learn to use their race to get Democratic-supported affirmative action, and female workers could get Democratic support through gender-based affirmative action.

This appeared to provide new forms of political community, legitimated under the Democratic ideology of DEI (diversity, equity, and inclusion). But while racism and sexism are centrally important and dangerous, with people of color and women as central targets of white Christian nationalism and Trumpism, the anti-racist and feminist movements need to be integrated with a universalizing resistance to the corporate oligarchy and a revived class politics, building solidarity with white workers and the broad working class of America as FDR did in the New Deal. Siloed identity politics, divorced from a unifying class politics, endangers the people it claims to protect. Without universalizing resistance, it has undermined the class-based solidarity that had begun to unite workers during the New Deal. Divided by race and gender, workers began competing against each other for whatever benefits the corporate elites were willing to dole out.[14] Moreover, siloed identity politics, in the name of protecting them, has put people of color, women, immigrants, and other "identity communities" at extreme risk. In the Trump era, all of these groups have been subjected to cultural, political, and physical repression and violence, as witnessed in authoritarian regimes throughout history in the US and Europe.

***

The Democratic Party's embrace of siloed identity politics has led millions of workers to hate the post-New Deal Democratic Party. Its liberal identity politics were turning them against each other and blaming white workers for Black workers' problems while global corporate neoliberal policies were stealing their jobs. This was political suicide for Democrats.[15] GOP identity politics promised white workers a new sense of belonging and community, uniting white workers and white business people together in a white Christian nationalist state that would concentrate police and military power to fight enemies at home and abroad. Masked partly by populist rhetoric against the corporate Establishment or "the swamp," Trump made Republican politics increasingly authoritarian. It evolved from the Moral Majority under Reagan and Bush into a looming neofascist policide promising to unite true American patriots under Trump. The people the Democrats claimed to be defending in its siloed identity politics, especially people of color, women, and immigrants, have already been highlighted as the first victims of the Trumpist second term. As his second term unfolds, they face deportation, loss of freedoms over their body and of speech or protest, as well as jail or death.

Trump himself promised white working people a new "we" coalescing together in a politics for "the forgotten working man" and revenge and "retribution" against the enemies of white, Christian Americans. While many believe that Trump invented this specter of American neo-fascism, it has a long American history going back all the way to the Confederate slave South, where Southern elites won the support of poor whites or "white trash" by honoring their identity as the "true Americans" and giving them far more privileges than slaves who were brutally repressed.[16]

Racial division has always been a crucial vehicle for dividing working people in America. After the Civil War, Jim Crow Democrats won over white workers with an early version of white identity politics based on Jim Crow racial codes; these provided a worthy social identity and racially based community of poor whites who might otherwise turn against ruling corporations and "the system."[17] Race remained a central tool of

Southern and corporate Democrats; in the 1920s, the Democratic Party embraced the Ku Klux Klan and other white-supremacist violent groups in their post-Civil War new brand of neo-fascism ruling through the Deep South.[18]

In the 1930s Great Depression, the Republican Party began to discover its own interest in racially based identity politics. With the rise of the New Deal among Democrats, the GOP became the party challenging "big government" and championing capitalism, drawing its support in the North largely from large and small businesses. But since it could not win elections without attracting some workers, the GOP took a page out of the Southern Democratic Party Jim Crow playbook as well as drawing on the racist ideologies of authoritarian European parties, starting in the 1930s and 1940s with "America First" Republicans who aligned themselves with Mussolini and Hitler.[19] Hitler himself had long been interested in Southern racism and the American Jim Crow eugenics movement, telling German scientists to study it carefully.[20] Capitalists like Henry Ford and the DuPont family explicitly sided with Hitler's Nazis. They invested heavily in Hitler's building of the Autobahn and German arms industry, aiding Hitler's success in uniting despairing German workers in the collective "we" of a great fascist Germany.

Hitler had shown how to use fascist street rallies and political violence to rally German workers. "America First" Republicans turned to the openly fascist US radio broadcaster, Father Charles Coughlin, and another fascist celebrity, Charles Lindbergh, a leader of "America First" in this early fascist Republican movement, who tried to bring white workers into a new white-supremacist American "we."[21] Some Republicans in Congress, tied to a fascist Christian Front group, even attempted to rally their largely white base with an attempted coup in the early 1940s but were defeated and prosecuted by the FBI for sedition in 1944.[22] But the white nationalist identity politics of the GOP did not disappear, re-emerging in the 1950s in the McCarthy Era and the corporate Right led by Bill Buckley. This new Republican Party built a policidal "Southern strategy" to unite white business elites and white workers in a community of racial, blood-based nationalism, starting with Goldwater and Nixon, and culminating in Reagan and finally Trump.

* * *

The modern American form of fascism began to grow into a major political force with Reagan. Many Americans have forgotten how effectively Reagan used white Christian nationalism and broader white identity politics to begin winning over American workers, who were losing unions and labor or political solidarity. Nixon had mobilized a white, conservative "silent majority" to unite and fight against young people protesting the Vietnam War. Reagan relied heavily on his own version of the "silent majority" and Southern strategy, recruiting Evangelical leaders like Jerry Falwell, a founder of the Moral Majority, to build a coalition of the Christian faithful and white "true Americans" to wage spiritual and political battle against the enemies at home. Allying with white Evangelicals like Falwell and Pat Robertson, and conservative anti-feminist women like Phyllis Schlafly, Reagan preached the gospel of the free market and law and order, uniting white workers and business people against criminal Blacks and student anti-war rioters at home. He denounced Democratic support for affirmative action, women's rights, and welfare as anti-white and anti-Christian, newly solidifying white workers and their corporate bosses in the GOP identity politics of white Christian nationalism.[23]

The Evangelical movement was so passionately mobilized for Reagan that Rev. Falwell pledged that "the Moral Majority would get Christian Right voters to elect Reagan 'even if he had the devil running with him.'" Also rallying for Reagan, Phyllis Schlafly declared that "the true foundation of our constitutional republic is Christianity" and allied with Reagan in opposing the women's Equal Rights Movement and gay rights as an existential threat to marriage and women's natural role as mothers at home.[24] Meanwhile, Reagan furiously attacked rioters at radical campuses like Berkeley, California, who, starting in the late 1960s, he had condemned as "beatniks, radicals, and filthy speech advocates" and "this trash" on campuses, who were "rioting with anarchy" rather than pursuing "academic freedom."[25]

White identity politics was at the heart of Reagan's success in winning over white workers as he demolished unions and New Deal communities that had helped build worker social connections and economic security. Throughout the 1980s, Reagan raged against New Deal government programs, such as affirmative action for government contractors as well as in universities like Harvard and the University of North Carolina. Reagan combined his white Christian nationalism with an attack on the entire civil rights movement as a form of "reverse discrimination":

> More than any other modern U.S. president, it was Ronald Reagan who cultivated the concept of so-called reverse discrimination, which emerged in the 1970s as a backlash against affirmative action in public schooling as court-ordered busing grew throughout the country. During these years, a growing number of white Americans came to believe civil rights programs and policies had outstretched their original intent and had turned whites into the victims of racial discrimination.[26]

With his constant attacks on affirmative action and broader civil rights activism, Reagan won support from white workers who increasingly saw Democrats as undermining law and order and pouring billions of dollars into welfare for lazy and criminal Blacks at their expense. This became part of a broader culture war that would later be taken up and intensified by Trump and the MAGA Republican movement, based on the growing grievances and anger of a white working class, largely bereft of unions and labor solidarity, who felt abandoned and isolated as the New Deal faded. Workers facing sociocide and becoming an economic "precariat" – living paycheck to paycheck – became the perfect base for Trumpist policide.

Trump openly embraced authoritarian means to build his new community of white Christian nationalism. He encouraged political violence, most famously when he started his January 6 domestic coup by inciting armed militia supporters like the Proud Boys and Oath Keepers to keep himself in power after losing the 2020 election. Prosecutions by the Justice Department against Trump after the January 6 insurrection became the political foundation of his campaign for a second term in 2024, as he won over his MAGA base by uniting them in an all-out struggle to Make America Great Again as a white, Christian nation.[27] This call to save the country from moral and economic decay by purging aliens who were "poisoning the blood" of the true white Christians of the nation is a central foundation of classic fascist movements. In the spirit of all authoritarian movements, Trump was building his political power by bringing together economically insecure working people looking for power and community. Trump's huge political rallies offered a new way for working people to build new Far-Right religious and political communities, binding the white working patriots together – against immigrants and people of color, as well as liberal and Marxist federal bureaucrats - to make the nation great again and rebuild America's economy to restore the prosperity and culture of true Americans.

Trump offered just enough "pro-worker" rhetoric to mask the extreme authoritarianism that he was delivering as part of a populist attack on the globalizing corporate Establishment. Trump did, in fact, depart from Reagan and the traditional corporate GOP agenda, arguing for tariffs that Reagan never would have accepted and opposing NATO and traditional Cold War opposition to Russia. Trump's populism was a big part of his appeal to white workers who felt the Democrats were abandoning them for racial minorities – and that Harris, who repeatedly declared herself "a proud capitalist," was aligned with or part of the corporate oligarchy. But Trumpist populism was ultimately in the service of corporate power and wealth, tied to huge tax reductions for corporations and wealthy people, elimination of regulations, attacks on social welfare, and ending all government that could have helped the working class. Trump created his own coalition between the Far-Right and the corporate system, one that would be far more authoritarian than even Reagan had imagined possible.

Although Reagan had also attacked the administrative "deep state" and blasted judges hostile to abortion and voting rights, Trump moved toward a more overtly neo-fascist policide. He said he would be "a dictator on day one." The momentous July 1, 2024, Supreme Court decision that immunized Trump from prosecution for any of his official acts, even a potential assassination of a political rival, stamped constitutional approval on his dictatorial aims. Trump called for a police state that would eliminate the immigrants "poisoning the blood" of America, constantly using the language of Adolph Hitler, creating a great new community of true patriots by force.[28]

Trump's policide was built as a movement prepared to embrace militias and even civil war to fight the real enemies of the true American community. Resurrecting Hitler's language of "vermin," he attacked Black criminal gangs, women seeking abortion on demand, "lawless" protesters, and millions of immigrants allegedly moving into the heartland. Liberal Democrats allegedly encouraged the "invasion" of these vermin and Trump's regime change would bring together the real Americans to destroy them. Laying out his authoritarian agenda in Project 2025, a roadmap for a second term by the conservative Heritage Foundation, Trump promised he would subject the judiciary and the liberal "deep state" bureaucracy entirely to his own will, using his personal control to purge the government of more than 50,000 civil servants and replace them with Far-Right political allies, described as "Schedule F" politicized employees in Project 2025. They would help Trump destroy the deep state of the federal bureaucracy and rebuild a white Christian nationalist government and society, deregulating corporations and purifyingthe blood of the nation.

While Trump claimed in July 2024 that he was not involved in creating Project 2025, it was written by his former leading aides and leading conservatives. As discussed shortly, many of Project 2025's major architects, such as Russell Vought and Stephen Miller, were appointed to leading positions in Trump's second term. Project 2025 spelled out in 900 pages the personnel and policies Trump championed on the campaign trail. As detailed in Project 2025, he promised to create "deportation camps" filled with hundreds of thousands of immigrants who would be detained and then expelled from the country with the help of the National Guard and the military. Unions and labor rights would be severely weakened, with corporations freer to fire labor organizers and banning the use of pro-union cards that make it easier to organize; other anti-labor recommendations involve the abolition of public sector unions and of laws preventing child labor as well as legalizing state bans on all unions.[29] This would all be accomplished by Trump concentrating executive power in himself, contesting future elections that he didn't win, and firing thousands of "deep state" civil servants and prosecutors in the Justice Department, Pentagon, EPA, FDA, and other regulatory agencies who didn't do his bidding.[30]

Project 2025 made clear that the second Trump term was designed to be far more authoritarian and dangerous than his first term. Project 2025 archietects prepared a detailed list of the Far-Right personnel who have already been vetted and tapped to carry out extremist measures like creating deportation camps and expelling potentially millions of immigrants. Trump's most loyal "yes-men" took over the Justice Department, the Pentagon, and other executive agencies, ensuring that the people and many checks and balances restraining Trump in his first term were all gone.

Even before the 2024 election, the GOP had already moved forward with many of the more extreme second-term agenda promises, especially regarding election subversion. In 2024, before the election, MAGA Republican officials were training local officials administering elections in red states and areas they controlled in blue states in the arts of decertifying elections. Local voting officials were instructed to stop counting ballots and bring in MAGA lawyers to argue that irregularities required delaying the count and certification further, throwing the election into chaos. Meanwhile, they were also implementing more restrictive rules on gerrymandering, voter registration, and how to make Black and Brown voters afraid to vote. The fake electoral scheme of January 6 – and Trump's immediate pardon of the January 6 rioters after his re-election – was updated as part of detailed plans to prevent the certification of democratic election results.[31]

In the most authoritarian Supreme Court decision since before the Civil War, the Trump-appointed Roberts Court delivered decisions in the summer of 2024 that enacted much of Trump's agenda for his second term. The Court's Chevron decision overturned much of the authority of government agencies such as the Environmental Protection Agency and the Federal Drug Administration to regulate corporations, arguing that this usurped Congressional authority to make law which could only be changed by courts. The Presidential Immunity decision, the Court's response to Trump's argument that he could not be prosecuted for any of the serious legal cases related to insurrection and fraud, declared that Trump was immune from prosecution for all "official" acts and many acts on the "outer perimeter" of his official duties. This effectively freed Trump – and all future Presidents – to instruct the Justice Department to prosecute political rivals or even use the FBI or military to assassinate them. Justice Sonia Sotomayor, in her outspoken dissent on the Immunity decision, said the Court had made "the President a king":

> The Court effectively creates a law-free zone around the President, upsetting the status quo that has existed since the Founding ... "This new official-acts immunity now 'lies about like a loaded weapon' for any President that wishes to place his own interests, his own political survival, or his own financial gain, above the interests of the Nation."
>
> The relationship between the President and the people he serves has shifted irrevocably. In every use of official power, the President is now a king above the law[32]

Other critics joined Sotomayor in saying that the Supreme Court had turned the US into a "*constitutional monarchy*."[33]

The Roberts Court defined the President as the one person in America who the Constitution dictated was above the law, free to order any executive agency or official to do whatever he demanded, even if it involved acts of bribery, violence, or pardons in exchange for money. The Court essentially implemented significant parts of Trump's authoritarian agenda before he took office again, enshrining Trumpism in the Constitution. Moreover, it laid the ground for Trump in his second term to carry out parts of a neo-fascist program. This included not only the concentration of all executive branch authority in himself, the prosecution of political rivals, and purging of the civil servants in the administrative agencies of government, but also many other acts of retribution, including legal and violent threats of revenge that he promised in his campaign and spelled out in Project 2025.

Trump's pick of J.D. Vance as his Vice President confirmed the existential threat to American democracy. Vance has said that he would not have certified Biden's election had he been Vice President on January 6, ready to carry out the coup that Mike Pence prevented. Vance also said that he thought the President should carry out orders that the Supreme Court ruled as unconstitutional. He fully supports the authoritarian Immunity, Chevron, and Dobbs decisions. Vance will lead much of the implementation of Project 2025, making clear he agrees the President should purge thousands of career civil servants in the Justice Department, Department of Defense, and regulatory agencies, and replace them with political cronies. A graduate of Yale Law School, he cloaks Trump's neo-fascist agenda with a veneer of intellectualism, making him even more dangerous than Trump. As a Silicon Valley venture capitalist, closely tied to the billionaire financier Peter Thiel, he also is a perfect liaison to the corporate world, a key figure at the center of the authoritarian capitalist – Far-Right coalition which the second Trump term aims to cement.[34]

Trump's policidal agenda kept getting more explicit after January 6, with a four-year campaign for re-election amped up by calls for political violence and culminating in his pardon of more than 1500 jailed January 6 armed insurrectionists as one of his first acts of his second term. He had long promised supporters at his rallies that he would pay their legal bills if they "beat the crap" out of left-wing protesters. He told his supporters to surround election centers and intimidate "cheaters" going to vote. He also told his base to "rough up" liberal protesters in the streets. Trump praised armed and violent neo-fascists with swastikas at a 2017 Charlottesville, Virginia, rally as "some very fine people".[35]

All this encouraged many of his supporters to carry out political acts, including members of a Far-Right militia, the Wolverine Watchmen, in Michigan who were arrested by the FBI on October 8, 2020, for plotting to kidnap and kill Michigan governor, Gretchen Whitmer.[36] On October 28, 2022, a Trump supporter, David DePape, broke into Nancy Pelosi's home and brutally beat her husband, Paul Pelosi, with a hammer, almost killing him, claiming that Pelosi had conspired to steal votes from Donald Trump.[37] The attempted assassination by Thomas Crooks of Trump, himself, on July 13, 2024, at a Butler, Pennsylvania, campaign rally reflected, ironically, the political violence that Trump had normalized beginning in his first term, when a Florida Trump supporter, Cesar Sayoc, in 2018, sent mail bombs to the houses of Trump critics such as Barack Obama, Hillary Clinton, John Brennan, Robert De Niro, Alexandria Ocasio-Cortez, and Joe Biden.[38] As journalist Moira Donegan writes:

> Trump's own authoritarian politics have been accompanied by bigotry, virulent political tribalism, and a willingness to allow his preferences to be enforced and his enemies punished through physical violence. His rallies, for instance, have been sites of violence since his first campaign for the presidency in 2016, when supporters would frequently attack protesters and members of the media …

Trump's enthusiasm for a brutish and at times outright violent politics of domination appears to be infectious, and has spawned imitators throughout the Republican party: in 2018, then representative Greg Gianforte, of Montana, was charged with assault in the midst of his congressional reelection campaign after body-slamming a reporter, a move that Trump praised. "Any guy who can do a body slam, he is my type!" Trump said. (Gianforte pleaded guilty to a misdemeanor assault charge, and has since become Montana's governor.)[39]

Dornegan notes that after Trump was shot at his political rally, his response appeared to call for violent retaliation:

> After Trump ducked to avoid the bullets, he was immediately surrounded by Secret Service agents, who closely surrounded him as a human shield. But he rose from the stage, apparently in defiance of their wishes, to raise a fist in the air and yell "Fight!", Trump was defiant, and calling for revenge. The risk of vigilante violence by Trump supporters, meant to avenge their leader or punish his perceived enemies, will be high. There is no sign that Trump or his surrogates will disavow this, or make any effort to call it off. And why would they? They never have before.[40]

Political violence is an especially powerful tool for bringing together people atomized by sociocide. Trump encouraged his armed supporters to band together near election centers to intimidate "cheaters." MAGA rallied Trump's base into a political community to induce fear in their political opponents. In street militias and online MAGA networks, they rallied together to scare Democratic voters and Democratic candidates. Far-Right militias, local Christian MAGA groups, and Far-Right online activists sent death threats to numerous federal Democratic candidates in 2022 and 2024, scaring them enough to pay for bodyguards to protect themselves and their families.[41] GOP dissidents received the same threats, with Senator Mitt Romney announcing in 2023 he would not run for office again because it was too dangerous for himself and his family.[42] Thousands of election officials and volunteer election workers from Georgia to Arizona to Michigan, most often in Black urban centers, received death threats for allegedly monkeying with election machine software or "stuffing" the ballot boxes with phony votes. Between one-third and one-half of election workers and town officials had already received threats before the 2024 election; the MAGA forces were working feverishly to challenge legally and physically Democratic victories at local, state, and federal levels. In late April 2024, the Brennan Center for Justice released a report showing that:

> Most local election officials fear for their colleagues' safety and 62%, almost two-thirds, are concerned about politicians trying to interfere in how they or others do their work. More than one in three respondents said they had been harassed and abused because of their work as a local election official, and 16% said they had been threatened. Of those that had faced threats, 61% said they had been threatened over the phone, and the same number had been threatened in person.[43]

The Supreme Court's Presidential Immunity decision ensured that January 6 and many continuing efforts to subvert elections were now constitutional. Trump made election denialism a centerpiece of his 2024 campaign. He encouraged his base to come together in strong local Far-Right communities solidifying between 2020 and 2024 to prevent more "stolen" elections. MAGA Republicans in Congress bought into this frontal attack on elections and democracy, with 147 GOP Congressional Republicans raising objections on January 6 to certifying Biden's election as President, and many continuing to say Biden was not a legitimate President. [44] This rejection of Biden as a legitimate president had spread by August 2023 to almost 70% of Republican voters. This all helped build a new sense of community and social connection among Trumpists who had long felt politically abandoned and isolated by liberal Democrats.[45] The Supreme Court declared effectively that Trump's election subversion and larger Project 2025 agenda in a second term was constitutional. The threats and often violent attacks on the people administering voting centers, as well as Democratic candidates for office, escalated all through Trump's race for a second term. This began to look like child's play compared to the "revenge" and "retribution" that Trump enacted after being elected to a second term. Anybody openly opposing Trump in his second term became vulnerable to the political and sometimes violent repression characteristic of neo-fascist regimes – most notably immigrants, people of color, women, liberal journalists, leftist or Marxist academics, civil servants, and Democratic Party activists.

Demographic shifts helped fuel Trump's white Christian nationalism. As racial minorities move toward becoming the majority in the US by 2040, whites face minority status for the first time in modern American history. Such demographic turning points do not necessarily or automatically create policide and neo-fascism. But Trump and MAGA Republicans, including leading Far-Right media figures such as Tucker Carlson, weaponized the "minority majority" as a terrifying threat to whites, codified in the Republican "Great Replacement Theory," as reported by one journalist:

> "The great replacement? Yeah, it's not a conspiracy theory. It's their electoral strategy," the Fox News host said, as the words "Democrats often celebrate demographic change" appeared on screen.
>
> The racist conspiracy theory claims that white Christians are being intentionally replaced by immigrants, people of color and non-Christians …[46]

The "Great Replacement" trope has become a staple of GOP white identity politics, providing new mass support for Trumpist policide. In May 2024, in a *Time Magazine* interview, Trump became very specific, announcing he would be building mass deportation camps for 11 million illegal immigrants that he would expel from the country using police, state National Guards, and the US military.[47] This was embraced by his huge base as the only way to save America from descending into the hell of a nation dominated by immigrants and people of color, while unifying white Christians into the new great racialized spiritual community that is at the heart of all authoritarian politics and has long defined American fascism.

***

Trump's presidential victory in 2024, with GOP majorities in both the Senate and the House, made it clear that Trump's threats to democracy, especially those embedded in Project 2025, had to be taken with the utmost seriousness. Trump made explicit the way forward in his November 6, 2024, victory speech: "I will govern by a simple motto: 'PROMISES MADE PROMISES KEPT.'"[48]

The promises – in the tangible forms of personnel and policies specified in Project 2025 – began to take shape immediately after his re-election as Trump and his top political operatives began to announce staff and programs. The Pentagon leaders and Justice Department attorneys who had helped to stave off the most authoritarian of Trump's initiatives in his first term, such as using the military to police protests inside the US or to prosecute Trump's enemies, were being replaced by vetted Trump ultra-loyalists. They included Tom Homan as his "border tsar" and Stephen Miller, his extremist anti-immigrant hawk, as Trump's new deputy chief of staff. Moreover, Trump tried to make the Senate relinquish their traditional constitutional function of approving his cabinet selections, so he could select his leaders as "recess appointments." This was a clear signal that Trump's authoritarian impulses to govern the nation personally, minimizing Congressional checks and balances on this power, would fuel his form of governance. Trump also supported the restoration of Presidential "impoundment," which gives the President the right to withhold funds appropriated by Congress, another serious infringement of US checks and balances.[49] Moreover, Trump supported the Republican House's law, passed on November 22, 2024, after Trump's re-election, that would allow the Treasury to strip the tax-exempt status of any non-profits that it deemed as supporting terrorism. This meant that any civil society group that the President saw as disloyal to him could effectively be financially destroyed and eliminated, a measure by which the President could further intensify the sociocide – or erosion of voluntary associations and other social relations in civil society – that helped give rise to Trump's authoritarian appeal and re-election.[50]

In the same authoritarian spirit, 50,000 "Schedule F" high-level civil service positions discussed earlier were newly designed to be subject to Trump's direct orders. This was the assault on Trump's "deep state" which now, like Congress, would see its checks and balances on the President deeply eroded in the executive branch itself. Trump affirmed his view of the "unitary executive" – fully fleshed out in the proposals of Project 2025 that argued all executive agencies, including the Justice Department and Pentagon, were subject to the direct personal control of the President and could not exercise any constitutional checks and balances overriding the President's will.

Trump's appointment of Russell Vought as Director of the Office of Management and Budget (OMB) made clear that he would use his top picks to enforce many of the most authoritarian Project 2025 proposals. Vought was a leading architect and author of Project 2025. In an interview with Tucker Carlson, Vought made clear that he would move quickly to eliminate the independence of all federal agencies from the President and fire thousands of career civil servants in the deep state:

> "The president has to move as fast and as aggressively as possible with a radical constitutional perspective to be able to dismantle that bureaucracy in their power centers," said Vought. "Number one is going after the whole notion of independence. There are no independent agencies."[51]

In other interviews, Vought argued that Trump should bypass the Senate to make recess appointments and argued he would help Trump enact the most authoritarian of Project 2025's proposals; in videos obtained by ProPublica:

> Vought describes invoking the Insurrection Act to compel the military to crack down on protests and intentionally demoralizing career federal employees to push them

out of their positions. Vought has openly promoted elevating Christianity in government, complaining in speeches about "secularism" and "Marxism" in America.[52]

This is not to say that Trump's most authoritarian and neo-fascist policies will all be
enacted or implemented in his second term. Many potential hurdles could stand in the
way, including adverse court decisions by federal and state judges, opposition by small
numbers of Congressional or Senate Republicans allying with Democrats, and opposition
by state governors, local officials, and thousands of ordinary Americans mobilizing in
street and town hall protests to stop Trump. All these forms of resistance began to grow
in the first few months of Trump's second term. Moreover, in the 2026 Congressional
elections, backlash to extremist or failed Trumpist measures could change the balance of
power in the Senate, House, and nation.

Nonetheless, as Trump began to take the reins for his second term, it was clear he
meant to keep his promises. At the very top of his priority list was the mass deportation
of potentially millions of undocumented immigrants at the heart of a larger campaign to
shut down the border. Building mass internment camps, separating families and removing them from their homes, mobilizing the funds for construction and organization of the
land, building of the camps, and galvanizing the police and National Guard to carry out
the purge of millions of people would require a massive effort taking months or years; it
could take years of bureaucratic litigation and court cases. Nonetheless, the fear of this
unprecedented 21st-century vision of millions of people forced into camps evoked terror
in immigrant communities before and after Trump's re-election. It also created a specter
of American fascism among those who remembered the mass internment of the Japanese
by the US government in World War II, as well as the collective memory of the horror of
the German concentration camps, the ultimate symbol of the worst horrors that fascism
has created.

The fear of a more explicit police state or neo-fascist order was reinforced in the early
days after Trump's re-election. Beyond hard-line Far-Right appointees like Tom Homans
and Stephen Miller, Trump announced a few days after his re-election that he would
issue an executive order to create a "warrior board," composed of his most trusted aides,
with the mandate to review the loyalty of all 3-star and 4-star generals to Trump personally, opening up a new institutionalized mechanism to ensure that the military would face
ongoing threats of demotion or firing if they refused Trump's orders, constitutional or
not. Media reports indicated that the executive order and the warrior board could:

> fast-track the removal of generals and admirals found to be "lacking in requisite
> leadership qualities," according to a draft of the order reviewed by *The Wall Street
> Journal*. But it could also create a chilling effect on top military officers, given the
> president-elect's past vow to fire "woke generals," referring to officers seen as pro-
> moting diversity in the ranks at the expense of military readiness.
>
> As commander in chief, Trump can fire any officer at will, but an outside board
> whose members he appoints would bypass the Pentagon's regular promotion sys-
> tem, signaling across the military that he intends to purge a number of generals and
> admirals.[53]

CNN reported that the military was discussing how to respond to Trump giving illegal
orders, giving more credence to the fear that Trump was preparing to use the military
against US citizens and protesters at home; at the same time, the Pentagon was also

making plans about how to respond to Trump's stated plans to fire "scores of civil servants" in the Pentagon itself, while also potentially illegally deploying the military against
migrants on the border.[54]

Trump's selection of Pete Hegseth as his Secretary of Defense magnified the fear that
the military would be used to oppose the Left and shut down domestic protests. Hegseth,
a veteran and former Fox News television personality, is a vocal supporter of the January
6 insurrection and wrote that the Democrats were an enemy who could only be defeated
by a civil war in which the military would have to intervene to ensure that Trump was
put in the presidency. He repeatedly called for a holy American crusade against the
enemy within.[55] Hegseth promised to purge the military of "woke" generals and admi-
rals, whether because of their commitment to diversity, women in combat, or "Marxist"
ideology. Like many of Trump's cabinet picks, Hegseth had been investigated for sexual
assault and was known for his extremist MAGA views. He had a tattoo of an American
flag with an A15-Assault rifle as the lower stripe of the flag.[56] His extremism meant that,
like Matt Gaetz, he might face confirmation problems in even a Republican Senate, but
Republicans overwhelmingly confirmed his nomination.[57]

The fear of police or military violence spread from immigrant communities to people
of color, who knew that fascist measures against immigrants historically had been linked
to violence against themselves. Trump's open embrace of white Christian nationalism
and militant Far-Right white-supremacist militias and podcasters began to take on even
greater concern after his re-election. As he moved into his second term, promising a
kind of immunity for police seeking to protect Americans against crime and anarchy,
Trump's re-election reinforced fears of his threats of fascist-style revenge and retribution
against what Trump was now calling "the enemies of the people." In Trump's words,
this included the mainstream media and Democrats who had prosecuted him and what
he called the "great patriot" insurrectionists rioting in the Capitol on January 6.

As noted earlier, Trump promised even before his re-election that he would be a "dictator on day one." He talked after his re-election about firing special prosecutor Jack
Smith" in "two seconds," as part of his top priorities to keep himself out of prison and
exact retribution on all those who had prosecuted or convicted him of 34 felonies; Smith
quickly resigned after Trump's re-election but faced potential Trumpist law-suits and
other threats. Not only was Trump freeing himself from all possible federal prosecution, but he was also letting Americans know that there would be a new "rule of law" in
which the Attorney General that he selected would act like his own personal attorney and
carry out appropriate retribution against all those attacking him. Rolling Stone reported
accounts that Trump was making plans not only to possibly prosecute Biden's Attorney
General Merrick Garland or Alvin Bragg, the New York Distrcit Attorney who convicted
him of 34 felonies, but even his own aides, like his former top Republican aides such as
his Attorney General William Barr and his former chief of staff, 4-star Marine General
John Kelly, who had called him in the week before his re-election "a fascist to the core,"
a charge echoed in the same words by Trump's former military chief of staff, General
Mark Milley. As he prepared to staff his new Justice Department and begin his second
term, the greatest fear voiced by many was Trump's repeated vow to take complete control over the Justice Department and turn it into an instrument for enforcing his own will
and revenge.[58]

Trump's selection of Florida Attorney General Pam Bondi as US Attorney General
made clear that Trump wasn't joking about turning the Justice Department into his own
personal law firm. Bondi was an ultra-Trump loyalist, helped lead a hard-right America

First Trumpist political group set up by Trump's chief anti-immigrant hawk, Stephen Miller, and was one of the prime Trump litigators challenging the 2020 election of Biden. She had promised to help "prosecute the prosecutors" after Trump's re-election, and did nothing after becoming his Attorney General to stop Trump's war on government, firing of civil servants, or arbitrary executive orders.[59] Bondi had led legal suits against Pennsylvania in 2020 for electoral fraud which were based on lies and were dismissed by the courts. She had represented Trump as his personal attorney in business and political cases, including his impeachment trial, since 2016.[60] Her selection made clear that Trump was serious about turning the Justice Department into his own personal law firm. After nominations of extreme MAGA Attorney General choices like Matt Gaetz, followed by selection of Bondi, career lawyers in the Justice Department were reported in the media to be "lawyering up," with many hoping to stay in the Trump Justice Department and do their best to fight in the courts to ensure as much traditional independence of their work as possible. There are major legal hurdles to Trump simply firing thousands of career prosecutors in the Justice Department, but he has other ways to force them out, such as reclassifying them to work in legal areas they have no experience or interest in and sending them to work in other jurisdictions. Fear reverberated through the coteries of thousands of civil service lawyers that the rule of law was in deep jeopardy as the Justice Department was transformed into a "Trump law firm."[61]

***

Concerns about a neo-fascist Trumpist second term focused most heavily on his plans for concentrating his personal control over the military and judiciary, as well as his Project 2025 plans for mass deportation of immigrants, racial vendettas involving rolling back minority rights, police immunity, and election denialism. But there were other worrisome signs of corporate oligarchy, a classic dimension of fascist regimes that aligns government with huge corporations to help impose other socially harmful policies by executive order or force when necessary. In classical fascism, the sociocidal breakdown of social relations and solidarity in the workplace and civil society creates powerlessness and isolation, emboldening the government to authorize policies favoring big business at the expense of an atomized public. Fascism breeds such transactional systemic corruption between government and corporate elites.

When Fox News star anchor, Sean Hannity, asked Trump what he would do on the first day of his second term, he said "drill, baby, drill." The promise to end all environmental regulation and abandon the fight against climate change was launched in Trump's first term – when government scientists were forced to purge the words "climate change" from all official government research and documents. The attack on the "hoax" of climate change, as Trump often mocked it, was almost certain to be intensified in his second term, empowered by the Supreme Court's Chevron decision that undermined much of environmental regulation. Plans to turn over millions of areas of public land to the "carbon-industrial" corporate complex (the CIC) of Exxon, Chevron, the Koch Brothers, and other energy giants were a near certainty. *The Washington Post* reported that Trump promised oil executives of the CIC that if they gave him a billion dollars before the election, he would immediately sign executive orders that would expand drilling and approve other fracking and carbon projects; Trump got the money from Big Oil and Gas and did exactly what he promised, opening up public lands and shorelines to driling and fracking. At the very time that global scientists were expressing fears about the failure of climate efforts to stave off disaster in the first Trump term, with concerns mounting as the pace of horrific fires, hurricanes, and warming intensified virtually every year, Trump's getting into bed with oil and gas companies and fomenting ever more climate denialism could ultimately be the most catastrophic consequence of his second term. Even as the public, especially young people, grew more fearful of climate catastrophe and the environmental bonfire too big and hot to stop, the shut down of public voice and protest in a more authoritarian second Trump term could emerge as the true "holocaust" of 21st century American fascism.[62]

The success of all of Trump's neo-fascist promises and programs will depend in large measure on the role played by large and powerful US corporations and banks, including those in the carbon-industrial complex, the Military-Industrial Complex, the Big Tech titans of Silicon Valley, and the biggest moguls on Wall Street and private equity, including J.P. Morgan Chase, Goldman Sachs, and Blackstone, as well as billionaires like Elon Musk, Jeff Bezos, and Vance Silicon Valley patron Peter Thiele. During his re-election campaign, most major corporate CEOs remained neutral, other than Musk; many were privately concerned about Trump's authoritarian impulses and populist economic policies but fearful of alienating Trump. After Trump's victory, large numbers came out and supported his victory, sending him texts or visiting him at Mar-a-Lago to congratulate him. This immediate desire to get on the re-elected President's list of favorites is, based on historical precedent in authoritarian and fascist regimes, just the beginning of a more open and corrupt alliance between the corporate world and Trumpist authoritarianism, already clearly in view in the first few months of Trump's second term. Trump appointed a new Cabinet of billionaires and an Administration inseparable from a more empowered and entitled corporate oligarchy.

Corporations depend on government for billions of dollars in contracts, subsidies, and other forms of corporate welfare. During European fascist regimes in Germany and Italy, corporations quickly rallied behind fascist leaders, recognizing that fascism, unlike communism, was a form of authoritarianism in which corporations and capitalism itself could flourish. Both German and American corporations aiding Hitler profited substantially from the *great leader*'s rebuilding of the autobahn, the German military, and the kind of broader military Keynesianism that helped bring Germany out of its Great Depression. US corporate leaders clearly welcomed the immense tax benefits for corporations and billionaires that Trump promised to renew in his second term, as well as his plans for deregulation and shrinking government under a Musk-supervised "efficiency" tsardom. Musk himself, after Trump's second-term electoral victory, joined with Trump as a new "co-president" to say their new war on government would bring significant short-term "hardship" to ordinary Americans. Fiscal sanity, Musk announced, required major cuts in Medicaid, Medicare, Social Security, public education expenses, welfare programs, and much more, adding up to more than a trillion dolllars in cuts in government spending, When Trump appointed him head of the Department of Government Efficiency (DOGE), Musk waged his famous war on "waste and fraud" that led to mass firings of tens of thousands of federal workers and unconstitutional moves by Trump toward abolition of entire government agencies such as the Department of Education, USAID, and the Consumer Protection Finance Board. Trump and Musk said mas cuts and firings were the precondition for efficiency and an eventual US recovery, a claim that most mainstream economists rejected. Nonetheless, Trump's and Musk's all-out attacks on government and social welfare were a dream come true for America's corporate oligarchy. The US stock markets jumped immediately after Trump's re-election to record highs, reflecting corporate confidence that this was a billionaire President on whom they could rely for protection from government regulation and future profitability.

Concerns about too much authoritarianism receded in the corporate world as they welcomed Trump into office and jockeyed for the contracts and policies that would lead to a new era of profits and corporate rule, even if enforced by the iron hand of an opnely authoritarian a government that they traditionally prefer to limit and disguise under the long-standing veneer of popular rule and democracy. Trump's chaotic tariffs policy began to destabilize the markets, but the fear of a "Trump-recession" did not lead most big companies to oppose him. More and more companies endorsed him and went to Mar-a-Lago to fund him. They embraced policies that would deregulate them, abolish unions, and lower their taxes, massively increasing their power and profits while entrenching a new corporate and state authoritarianism.

Trump's second term is an intensification of corporate oligarchy in the US, linking the anti-democratic power of the billionaire and CEO corporate class with authoritarian strong man political governance. Beyond Musk at least nine other billionaires were appointed to Trump's second-term cabinet, including hedge-fund owner Scott Bessent as the Secretary of the Treasury and Howard Luttnick as Secretary of Commerce. American fascism does not replace American capitalism but rather enriches dominant corporate elites through strong transactional ties between leading corporate oligarchs and Trump. While there will be conflicts over the scale of tariffs and other possible limits on trade, both the oligarchs and Trump will enrich each other by institutionalizing mutually beneficial relations that eliminate potentially more than a trillion dollars in government social welfae spending and send billions of government aid and contracts to big business, led by allies such as Musk, and return billions more in corporate donations to Trump and his top political aides. The rise of 21st-century American fascism will not replace capitalism but empower and enrich it at the expense of ordinary workers who voted Trump back into office. The ultimate victim of this melding of corporate power and fascism – in what can be called fascist capitalism – is US democracy itself. Resisting and overthrowing this new regime requires rebuilding personal and social relations in civil society, the labor movement, and other anti-corporate social networks and advocacy groups in the economy, as well as pro-democracy local to global groups in a global anti-fascist politics. As shown in the next chapter, this starts with small acts of personal reconnection, kindness, and solidarity, the beginning of the sociocidal assault on the breakdown of social relations that is the breeding ground of fascism itself.

* * *

The Military Spiral is a second policidal American dynamic, intertwined with the Neoliberal Spiral, where the breakdown of social relations and decline of trust fuels wars that unite the fractured population around defeating the "enemy." Defeating the enemy abroad has always been the twin pillar of fascist politics along with destroying "the enemy within." While Trump was branded by mainstream media as an "anti-war" candidate because of his rhetoric against NATO and the war in Ukraine, his victory and policy in his second term are likely to stir conflict and war in the classic vein of authoritarian strongmen such as Hitler and Mussolini. As Trump was being re-elected, it became clear that his long-standing hostility to Iran and support of Netanyahu's policies could draw the US into a new major Middle Eastern war, potentially engaging the US itself in a frightening war with Iran and its surrogates, likely billed as the decisive war on terrorism. Trump's hostility to China also could breed tension and possible war over Taiwan, should the Taiwanese leadership view Trump's return to the presidency as a license to declare full independence from China.

The US has always been expansionist and militarist, creating a national security state that traditionally has fostered sociopathic relations toward other nations in the spirit of gaining geopolitical power and raising profits, while also mobilizing a population divided by class and racial caste to come together to destroy the enemy. This dynamic, associated with long-standing imperial war policies in the US, is particularly strong in authoritarian states, as memorably described by George Orwell in his classic dystopian novel, *1984*.[63] Big Brother unifies the country under his control by invoking the "three-minute hate," where the whole public stops what it is doing during the day and comes together to watch the "telescreens," where they scream a collective rage, revenge, and violence against the enemy.

US militarism has long been a major bipartisan force to unite a fractured, atomized population around defeating the enemy. In 1980, Reagan amped up this agenda by intensifying the Cold War and vowing to destroy and eliminate the Soviet "Evil Empire." His militaristic agenda was fueled further by George W. Bush after 9/11, as he waged a new age of "war against terror" in the Middle East, notably in Iraq, after initially invading Afghanistan.[64] Terrorism provided a global war against relatively faceless enemies that could never be decisively defeated, a kind of war designed partly to unify an increasingly polarized and atomized nation. In the 2020s, such "unifying" war got turned partially inward against domestic enemies and "terrorists," including against largely peaceful students protesting against war on their campuses, while also directed outward against foreign enemies such as Hamas and Iran, now highlighted in the evolving war against terrorism as well as against Russia and China in two new Cold Wars.[65]

Extreme militarism has been both a response to and cause of the 21st century transition from a sociopathic to a sociocidal society, for all the reasons discussed in earlier chapters. The breakdown of trust and social relations in multiple spheres helped give rise to the militarization of rage and fear in Trump's first term, as he repeatedly denounced Iran and China as enemies, along with the immigrant and racial enemies at home. At the same time, Biden embraced the historic Democratic Party's bipartisan support of US militarism, supporting the war on terrorism and the Israeli war in Gaza, even as famine and evidence of war crimes by the Far-Right Israeli Netanyahu government were collected by the State Department, leading some US diplomats to resign in protest.[66] While both the Biden and Trump Administrations strenuously objected, claiming anti-semitism on the part of Israeli critics, many international leaders at the UN and in regional conferences and international courts called the Gaza war an unfolding "genocide," with Samantha Power, Biden's head of the US Agency for International Development and the most authoritativedocumenter of the Rwandan genocide, warning of the spread of famine already killing thousands of Palestinian children.[67]

The Democrats were entirely complicit in the Military Spiral, not only in what many in the international community was describing as a policide in Gaza, but in their call for NATO expansion and full-scale military support for Ukraine, as well as the new Cold War with Russia and with China. While partially united by substantial bipartisan militarism, the US polarized between the Trumpist authoritarian GOP and the Democrats trying to hold on to their weak democracy. Social divisions became so intense that fear of a second Civil War mounted, and the Military Spiral became a key national political instrument for binding the country together.

While Trump's isolationist and anti-NATO rhetoric seems to make him less complicit in the Military Spiral, the reality is somewhat different. It is true that Trump's admiration of Putin's "strongman" rule makes him appear less of a Cold Warrior against Russia than the Reagan or Bush earlier GOP Establishment. Far-Right Republicans, such as the 1930s and 1940s America Firsters, have historically used isolationist policies to oppose unpopular Democratic war policies. Trump acted in the first two months of his re-election to bring a more rapid end to the war in Ukraine and curb the expansion of NATO beyond the defense of Europe. But the notion of Trump as a peace candidate or President is misguided. In Trump's first term, he pulled out of the nuclear agreement with Iran while dramatically building the US nuclear arsenal, and laying the ground for a greater Middle Eastern war pitting the US and Israel against Iran and its proxies. Meanwhile, Trump also stoked aggressive economic and military policies against China, funding a US military build-up in the Pacific Theater and boasting of readiness to fight to protect Taiwan.[68] While Trump signaled a clear desire to imitate and ally with Putin, who was becoming the idolized authoritarian of the US Far-Right, even much of Trump's MAGA party would end up supporting the huge US military aid to Ukraine in 2024, as the US built up its military presence in the Middle East and on the Russian border from Ukraine to the Baltics, Poland and Finland.[69] Two days after his re-election, Trump and his new major ally, Elon Musk, spoke with Volodymyr Zelenskyy, the President of Ukraine, on the phone, with Musk promising to offer Zelenskyy satellite services and other aid that would support Ukraine's defense, though in an infamous Oval Office meeting with Zelenskyy two months later, Trump shamelessly bullied and humiliated Zelenskyy, appearing prepared to force a territorial settlement on terms acceptable to Putin while demanding that Zelenskyy fork over 50% of future revenues on Ukranian sales of its rare earth minerals.

The contemporary form of the sociocidal Military Spiral arises when greater social division leads both the GOP and Democrats to unify the country with sociocidal wars against more frightening "enemies." Militarist propaganda about enemies abroad and actual wars on terrorists redirect public anxiety and rage at the enemy abroad. This, in turn, spirals up efforts by political parties to gain support and public unity through more dangerous and endless wars. The Military Spiral unleashes a never-ending sequence of political rage against the enemy abroad, normalizing and breeding more political rage and violence against enemies at home, including Black activists against police violence deemed "terrorists" and student protesters on campus deemed lawless. Anger against these domestic enemies fuels yet another round of war against the terrorist enemy abroad, and onward toward more sociocide against other nations linked with sociocide at home.

The Military Spiral radiates into culture and personal life while fueling values of power and dominance in politics itself. People raised in military cultures, and especially those trained in the military or police, learn to value command and power itself. In a society filled with more disconnected, angry, and fearful people – and a working class feeling less empowered at work – the sense of powerlessness and the psychological need to be and feel powerful becomes intense. People pursue power both in private personal relations and in public settings, and many people become bullies as a form of intimidation and self-defense. This sets the stage for authoritarian politicians or "strongmen" such as Mussolini and Hitler, whose autocratic personalities become a model for sectors of the public feeling disempowered and desperately seeking to feel a sense of their own power.[70]

This helps explain the attraction of political personalities like Donald Trump, himself both a personal and political bully, who openly glorify naked power and embody it in their personal behavior and policies.[71] Popular disempowerment at work or in the community spirals into an attraction to political leaders who act out the power that disempowered people seek, which leads more disempowered people to offer even more support for authoritarian leaders, who then exhibit and execute even more autocratic or neo-fascist political power, with the spiral leading ever more toward both policide and sociocide. In Trump's case, he acted out extreme bullying in his political theater of machismo, running for his second term in the name of restoring traditional masculinity with political props like wrestler-entertainer Hulk Hogan and podcasts with macho figures like Joe Rogan, whose interviews with Trump just before his re-election reached millions of young and middle-aged men. As we show in the next chapter, both the neoliberal and Military Spiral are reversible and create conditions for more formidable movements for both economic and political democracy, despite the dire threat of looming American fascism mounting rapidly after Trump's first few months of unprecedented authoritarianism in his second term.

Notes

1 Alexis de Tocqueville, *Democracy in America*. Chicago: University of Chicago Press, 2002.
2 Steve J. Stern. *Remembering Pinochet's Chile*. Durham: Duke University Press, 2004. Michael Walzer, *Just and Unjust Wars*. NY: Basic Books, 2015.
3 Charles Derber and Yale Magrass, *Who Owns Democracy?* NY: Routledge, 2024.
4 Charles Derber and Yale Magrass, *Who Owns Democracy?* NY: Routledge, 2024.
5 Jessica Dickler, "61% of Americans Say They are Living Paycheck to Paycheck Even as Inflation Cools." *CNBC*, July 31, 2023, cnbc.com
6 Ronald Reagan, "The President's News Conference." August 12, 1986, reaganlibrary.gov
7 "Ronald Reagan Fires 11,359 Air-traffic Controllers." *History*, August 1, 2019, history.com
8 Jarrett Skorup, "Union Membership Reaches a 40-year Low." *Capcon*, January 24, 2024, michigancapitolconfidential.com
9 Ayn Rand, *The Virtue of Selfishness*, NY: Signet 1964.
10 Adam Smith, *The Wealth of Nations*. Thrifty Books, October 27, 2009.
11 Amy Chozick, "Hillary Clinton Calls Many Trump Backers 'Deplorables,' and GOP Pounces." *NYTimes*, September 10, 2016, nytimes.com
12 Charles Derber and Yale Magrass, *Who Owns Democracy?* NY: Routledge, 2024.
13 William Clinton, "Inaugural Address." January 20, 1997, presidency.ucsb.edu
14 Charles Derber, *Welcome to the Revolution*. NY: Routledge, 2017.
15 Charles Derber and Yale Magrass, *Who Owns Democracy?* NY: Routledge, 2024.
16 Nancy Isenberg, *White Trash*. NY: Penguin Books, reprint ed. 2017.
17 "The Black Codes and Jim Crow Laws." National.Geographic.ducation.nationalgeographic.org
18 David Pietrusza, "The Ku Klux Klan in the 1920s." *Bill of Rights Institute*, billofrightsinstitute.org
19 Robert Longley, "America First – 1940s Style." *ThoughtCo*, December 1, 2022, thoughtco.com Rachel Maddow, *Prequel*. New York: Crown, 2023 Charles Derber and Yale Magrass, *Who Owns Democracy?* NY: Routledge, 2024.
20 Stefan Kuhl, *The Nazi Connection: Eugenics, American Racism, and German National Socialism*. NY: Oxford, 1994.
21 David Gordon, "America First." A New York Military Affairs Symposium, September 26, 2003, bobrowen.com
22 Rachel Maddow, *Prequel*. New York: Crown, 2023.
23 Sidney Milkis and Daniel Tichenor, "Building a Movement Party: the Alliance between Ronald Reagan and the New Christian Right." UVA: *Miller Center*, millercenter.org. See also Randall Balmer, "Phyllis Schlafly: The Antifeminist Who Wanted a Job in the Reagan Administration." *LA Times*, September 18, 2016, latimes.com.
24 Milkis and Tichenor, "Building a Movement Party." See also Balmer, "Phyllis Schlafly."
25 History Resources, "Ronald Reagan on the Unrest on College Campuses." 1967, gilderlehrman.org

26 Justin Gomer and Christopher Petrella, "How the Reagan Administration Stoked Fears of Anti-white Racism." *Washington Post*, October 10, 2017, washingtonpost.com
27 David A. Graham, "Trump Says He'll Be a Dictator on 'Day One.'" *The Atlantic*, December 6, 2023, theatlantic.com.
28 Maggie Astor, "Trump Doubles Down on Migrants 'Poisoning' the Country." *New York Times*, March 17, 2024, nytimes.com
29 Steven Greenhouse, "Trump Claims He's Pro-worker. Project 2025 Will Gut Labor Rights." *The Guardian*, August 4, 2024, theguardian.com
30 Project 2025, "Building Now for a Conservative Victory through Policy, Personnel and Training," *Project 2025, Presidential Transition Project*, project2025.org
31 Jim Rutenberg and Nick Corasaniti, "Unbowed by Jan. 6 Charges, Republicans Pursue Plans to Contest a Trump Defeat," *New York Times*, July 13, 2024, nytimes.com
32 Sonia Sotomayor, quoted in Rebecca Beitsch and Zach Schonfeld, "Sotomayor Scolds Immunity Decision for Making Presidents "King Above the Law," *The Hill*, July 1, 2024, thehill.com
33 Colbert King, "Let Us Declare Independence from the Monarchical Presidency." *Washington Post*, July 3, 2024, washingtonpost.com
34 Martin Pengelly, "JD Vance Once Worried Trump Was 'America's Hitler'. Now His Own Authoritarian Leanings Come into View." *The Guardian*, July 16, 2024, theguardian.com
35 Rosie Gray, "Trump Defends White-Nationalist Protesters: Some Very Fine People on Both Sides." April 15, 2017, congress.gov
36 "Gretchen Whitmer Kidnapping Plot," *Wikipedia*, en.wikipedia.org
37 Brandon Drenon, "David DePape," *BBC News*, November 10, 2023, bbc.com
38 Moira Donegan, "The Trump Shooting is a Reminder: We Live in a Grim New Era of Political Violence." *The Guardian*, July 13, 2024, theguardian.com
39 Moira Donegan, "The Trump Shooting is a Reminder: We Live in a Grim New Era of Political Violence." *The Guardian*, July 13, 2024, theguardian.com
40 Moira Donegan, "The Trump Shooting is a Reminder: We Live in a Grim New Era of Political Violence." *The Guardian*, July 13, 2024, theguardian.com
41 Joseph Konig, "FEC Wants to Allow Campaigns to Pay for Security Amid Rising Threats against Politicians," *Spectrum News*, March 28, 2024, ny1.com
42 Joseph Konig, "FEC Wants to Allow Campaigns to Pay for Security Amid Rising Threats against Politicians," *Spectrum News*, March 28, 2024, ny1.com
43 Matt Shuham, "Nearly Two-Thirds of Election Officials Worry Politicians Will Interfere With Their Work: Poll," *Huffington Post*, May 1, 2024, huffpost.com
44 Karen Yourish, Larry Buchanan and Denise Lu, "The 147 Republicans Who Voted to Overturn Election Results," *New York Times*, January 7, 2021, nytimes.org
45 Jennifer Agiesta and Ariel Edwards-Levy, "CNN Poll: Percentage of Republicans Who Think Biden's 2020 Win Was Illegitimate Ticks Back Up Near 70%." *CNN*, August 3, 2023, cnn.com
46 Josephine Harvey, "Tucker Carlson All Out Embraces 'Great Replacement' Theory." *Huff Post*, July 19, 2022, sports.yahoo.com
47 Time Magazine, "How Far Trump Would Go." *Time*, April 30, 2024, time.com
48 NPR, "Exploring What the Early Days of a Second Trump Administration Could Look Like." November 7, 2024, NPR.org
49 Paul Krawzzak, "Trump Says He'll Restore Presidential Impoundment Authority." Roll Call, June 20, 2023, rollcall.com
50 Thalia Beatty and Farnoush Amiri, "House Passes Bill that Would Allow Treasury to Target Nonprofits it Deems to Support Terrorism." *AP*, November 22, 2024, apnews.com
51 Alice Herman, "Trump's Pick for Budget Head Worked on Project 2025 – and Wants to Bypass the US Senate." *The Guardian*, November 23, 2024, theguardian.com
52 Alice Herman, "Trump's Pick for Budget Head Worked on Project 2025 – and Wants to Bypass the US Senate." *The Guardian*, November 23, 2024, theguardian.com
53 "Trump Advisers Mulling "Warrior Board" to Organize Purge of top Military Offices-Report." *The Guardian*, November 12, 2024, Theguardian.com
54 *The Guardian* "Military Officials Discussing How to Respond to Illegal Orders Under Trump – Report by CNN." November 8, 2024, theguardian.com
55 Jason Wilson, "Trump's Pentagon Pick Hegseth Wrote of Us Military Taking Sides in 'Civil War,'" *The Guardian*, November 22, 2024, guardian.com

56 Jason Wilson, "Trump's Pentagon Pick Hegseth Wrote of Us Military Taking Sides in 'Civil War,'" *The Guardian*, November 22, 2024, guardian.com

57 Ama Marie Cox, "Pete Hegseth is the Perfect Trumpworld Monster." *New Republic*, November 25, 2024, newrepublc.com

58 Ryan Bort, "Every Awful Thing Trump Has Promised to do in a Second Term." *Rolling Stone*, November 8, 2024, rollingstone.com

59 Martin Pengelly, "Leading Republican Strategist Rebukes Trump for Bringing 'Chaos' Back." *The Guardian,* November 22, 2024, theguardian.com

60 Hugo Lowell, "Trump Names Pam Bondi As Attorney General Pick After Gaetz Steps Aside." *The Guardian*, November 21, 2024, guardian.com

61 Filip Timotija, "Raskin: DOJ Staff Worried It Will Become 'Trump Law Firm.'" *The Hill*, November 22, 2024, Thehill.com.

62 *The Guardian* "Military Officials Discussing How to Respond to Illegal Orders Under Trump – Report by CNN." November 8, 2024, theguardian.com

63 George Orwell, *1984*. NY: Harper Perennial, 2014.

64 Jonathan Steele, *Defeat*. London: I.B. Tauris and Co., 2008

65 Charles Derber and Suren Moodliar, *Dying for Capitalism: How Big Money Fuels Extinction and What We Can about It*. London: Routledge, 2023.

66 Emma Farge, "UN Expert, Says Israel Has Committed Genocide in Gaza, Calls for Arms Embargo." *Reuters*, March 26, 2024, reuters.com

67 Norah Lanard and Julianne McShane, "Samantha Power Confirms Famine Is Likely Underway in parts of Gaza." *Mother Jones*, April 11, 2024, motherjones.com. Fatima Al-Kassab, "A Top UN Court says Gaza Genocide is 'Plausible' but Does not Order Cease-fire," *NPR*, January 26, 2024, npr.org. Megan Lim, Justine Kenin, Mary Louise Kelly, "State Department Diplomat Resigns in Protest of US Policy in Gaza." *NPR*, April 29, 2024, npr.org.

68 Missy Ryan, Philip Rucker, and Karen DeYoung, "Trump Stokes Iran Tensions with Threats of Dire Consequences for Tehran." *Washington Post*, July 24, 2018 washingtonpost.com. Joshua Kurlantzick, "What a Second Trump Term Could Mean for Southeast Asia." *Council on Foreign Relations*, May 10, 2024, cfr.org

69 Greg Myre, "Biden Signs $95 Billion Military Aid Package for Ukraine, Israel and Taiwan." *NPR*, April 24, 2024, npr.org

70 Ruth Ben-Ghiat, *Strongmen*. NY: Norton, 2021.

71 Ruth Ben-Ghiat, *Strongmen*. NY: Norton, 2021. See also Charles Derber and Yale Magrass, *Bully Nation*. Kansas City: University Press of Kansas, 2016.

8 Beyond the bonfire

Historic lessons, sociophiliac movements, and creating deep democracy and community

Sociocide is dire but not hopeless. History offers examples of both sociocidal and politicidal societies that collapsed, broke apart, or turned to fascism but then found a way to reconstruct and democratize. Examples include Nazi Germany after World War II and the US after the Civil War. In both instances, reconstruction took place only with outside forces helping guide a new path toward a sustainable civil society and democracy. But internal social movements, especially among workers and the young, can also pull a society away from the sociocidal brink. While it may take years or decades and require building new social capital and solidarity – bridging communities of color, women, immigrants, workers, and liberal or leftist activists – both sociocide and policide can be successfully challenged.

People increasingly subjected to threats, prosecution, firings, and violence by a policidal Trumpist regime experience threats and fears for their jobs, safety, and survival. However, they can learn from the disasters of their forebears and rebuild society and democracy, as enough checks and balances remain in the US system to offer hope for building serious opposition and a post-Trump future. The resistance began early in Trump's second term with mounting protests by fired federal workers and citizens outraged by Trump's authoritarianism.

Resistance to fascism often starts small, building social relations among family, friends, and colleagues at work or school which can go unnoticed by political authorities. Such small-scale resistance then may grow both online and offline into large-scale movements for freedom and democracy that have historically emerged successfully against authoritarian regimes. Such resistance in the US was modeled in the New Deal, when FDR mobilized class politics to build a new labor movement, bring workers new jobs and social protections, and help create an emerging democracy in the workplace as in the political sphere. Other examples are the movements for multi-racial democracy in the violent Jim Crow regimes of the South, where Black communities and civil rights activists worked under the threat of death to build new relationships and movements to survive, make new loving social connections, and begin to overthrow the American neo-fascism of the Jim Crow era.

Sociocide and policide can lead to fascism and human extinction, a horrific threat that is very real in the 21st century. But the possibilities for reconstruction – even in the face of fascist victories and dire extinction threats – remain real and potent in the US today. There remain significant checks and balances in the system that leave openings for opposition at the local, state, and federal levels. Resistance can also emerge and succeed because sociocidal and policidal forces are so deeply contradictory that they can create new opportunities or motives for rebuilding social communication and relations even

DOI: 10.4324/9781003491798-9

as they destroy existing forms. A good example is social media, which is eroding face-to-face relations but also creating multiple new forms of social connection, both online and offline. Another is the revitalization of local and state-level civil society and activist groups, whether neighborhood and school associations, environmental advocates, and labor unions. Another example is the rise of 2024 left populist anti-fascist and pro-democracy coalitions to beat back the Far-Right populist threat in France and other European nations as well as the US, where the Harris-Walz Presidential agenda, fatally flawed though it was, offered hints of essential anti-sociocidal and anti-policidal values and possibilities. They were captured with simplicity by Walz:

> This idea of caring for our neighbor and kindness, and a hand up when somebody needs it. And just the sense that people go through things and to be able to be there when they need it, that's who we are.[1]

Sociophiliac social movements mobilize and grow as sociocidal and authoritarian emergencies intensify. They build desperately needed forms of social and worker solidarity to overcome fear and threats brought by increased personal isolation in the wake of rising Far-Right regimes. Building personal connections with family, friends and colleagues at work or school are early essential steps that help build new social capital among working people and create new larger movements and anti-fascist coalitions for rebuilding a deeper democracy both in the economy and the polity. These "deep democracy" movements in the US began to be built before the 2024 election and have become far more urgent after Trump's re-election. Before the 2024 elections, the extreme threat of climate change unleashed major new Gen Z and Green New Deal movements to change lifestyles, create new economic priorities for suffering workers, and curb the power of Big Oil and Big Gas. The threats of guns, political violence, and authoritarianism likewise mobilized public pro-democracy protests in town halls and on the streets. Peace movements and anti-fascist coalitions focused on democratic and voting rights mobilization at local, state, and national levels began to grow – led by labor and activist groups such as the United Auto Workers, the AFL-CIO, the Southern Poverty Law Center, Indivisible, Black Voters Matter, the National Organization for Women, and Leaders We Deserve.

Authoritarianism triumphed in the 2024 Presidential election by offering its own solutions to sociocide, uniting increasingly disconnected and angry working people into a political cult formed around Trump and his successful MAGA campaign. The anti-Trumpist assault on sociocide must become deeply political, because Far-Right populism fuels its own powerful anti-democratic political communities. The rise of new intertwined anti-war, climate, labor, feminist, and anti-racist social movements –all a form of left populism in the US today – is crucially important because they are essential to connecting an incresingly isolated citizenry and building sustainable community and deep democracy. Trump defeated Harris in large measure because she did not offer such a left populism that militantly challenged the entire system of the corporate oligarchy, leaving Trump to become the "change" candidate and exploit the anger of the public against a sociocidal failing system.

Political scientists have debated whether anti-authoritarian elites or popular mobilizations are more effective in defeating sociocide and building democracies. In a comparative study of 115 nations since 1950, many run by authoritarian leaders, political sociologist Mohammad Ali Kadivar has shown that popular mobilizations by labor, youth, and pro-democracy social movements have been the most successful path to creating and sustaining democracy in autocratic regimes. He found that the longer and more sustained the pro-democracy movements, the more sustained the democratic outcome.[2]

I suggest here that sustaining and deepening democracy – and moving beyond both sociocide and policide – requires a new integration of class and caste politics. Fascist authoritarianism must be defeated in part by strong anti-caste movements led by women and people of color. But such anti-policidal movements require a universalizing of caste resistance beyond siloed identity politics into class politics that challenge neoliberal capitalism and its hyper-individualistic culture. A Harris-Walz Democratic Party of siloed identity politics based on race, gender, and other caste issues – and embracing Republican anti-government and pro-capitalist discourse about freedom – will lead to more siloed identity politics and more Democratic defeats after 2024. To defeat Trumpism, Democrats must embrace a new 21st-century class politics and reconstruct a different kind of "deep democracy" struggle to democratize the economy as well as the political sphere. This requires a challenge to the neoliberal and increasingly oligarchic and fascist capitalist system led by labor movements, progressive Democrats, and social justice movements.

As noted above, resistance in the first few weeks of Trump's re=election started with law suits against Trump and mounting public protests by fired government workers and citizens alarmed by Trump's authoritarianism. Resistance often started for many people in more small and personal ways. Each of us must try to help rebuild local and state-level civil society groups that knit people together, moving ourselves out of isolation and into stronger direct relations with family, friends, and neighbors. This must happen both online and offline. As civil society relations, associations, and communities grow, and our personal relations grow stronger and create more solidarity, we can expand our networks to larger and broader social and political networks, labor and other social justice movements, and political parties with the capacity to challenge the Trumpist regime and its corporate oligarchy.

One example of starting locally is the US citizens' group, Indivisible. It organizes locally, building the social capital and networks that have grown since its founding at the start of Trump's first race for President into a national movement of progressive activists seeking to build local, state, and political power to counter Trumpist authoritarianism. Immediately after Trump's re-election in 2024, it doubled down with rallies at town halls, meetings with local Congressional Representatives, and new efforts to mobilize resistance on the streets at all levels, simultaneously building social capital and the political movements that are essential to building democracy in the neighborhood, the economy, and the political sphere.

Countering Trumpism and American fascism – a system that can be called fascist capitalism – is a long-term process. It must build on historical lessons from the past. In the rest of this chapter, we look at historical experiences, both in the US and Europe, that offer clues about how to rebuild our social relations and civil society as part of a broader movement to challenge authoritarianism and build a deeper economic and political democracy. The aim after Trump's re-election is to expand from local resistance and the rebuilding of civil society to state and federal social movement and political party rebuilding, preparing for elections in 2026 and 2028. The foundation for success is a reconstruction of social capital and of a renewed potent civil society network in America that unites and galvanizes working people across race, ethnicity, and gender in sustainable social and political relationships and movements. Public outrage about Trump's policies will grow and offer larger and larger spaces for resistance and major democratic change.

* * *

We start by looking briefly at historical examples of societal reconstruction both in Germany and the US. German reconstruction after World War II was only possible because of strong limits and new policies imposed by the victorious Allies. These banned the Nazi Party, put constitutional limits on German re-militarization, and incentivized civilian German re-development, replacing Hitler's fascist economic policies that relied on military spending, war, and violence to bring Weimar Germany out of Depression.[3]

The armed presence of foreigners was necessary to ignite this rebuilding of German society, but it could not have happened without a domestic transformation of education, culture, economy, and politics, especially among German youth.[4] It took two generations of deeply introspective German young people to come to terms with what their Nazi forbears had wrought, and to come together and create a drastically different society. It required immersion in a new German education and political worldview that was culturally challenging and personally painful. The young had to reject what their parents and grandparents had helped create and to remake their own personal and political identities and social relations.[5] While this was a Herculean enterprise, two generations of young Germans eventually succeeded in helping create their own brand of democratic Germany, including a social democratic economy that rejected neoliberalism and helped bond together working people and youth seeking a new civil society. The strong value of community in European culture – as highlighted by Jeremy Rifkin in his book, *The Euroepan Dream* – helped lay the foundation for rebuilding civil society and democracy in Germany and other post-war European nations. Americans need to consider how the communitiarian values of European natons have contributed to Europeans' democracy. The Europeans value individuality but recognize that social relationships and strong communities are the only way to ward off both sociocide and policidal fascism.[6]

The resurgence of Far Right and neo- fascist parties and voters in German society and politics in the 2020s shows that sociocide and policide always lurk as threats in democratic societies. They lie latent in German history and can be warded off only by cultivating a clear view of German history and its lessons about fascist horrors. After the rise in votes for the Far-Right AfD party in German elections, which came in second in 2025 German elections, German social democratic and mainstream leaders, parties and left-leaning movements began to bring workers and young people together into a new anti-fascist democratic coaliton. It is enabled by the communitarian values of European society and the sustained social movements and politics for peace and democracy that their long-standing commitment to community in the European Dream helps fortify.[7]

A second example is the Reconstruction era in the US after the Civil War. Sociocidal forces and divisions that intensified in the decades leading up to the Civil War became catastrophic, preventing the US from holding together. When the country collapsed into Civil War, it took a major new effort to rebuild the nation that got its start in the Reconstruction period right after the Civil War and lasted about 12 years until 1876. There are important successes and failures of this short Reconstruction era that are useful in considering how to create a second American Reconstruction.[8]

As in Germany, Reconstruction could not have occurred without outside force, in this case exerted by the Northern Army over the defeated South. The North occupied the defeated Southern states and re-imposed a new constitutional order on the Confederacy. Slavery was constitutionally banned; Confederate political leaders and parties were banned as well. These changes were part of a broader social and political shift directed by

Northern occupiers and supported by Southern freed slaves and a small sector of Southern white allies toward a multi-racial democracy in which Black citizens were protected in new constitutional rights to vote, own farmland and other property, and become elected officials ruling local, county, and state governments. Blacks organized new democratic and civic associations at local and state-wide levels. Public schools played an important role in helping build this new South since both white and Black young people were offered a new vision of their history and culture. This had a major catalyzing effect on the new Black generation who began to build community and civil rights movements. It had very mixed results on young whites, many of whom would aggressively seek to build a new version of the old order in the Jim Crow regime that began to take root shortly after the North withdrew forces and allowed whites to take back control.[9]

The brevity of Reconstruction – and the resurrection of a new brand of Southern neo-fascist Jim Crow – showed how difficult it is to combat authoritarianism.. The North lacked the will and resources to maintain a longer presence, which might have gained the support of more Southerners and moved the South in a more fundamentally new direction. But despite this lack of success, Reconstruction was not a total failure. The Confederacy was dead. The new South had to live within the Constitutional order of the larger nation and could not legally or politically return to the *ante-bellum* slave caste era. Economically, the larger capitalist forces would move into the South and West as well as grow in the North, bringing a new industrializing force into the South that would partly re-bind it to the Union. This had obvious sociopathic limitations, rooted in capitalism itself and the resurrection of Jim Crow in the South. But it created new free and civil associations in a new generation of Blacks, helping inspire a centuries-long struggle for a multi-racial democracy.

Both the historical German and American cases show the enormous challenge of rebuilding society and democracy when subjected to sociocidal and policidal assault, as the US is today. But the US, while moving closer to the precipice with the 2024 re-election of Donald Trump, has not collapsed at this writing into complete fascist rule or total destruction of social relations. All the sociocidal system drivers we have explored in earlier chapters are accelerating alarmingly, especially with the rise of MAGA and Trumpism. Political repression against sociophiliac and pro-democracy movements will likely become increasingly violent and deadly. Nonetheless, because of the contradictions built into many sociocidal systems and forces – and the social space that still remains in the US for civil society renewal and democratic social movements to grow, there is reason for hope.

The US faces a sociocidal and policidal emergency. Defeating both sociocide and poli-cide requires social and political solidarity that can unite students, workers, women, and people of color in new communities and in a multi-racial anti-fascist, pro-democracy movement. If the fascist threat is beaten back, emergency political mobilization is still necessary to build stronger movements to deepen democracy and strengthen social soli-darity, uniting Americans against the extreme perils of social, political, and environmen-tal breakdown.

Our new "constitutional monarchy" put in place by the 2024 Roberts Supreme Court, ensures a strong Far-Right politics and a crisis of democracy enduring through the second Trump term. With constitutional authoritarian seeds already planted, the fascism that thrives in a sociocidal environment, where people's perilous economic condition and social isolation draw them to the perceived power of an authoritarian leader like Trump, will only grow stronger. This can only be countered by *an extremely broad and wide anti-fascist coalition for economic and political democracy*, uniting neighborhood and local civil society groups, state and federal left movements, progressives, labor, women's groups, civil rights and voting rights groups, centrist Democrats, and Independents. It has to unite class politics challenging the US corporate oligarchy with strong feminist and anti-racist forces, since women and people of color have the most to lose with the triumph of white Christian nationalism. Creating a broad anti-fascist and anti-corporate pro-democracy movement is the most urgent need in the US.

The watering ground of fascism and the Far-Right is always the fear and anger of a population facing the breakdown of sustainable and nourishing social bonds. The MAGA Republican Party, like earlier American and European authoritarian and fascist movements and parties, attracts millions of ordinary Americans losing social relations and support. Right-wing nationalism brings them together with others in an angry but emotionally reassuring community seeking retribution against those who abandoned them. The only way an anti-fascist and deep democracy politics can defeat Far-Right power in the short and long term is to offer the real deal: genuine community to overcome the sociocidal threat. And this ultimately depends on success in building the widest possible anti-authoritarian and deep democracy movements and communities, inside and outside of politics itself.

In Europe, facing similar anti-democratic catastrophes, we saw the stirrings of such political movements in the 2024 rise of the broad anti-fascist New Popular Front, a coalition of four left socialist and green parties in France, which beat back the Far-Right populism led by Marie Le Pen and her National Rally neo-fascist party. The New Popular Front showed the power of a left populist movement that builds a broad anti-fascist coalition that not only united leftist parties but also organized a tactical voting strategy with Macron's center to ensure the defeat of Le Pen's fascist candidates. Building a broad anti-fascist coalition is essential to defeat authoritarian parties everywhere, but the tactical breadth of the coalition uniting the left and the center does not imply abandonment of a transformative agenda either in Europe or the US. To abandon populist anti-corporate goals and embrace militarized capitalism is a sure recipe to empower Far-Right populism, which always awakens to fill the void created by the Democratic Party's abandonment of left populism, an abandonment that doomed the Harris 2024 campaign.

* * *

Prior to the 2024 Presidential election, unexpected sociophiliac domestic economic policies by the Biden Administration, as well as new anti-war and labor movements, got a foothold in America. Despite Biden being forced to drop out and despite his unchecked militarism, his first term after his election in 2020, as we show later, did break with neoliberal economic orthodoxy and made initial steps toward greater economic as well as political democracy. Progressive Democrats started to create new social capital in unions and political communities that could rebuild social relations. They coalesced to try to build a new anti-fascist, pro-democracy coalition for both the short term and the long term, recognizing that success in defeating Trumpism is the precondition for solving all our other existential crises.

Building sociophiliac movements has become an urgent necessity. As long as Trumpists and MAGA exercise power at either federal or state levels, allied with and funded by sociocidal corporate elites, the relentless attack on free communities, civil society groups, and democratic government will persist. In the rest of this chapter, we look at how anti-corporate and anti-fascist movements can grow and succeed, starting with a deeper look at the experience of Europe and then returning to the US, building on our own history of struggles for a vibrant civil society and deep democracy.

Through much of the 20th century, after disastrous capitalist wars and the destruction of European fascism, the Europeans built social democracy - their version of what I am calling deep democracy – with strong labor unions, labor parties, and big investment in public goods and services. European fascism was not destroyed forever, but it was defeated for decades by anti-sociocidal left populist forces that built a new post-war European social democracy, elements of democratic socialism, and a collective "we."

Despite the rise of Far-Right neo-fascist European movements in the early 2020s, fueled by mass immigration and neoliberal European Central Bank policies, the US can learn much from the European experience. Rejecting their long nightmare of European fascism after the tyranny of Hitler and Mussolini, the Europeans created a new democratic "we."[10] Post-World War II social democratic governments in Europe decisively rejected neoliberalism, militarism, and fascism. Fueled by strong labor parties and unions, European governments shifted their huge investments in war and imperial expansion into job creation at home and universal and generous social welfare programs for affordable healthcare, childcare, and higher education, knowing full well how an insecure working class could be seduced by fascists. Public goods, funded by governments and communities at all levels, created the infrastructure and safety nets for a new European sociophiliac society, connecting workers to each other, their unions, and to labor parties. Europe's powerful unions organized to increase wages and improve working conditions, building new social capital and solidarity among labor and helping prevent sociocidal racial, ethnic, or religious division of workers. They invested heavily in vocational education for all workers. All these programs were made possible by shifts away from huge militaries toward investment in a peaceful, social democratic "we" symbolized by a generous and expansive welfare system at home that ordinary European workers could viscerally feel as an investment in and safety net for themselves and their family, friends and community.[11]

Despite the rise of new Far-Right poliitics across much of Europe, the European public goods economy has been, thus far, a successful approach for ending sociocide, beating back new fascist forces, and building democracy. Public investment in affordable community health care brings people together in a shared set of public health care community-based institutions and providers. Public investment in free public schools and universities offers a key public space where young Europeans of all backgrounds are given the means to come together in affordable and safe educational settings. European governments have also invested heavily in public transit and affordable urban housing, bringing people together in shared subways, trams, and buses rather than atomizing people into separate, private cars driving into individualistic suburbs that wall people off from each other in the US. The European experience, even in the wake of neo-fascist resurgence, shows how public goods and services can gain public support and help renew sustainable face-to-face social relationships and be part of the fight for rebuilding democracy.

The victory of the 2024 anti-fascist French New Popular Front in defeating Le Pen's Far-Right populism shows the strength of the anti-sociocidal social democratic embrace in Europe of labor parties, government, and a collective "we." Left populist movements in Spain, Greece, and other European countries suggest that positive populist movements are crucial ways to wagel anti-fascist politics. The question remains whether the European approach can find success in the United States – and how anti-fascist movements can find the skills and tools to survive brutal repression as they seek to roll back

Trumpism. We need to reconsider relevant, recent US history, where the corporate elites and Far-Right gained power under Reagan but then eventually had to yield some power during the Biden era, which continued Reagan's global hegemonic militarism but planted some seeds at home of economic as well as political democracy.

***

The Reagan revolution prevented the US from embracing sociophiliac European social democracy. But after 40 years of the Reagan era, from 1980 to 2020, an American shift from the neoliberal "me" to a new "we" – with some similarities to the European model – seemed to have begun. As noted above, it came from an unlikely source: the mainstream Biden Administration, linked to a new activist labor movement and anti-war youth movement.

In 2021, Biden took the first steps toward a new sociophiliac public goods economy that rejected the neoliberal values and policies not only of Reagan but also of Democratic Presidents Clinton and Obama. "Bidenomics" represented the biggest public investment in America since LBJ's Great Society and FDR's New Deal.[12] Biden passed the largest infrastructure, climate, and jobs bills in more than half a century. In his own version of a 21st-century New Deal, he relied on government to create or subsidize jobs at home: to build clean energy in West Virginia and Texas, semiconductor manufacturing plants in Arizona, New York, and Ohio, and new auto and steel manufacturing jobs in Michigan, Ohio, and Pennsylvania.

At the same time, the Biden Administration became the strongest supporter of unions since FDR, backing the UAW, steel unions, and progressive unions for teachers, nurses, and Hollywood screen actors and writers. Biden helped union organizers in Big Tech companies, such as burnt-out, contingent warehouse Amazon workers, as well as service workers organizing baristas at Starbucks and stewardesses striking for better wages and safer skies. Biden is the only US President to walk the picket line with striking workers, joining UAW workers in their union drives in Michigan and Tennessee with Shawn Fain, one of the most creative labor organizers since the CIO's John Lewis during the New Deal. Moreover, Biden invested in new and expansive social welfare. His move toward European-style universal sociophiliac welfare protected Social Security and Medicare, expanded Obamacare to more needy people, and began to provide the community safety net that can bring people back together and protect them in a still turbulent global economy.

Biden's large public investment in jobs and climate, as well as his activist support of a growing union movement, were a clear and unexpected rejection of the Reagan Revolution and Reagan's attack on government and the very idea of a collective good.[13] It was just a beginning and will be largely reversed in Trump's second term, as Trump embraces corporate oligarchy despite his "pro-worker" and "drain the swamp" rhetoric and use of tariffs to reshape some corporate foreign investment. But it was the first stage of 21st century New Deal-style sociophiliac programs supported by the Progressive Caucus of Democrats; in 2024, this included 98 left-leaning activist Congressional Democrats who supported many "democratic socialist" programs and policies.[14] The Progressive Caucus wants to move beyond Biden in a more progressive post-Biden Democratic Party and create a new sociophiliac economy and populist politics that bring all workers together in strong unions and offers more secure and higher-wage jobs, with universal cradle-to-grave social support. The continued push for such left populist programs is essential to defeating Trump's Far-Right populist agenda in his second term.

Biden's strong support for unionism was an important first step in building new worker social capital and an American anti-sociocidal and anti-fascist movement for both economic and political democracy. At Amazon warehouses, auto manufacturing plants, and hospitals, unions mobilized to end the sociocidal division of workers by race. The new progressive unions are multi-racial forms of solidarity, unlike earlier American craft unions, and help connect Black and Brown workers with white workers in "universalizing" workplace and political struggles.[15] In 2023 and 2024, we saw some union victories even in Southern factories, such as the UAW's successful organizing drive at a VW plant in Tennessee, long a Southern bastion of anti-unionism and American fascism.[16]

Biden's social welfare programs, supported strongly by labor and a broader Democratic coalition, were another first step away from neoliberalism. But to be truly sustainable and anti-sociocidal, they have to shift from the American-style means-tested "welfare," easily stigmatized as handouts to "welfare queens" and criminals, toward the universal welfare model of Europe, which has proved its ability over decades to help build solidarity and social cohesion across income, race, religion, and ethnicity. Biden's program was fiercely attacked by Trumpism and can only be advanced as part of an anti-fascism resistance – especially when linked with European insights. The European universal welfare model destigmatizes welfare and women's rights, making them universal rights for all citizens.[17] It is one of the best ways to challenge and ultimately defeat Trumpist white identity politics that have fueled white workers' migration to the GOP and its authoritarian populist appeals.

Biden's steps toward building solidarity among working people were all compromised by his militarism and wars, which angered many Americans and helped secure Trumpist and MAGA victories. Long before he became President, Biden was a stalwart member of the bipartisan American military and national security establishment, supporting global interventions – many of them anti-democratic and supporting dictators. These included wars in Nicaragua and El Salvador, the wars in Iraq and Afghanistan, and most recently the wars in Ukraine and the Middle East, which are legitimized as part of the war on terrorism and the two new Cold Wars pitting the US against Russia and China. The scale of brutal and violent killing of civilians and destruction of communities in both Gaza and Ukraine is hard to exaggerate. They have also fueled authoritarianism in the US, as Trump wins over workers partly by arguing that the billions of dollars for war in places like Ukraine should be invested in jobs at home.

War and militarism are systemic drivers of sociocide. They not only create hatred of and violence against other nations but infuse these poisons into sociocidal wars against enemies at home. Militarized imperial societies usually create violence and polarization at home, mobilizing hatred and violence against competing parts of their own citizenry based on income, race, religion, or ethnicity. European history shows how militarized empires only began to reject both policide and sociocide after rejecting their war systems. Yes, war allows the Orwellian building of social cohesion and solidarity by hating the foreign enemy on the tele-screen.[18] But that almost always ends us in wars at home against domestic enemies, as illustrated by Hitler, Mussolini, and other fascist leaders in imperial European nations, and by Trumpism in the US.

But out of the horrors of war often come struggles for peace, illustrating the contradictions of sociocidal forces. American militarism is sociocidal in much the same way that European colonialism was in earlier centuries, fueling the Military Spiral discussed in the last chapter. But it is also producing, contradictorily, peace and justice movements, especially among young Americans.[19] Such movements have historically been among the most sociophiliac forces in any society. They bring people together in a common cause for peace and justice. Social movements create friendships, solidarity, and a collective identity built around new communities formed on the streets, in workplaces, or campuses. Activists become activists partly by discovering the pleasures of shifting from the "me" of American life to the "we" of the collective movement for peace and democracy, all part of a larger anti-fascist politics critical to defeating both sociocide and policide in the second Trump term and beyond.

* * *

In mid-2024, before the crucial 2024 Presidential election, Gen Z in the US was rediscovering the sociophiliac power of mass protest and anti-war movements, which were arising along with a populist and energized new labor movement. The only way to counter and defeat the authoritarian threat created by Trump's re-election and the Roberts Supreme Court in the 2020s and beyond is to move the Democratic Party toward the broadest and most powerful anti-fascist coalition in America. This will require uniting progressives and positive populists within the Democratic Party with centrists and Independents who want democracy, while also building a new pro-democracy and left populist coalition with the anti-war and climate social movements beginning among young people and rising in the new labor movement.

In the Spring of 2024, a new anti-war movement embraced by young people exploded on campuses across the country. Just months before the 2024 elections, famine and a humanitarian catastrophe in Gaza, shown on TV and social media in daily images of starving children and bombed-out hospitals, schools, and shelters mobilized college students into new networks of solidarity. The anti-war movement was based on shared horror at the violence and injustice of the long denial of Palestinian statehood and human rights, and solidarity with fellow campus activists subject to police violence and university sanctions. While this sociophiliac new movement and politics, especially among the young, was quickly attacked and weakened Trump, we need to explore it as a foundation of broader anti-fascist resistance and pro-democracy movements led partly by young people and labor, that are crucial to defeating Trumpism.

The large-scale anti-war movements of Gen Z emerged as part of a broader anti-sociocidal mobilization among young people in the 21st century against racism, sexism, gun violence, police violence, climate change, economic inequality, and fascism. These movements begin to bring together millions of young Americans to fight for their survival together rather than compete against each other, Ik-like, for individual survival. Young people fearing shooters in their schools can personally connect with civilians in war zones fearing for their lives. Young people horrified by wartime violence can connect with other young people grieving the violence against the environment perpetrated by Exxon drilling for oil or Cargill clearcutting virgin forests. Young people suffering racial, gender, or racial discrimination or violence share visceral experiences of isolation and powerlessness with burnt-out, badly paid workers, poor people, or immigrants. All these intertwined crises experienced by Gen Z can help bring them together during the second Trump term in a new multi-racial anti-fascist coalition, often led by young women and students of color with personal experiences of discrimination or exclusion, emerging on college campuses despite brutal state and police repression.

Pro-democracy youth movements always face violent repression by elites. The brutal police attack on pro-Palestinian student activists was widely reported and became part of a broader political movement of MAGA Republicans to define the protest as anti-Semitic and violent.[20] Largely peaceful students were sometimes treated as terrorists on their own campuses. This is all part of elites seeking to limit dissent and curb the solidarity of young people. Trumpists and corporate elites worry that students are learning in classrooms and protests about the causes of violence, injustice, and American authoritarianism – and that campus protests are a gateway to protests against militarized capitalism and the roots of authoritarianism itself.

This points to education as a major sociophiliac force. Education is the most important way that young people learn how power is created and how neoliberal capitalism, militarism, and fascism are intertwined. Moreover, schools and universities bring young people together in a collective space; this is inherently sociophiliac, much in the sense that that collective workplace space inherently opens up avenues toward workplace solidarity and action..

The sociophiliac nature of education, bringing young people together in critical thinking and studies, helps explain why universities in the US have now become the target of Trumpist elites.[21] Far-Right GOP Speaker of the House, Mike Johnson, went to Columbia University at the height of the April 2024 protests against the war on Gaza, calling the largely peaceful protesters anarchists and criminals who should be arrested. They were, indeed, arrested shortly after, not only at Columbia but at UCLA, the University of Wisconsin in Madison, Tulane, the University of Texas in Austin, Northern Arizona University, and scores of other universities across the country.[22] The attack on universities as "woke" centers of indoctrination and social agitation is a barely disguised assault by MAGA elites, who fear a new generation coming together in peaceful action against the military-industrial complex and authoritarian, political violence.

MAGA Republicans today are exploiting the memories of the anti-war movements in the 1960s and 1970s, when Nixon and Reagan successfully turned much of the public against civil rights and anti-war protesters, especially on campuses, turning the entire country to the right.[23] This is a reminder that while social movements are essential sociophiliac forces, they run the danger of allowing authoritarian and violent elites to mobilize their own Far-Right base. Young people and other activists need to be extremely aware of this danger, always maintaining non-violence and protesting in ways that reach out to the larger public. Failure to do so allows the Far-Right to polarize much of the public against protest itself and to use violent repression against student protests, sure to be wielded against them by Trump throughout his second term. Trump's withdrawal of $400 millions dollars from Columbia University in March, 2025, early in his second term - for permitting student protest against the war in Gaza which he called anti-Semitism -was just the first sign of how Trump would continue to punish students and their universities for political dissent.

* * *

In May 2024, America's UAW labor leader, Shawn Fain, speaking for millions of ordinary workers, threw his support behind the Gaza campus protesters.

> The UAW will never support the mass arrest or intimidation of those exercising their right to protest, strike, or speak out against injustice. Our union has been calling for

a ceasefire for six months. This war is wrong, and this response against students and academic workers, many of them UAW members, is wrong. We call on the powers that be to release the students and employees who have been arrested, and if you can't take the outcry, stop supporting this war.[24]

This is potentially transformative. A coalition between students and a new labor movement for peace and justice began to take a modern 21st-century form in the Biden Administration. The resurgence of a vibrant labor movement is central to defeating American fascism and building a long-term pro-democracy movement challenging militarized capitalism and corporate oligarchy. While labor will face repression from Trump throughout his second term, there will still be space for unions to organize. At the Republican Convention in July 2024, Trump explicitly denounced Shawn Fain, urging auto workers to kick him out and get out of the union, a sign of the repression that the labor movement, after Trump's re-election, began to prepare for in alliance with other unions and pro-democracy movements.

Unions are now growing not only in Rust Belt manufacturing strongholds among auto, steel, and railroad workers, but also in the huge service sector where most Americans work. Some of the most progressive and pro-democracy unions are rising among baristas, hotel workers, stewardesses, nurses, physician associations, actors and scriptwriters, university graduate student and faculty unions, and government unions. They unite auto workers, steel workers, and railroad workers who are fighting for both economic and political democracy. The AFL-CIO, the American national labor federation, is itself becoming a pro-democracy movement, throwing its substantial fund-raising and political clout into 2024 Democratic campaigns. While it failed to defeat Trumpism at the ballot box related to the failures of Harris to run a strong and clear anti-corporate, pro-labor campaign, it set the stage for populist labor challenges to the anti-unionism of Trump in his second term.

What is most important here is not just the sharp rise in the number of workers being organized but the new vision and militancy of the movement central to building a new class politics led by "deep democracy" leaders like Bernie Sanders. Labor's alliance with populist left politicians like Sanders is crucial to curbing Trump in his second term. Fain's anti-war solidarity with student protesters reflects a major change in the conservative Cold War politics of 20th-century labor. Pro-Vietnam unions in the 1960s joined Nixon's silent majority against the anti-war youth movements. Today, the new anti-war position of unions like the UAW is making possible a new progressive coalition of students and workers. During the 2024 student peace protests, a number of UAW members were arrested by LA Police for protesting the Gaza war in solidarity with student protesters at UCLA and other LA schools.[25]

The new anti-war politics of this new labor movement is part of a broader union shift away from bargaining for one's own members while accepting the larger corporate system. Well before the Harris campaign, unions were joining with activist students, community organizers, and political groups to fight poverty, racism, climate change, war, and neoliberal militarized capitalism itself. Sociologist Ben Manski writes that this new labor movement rose during the 1999 Battle of Seattle, when union and environmental groups came together in massive street protests to fight corporate globalization and the World Trade Organization. It kept growing in the anti-capitalist Occupy movement and beyond, starting with:

the participation of unions in Occupy Wall Street and Occupy everywhere. We saw unions grappling with police brutality and white supremacy and deciding what side they were on as tens of millions declared that Black Lives Matter. We saw general strikes and wildcat strikes in public education from Chicago to California and West Virginia to Oklahoma. We saw the railroad unions prepare a national strike to demand public ownership of the railroads. And this past year we've seen a new UAW promising to "Unite All Workers for Democracy ..."[26]

Manksi sees the new labor fight for militant strikes, worker ownership, and democracy as a version of the socialist and pro-democracy labor movement led a hundred years ago by the Gilded Age's labor leader, Eugene Debs. Debs was in prison for his opposition to World War I when he ran for President on a socialist ticket and got over a million votes from jail. Manksi notes that just as Debs' labor movement supported a "Cooperative Commonwealth," today "the union movement is finally getting past its 20th century addiction to state-sponsored collective bargaining and beginning to back economic democracy: worker and community ownership."[27]

Economic and political democracy go together. Sean Fain's call for a 2028 national strike of all American workers targets both corporate elites and MAGA political authoritarianism. Fain describes the working class as "the arsenal of democracy" and is joining other labor movements and the AFL-CIO to help labor lead the American anti-fascist and pro-democracy movements.

The strength of unions and labor parties is at the foundation of European social democracy and its success in building worker solidarity against neoliberal corporate rule. In the US, it was also the rise of unions in the New Deal that led the fight for both economic and political democracy. While Trump in his second term will do all he can to repress and destroy militant pro-democracy unions and labor movements, they are the crucial seeds of anti-sociocidal and anti-fascist resistance.

Unions will now play an even more central role in universalizing resistance, moving the left and Democratic Party beyond their current embrace of siloed identity politics and militarized capitalism. Reaganism and Trumpism, as discussed in the last chapter, ended the anti-sociocidal class politics of the New Deal that began to bring together workers across race and gender. Unions speak for the interests that all workers share and prevent the division of the working class by race and gender – and the larger sociocide – that breeds resonance with Trumpist white Christian nationalism and neo-fascism. But the assault on unions beginning with Reagan and reaching full force under Trump has been reinforced by the Democratic Party's movement toward siloed anti-racist and feminist movements, pitting different communities of color and different genders against each other as well as against the white working class.

Organized labor must, in addition, help recruit ordinary workers into the Democratic Party and encourage them to run for local, state, and federal office. As long as Congress is made up mainly of millionaires, no outside pressure can create decisive change. Recruiting workers to run for office should become a major concern of organized labor, working alongside groups like Indivisible that mobilize people at the local level, street by street, to register, vote, and run for office. Unions could recruit political candidates in tandem with Indivisible in communities, while also mobilizing in the workplace ordinary union members or other workers to run for local, state, or federal political office. Only when we have a more class-diverse Congress and political class will we have any real chance of building a labor-friendly political democracy.

***

The need to move beyond siloed identity politics – and the central need for a broad class-based movement to dismantle corporate oligarchy and curb Trump's authoritarianism in his second term – does not mean abandoning the crucial importance of race and gender. People of color and women are the most exploited groups in neo-fascist capitalism. Moreover, they have the historical experience and values central to repairing social relations, building social solidarity, and helping lead a truly anti-fascist and anti-corporate coalition to defeat Trumpism at the ballot box in 2026 and beyond.

Women and people of color have long been among the most organized and militant groups seeking to fight Trumpism and earlier forms of American fascism. The Democratic Party's siloed identity politics actually weakened women's and people of color's ability to coalesce, not only with each other but against the neo-fascist corporate Trumpist regime. Harris' campaign appeared that it might try to bridge earlier divisions, beginning to universalize anti-racist and feminist movements by tying them closely to the broad labor and class solidarity of unions central to the Democratic Party and supportive of Harris' 2024 race. Civil rights and feminist movements – such as Black Lives Matter and Black Voters Matter as well as Planned Parenthood, the National Organization of Women, and the League of Women Voters – found receptive and powerful allies among Sean Fain's UAW, as well as socialist-leaning unions of teachers, nurses, government, and service workers, many led by women and people of color. But the Harris campaign's abandonment of a robust class politics doomed her chances as she declared herself "a proud capitalist," embraced wars in the Middle East and Ukraine, and increasingly adopted a pro-corporate and pro-war stance that reversed traditional partisan ideologies. It all made her sound like the traditional Republican Party establishment that Trump himself was challenging. This political "twist" undermined the promise of a clear and forceful anti-corporate politics and doomed the Democratic Party's prospects of rallying workers back to the Democrats and away from Trump. It led in 2024 to Democratic defeat and Trump's win, undermining the initial promise of a new anti-corporate Democratic Party linking labor and class politics to women and people of color.

When Trump was elected in 2016, it was women who poured out into the streets in mass protest after his inauguration; they continued to mobilize to try to vote out Trumpism after the Dobbs decision and the elimination of women's most important freedoms. They were successful in constitutionalizing reproductive rights in multiple state elections before 2024 – reflecting not only the profound attacks on their freedom and rights but the values of solidarity and community that are more deeply socialized among women, as Katherine Adam and I showed in the book, *The New Feminized Majority*.[28] The tendency of women to support values of connection and community more strongly than men makes them a key force in fighting both sociocide and neo-fascism. However, this can be fully realized fully only when feminist values and women, who are the majority of the working class, can express their values not in siloed identity politics but in the universalizing politics of a pro-labor democracy movement seeking democracy in the economy and workplace as well as the corridors of Congress and the White House.

The same is true of anti-racist movements. People of color have suffered the most brutal experience of American fascism, going back to the founding in the proto-fascism of the Confederacy slave state. As with women, this has generated a historical experience that has bred social solidarity in their own communities and broader pro-democracy movements to protect themselves and their freedoms. But as with women, today's siloed identity politics has limited the power of people of color to fully express their values of social solidarity and create a successful politics to defeat neo-fascist Trumpism and the corporate system that has always thrived by dividing workers by race. The rise of a new wave of populist class politics is central to bringing Black and Brown people together with white workers in a unified struggle for economic and political democracy. A leader in this movement today is Rev. William Barber, who has championed the struggle against poverty and is building a pro-democracy struggle uniting white, Black, Brown, and people in a new civil rights struggle that will help define the prospects of humanity and freedom in the second Trump term and beyond. Barber leads a populist mass anti-poverty campaign focusing on political mobilizing and registering to vote more than 80 million poor Americans who could tilt future elections away from Trump toward populist left Democrats like Bernie Sanders and AOC.[29]

To combat and defeat Trumpism and white Christian nationalism, anti-racist, and civil rights movements must be embraced by and embrace the new labor movement that is crucial to the larger anti-fascist and pro-democracy coalition. The historical experience of Blacks and other people of color makes them central, along with young people, labor and women, in any successful anti-fascist movement. Martin Luther King is the great historic symbol of that movement, building communities of resistance for voting rights and democracy in the neo-fascist Deep South. King knew that uniting with labor against militarized capitalism was crucial in winning civil rights; he opposed the Vietnam war and died while participating in a strike of Memphis garbage workers. If King were alive today, his civil rights struggle would be leading the fight, with economic democracy activists like Rev. Barber and Shawn Fain, against the Trumpist regime run by neo-fascist white Christian nationalists and corporate oligarchs.

* * *

Along with labor and workers, poor people, women, and people of color, young people are also critical to any anti-fascist and pro-democracy politics; they are both targets of Trump in his second term and carriers of democratic hope. The sociophiliac possibilities of the Gen Z movements are potentially stronger today than mobilizations of earlier generations because of their skills in using the internet and social media to connect and spread their message. This may seem to run against arguments in earlier chapters about the sociocidal nature of online relations and social media. But as we have also shown in earlier chapters, social media, like many sociocidal forces, are full of contradictions. Despite the ways they can undermine social relations and movements, they can also empower movements for change, connecting people and causes across space and time into rapidly accelerating global movements against both sociocide and policide, as well as national pro-democracy movements. Kamala Harrris's failed 2024 presidential campaign nonetheless made clear that youth and social media are emerging as one of the most powerful new forces shaping the prospects for democracy and community.

If you visited any of the encampments of Gen Z protesters on campuses, you would have seen that they were building new communities, sleeping together in tents, cooking and eating together, chanting and singing together, and hugging in expressions of care, fear, and excitement. I remember activist communities in the 2011 Occupy Movement, where intimate connections and solidarity were built in the heat of shared fear and hope, as armed police hovered all around Occupy protesters who had taken over public squares, pitched tents, and lived together for days, much like the students in protest camps on campuses.[30] In Vivian Gornick's classic book, *The Romance of American Communism*, Gornick showed that 1930s left-wingers built a new extended family, with activists living together, marrying and having "red diaper" babies, sending them to summer camps together, creating poems and songs that they recited or sang around small sociophiliac bonfires at night.[31] All these movements are prefiguring the society they want, creating the "we" that replaces the lonely "me" of ordinary life.

Of course, 1930s activists didn't have iPhones and social media, which were relatively new during the Occupy movements but became central to Gen Z when the Harris campaign exploded with its initial exuberance among millions of young people online and tuned into social media. The crucial question is whether social media, despite all its contradictions, may help a new generation build stronger communities and pro-democracy movements, overcoming the disastrous failures of the Harris campaign to barnstorm for systemic corporate change and anti-war policies in a revitalized left populist Democratic Party.

For activists, social media are connectors and megaphones, allowing them to get out calls for meetings and actions in split seconds, and now capable of communicating with activists around the country and the world. Gen Z activists couldn't organize at scale without social media, and they could never get their messages out to so many people, both inside and outside of the movements, without social media. As shown in earlier chapters, the Harris campaign could not have exploded without the millions of posts, memes, videos, and Zoom meetings powered by thousands of Gen Z Harris supporters and influencers online. Within the first week of her campaign, it became clear that young people were central to future politics – and despite her failed campaign, it is important to remember the sociophilic force of young people that came together to support her at the first stages of her candidacy and might have powered a campaign with a more universalizing and anti-corporate leader to victory.

The excitable mix of young people and social media became known as the "Kamalanomenon." Along with "brat," it became central to the Harris campaign, a meme repeated on TikTok and Instagram in endless designs, videos, clothing fashion, and pop culture symbols. It was all about the power and joy of community – young people most of all tuning into the web and saying they were an unstoppable force as they came together to change the world.[32] The "Kamalanomenon" in 2024 – at least for a short time – became arguably the most powerful anti-sociocidal eruption in modern American politics, even more intense than the millions of people coming together around Barack Obama in 2008. It showed how deeply social connections had been buried and how powerfully social media – which had helped breed that disconnection – could help bring young people together to create the hopeful and joyful community that they had hungered much of their life.

It was far from enough to overcome the profound weaknesses of Harris as a self-declared "proud capitalist," failing to bring a transformative anti-corporate economic message to the American majority in the vulnerable "precariat," who were suffering and feeling transformative rage toward the system that Trump articulated far better than Harris. A major lesson of the 2024 Democratic defeat is that using pro-corporate and pro-war strategies to build a new "center" is a recipe for the Democratic Party's continuing disaster. Harris used Republican rhetoric against government – saying women's freedom rested on keeping government out of the bedroom – which bled into the larger Republican discourse about freedom as inherently rooted in small government and a society based on the "free market." Harris rejected the militant class agenda for working people that would have brought blue-collar workers back into the Democratic Party. For Democrats to become a governing party, they have to reverse the "twist" that the Harris campaign disastrously introduced. She embraced much of the corporate and war policies of traditional Republicans, making them new Democratic Party orthodoxy while Republicans became the party of "change," challenging the entire system that working people feel legitimately has abandoned them.

Trump's supporters' reactions to Trump's populist anti-establishment picks show how successfully Trump stole the "change" message from Harris, who voters saw as just one more Washington politician deep in the corporate swamp. As one Trump supporter, Neil Shaffer, a GOP county chair in Iowa, put it:

> I like the idea of bringing people from outside government to look at this with eyes from the real world not Washington DC. Washington DC is not the real world. It's a made-up puppet regime of dark shadows. You've got the military-industrial complex, big pharma, big agriculture pulling all the levers. They want all that money.[33]

After interviewing many Trump supporters, journalist Chris McGreal observed that:

> Shaffer offers a frequently heard view among Trump supporters that the former president was ill-prepared for his unexpected victory in 2016, and was then captured by big business and the Republican establishment in making cabinet appointments. That, he said, held back Trump's promise to "drain the swamp."
>
> "He was inundated with all these lobbyists and corporate interests and individuals who really were there more to perpetuate the system instead of reform the system," he said.
>
> This time, said Shaffer, Trump has the experience to put in place officials who will represent his ambitions.[34]

This reinforces the argument that Harris was perceived by voters as the candidate of "the swamp," allowing Trump to be seen as the anti-establishment change agent. Harris was perceived as comfortable with corporate power, as she repeatedly declared herself "a proud capitalist" and refused to speak out against wars in the Middle East and Ukraine. Trump supporters, McGreal found, applauded Trump's decision to bring billions of funds spent on wars abroad back to fund manufacturing jobs in America, rejecting Harris because of her failure to promise real change and "drain the swamp."[35] And while they failed to see how Trump was a creature of the corporate establishment who would enrich "the swamp," they were not wrong to see Harris as representing much of the corporate and military status quo and embracing much of "the establishment."

Nonetheless, despite these crippling failures of Harris and much of the Democratic Party, some of the initial sociophiliac moments of the Harris campaign demonstrate both the importance of a new generation raised on the internet and the political potential for a new sociophiliac anti-corporate and pro-democracy movement led by young people against Trumpism and future forms of sociocidal American fascism and corporatism.

This is not to dismiss all the earlier concerns about the sociocidal threats of social media and its dehumanizing impacts. Gen Z activists, like young people generally, have long felt that they cannot trust messages they get on social media, are suspicious of unknown influencers and fake news, and never rely on people they don't know personally to make important decisions about how to think about political issues and strategies for protest. But as authoritarianism grows and the Far-Right gains more power, social media may play a surprisingly important role in building an anti-fascist politics and a more connected and democratic society. Gen Z activists had to deal with all kinds of threats, deep fakes, and future recriminations launched at them online from MAGA and the Trump campaign in 2024. This had serious anti-democratic consequences – and will not go away in the future. But the excitement and political power of uniting and building anti-sociocidal community in a pro-democracy campaign – that speaks to young people's existential fears about climate change, extreme inequality, and nuclear war as well as their needs for secure jobs, good wages and solidarity in a more democratically controlled economy – and for their consitutional rights in a renewed deep democracy – are now clear. There remains the possibility that social media may become one of the next generation's most important tools in building new personal and political relationships as young people confront both the Trumpist second term and authoritarian as well as corporate oligarchic threats that will remain for decades.

The authoritarian bent of the second Trump term can bring the full force of the police and the courts against protesters. Rallying on the streets, as the anti-Gaza war student protesters did while it was still relatively safe to do so, could lead to arrest and jail time – or even a death sentence – in Trump's second term, as he promises to use the Justice Department to prosecute his enemies in universities or on the streets. Trump's promises to use the military to round up immigrants into deportation camps will test the boundaries of free speech and political activism like never before, exposing millions of young people horrified by mass deportation and threats to their own free speech and civil liberties to challenges they never imagined they would confront. Under those conditions, online organizing through social media may become a key survival mechanism for an anti-fascist movement. People skilled in online techniques and familiar with the dangers of surveillance from both commercial and political agents will find new ways to organize resistance through both secure online and offline forms of communication. The more power held by Far-Right leaders, the more resistance will have to emerge online. When in power, a neo-fascist American regime will make online organizing strategies more important, as online organizing is harder for elites and police to discover, track down, and eliminate.

But online sociophiliac movements can never succeed without offline anti-fascist and pro-democracy movements. For all the reasons discussed earlier, online solidarity is not sufficient to create the deep social and political communities that ultimately need to find expression face-to-face. Whenever the Far-Right is in power, much in-person organizing will have to take place behind closed doors, whether in campus dormitories, apartments, workplaces, or community centers. Learning how to connect and organize under a neo-fascist regime without drawing attention and violent repression by the National Guard, military, and other authorities will become important – and sometimes means going underground to avoid being arrested, jailed, or killed. Whenever possible, anti-fascist groups opposing mass deportation of immigrants or the use of the Justice Department to prosecute Trump's "enemies of the people" – including the mainstream media, Democratic politicians, anti-corporate, and anti-war activists on the streets – will have to coalesce in intense face-to-face relationships and groups, campus and street protests, and in unions and democratic political parties. Such organizing in-person and on the streets, as well as on campuses and in unions, will take courage and will require sacrifices, including the risk of being fired or jailed. The major structural changes to defeat fascism in the short and long term can only coalesce in deeply cemented face-to-face relationships, civil society associations and communities, and durable organizations like unions and movements that are the foundation of hope – and are also buttressed by mass online movements that can help shield in-person mobilizations facing violent repression on the streets.

At the same time, as noted earlier, the intense mobilization of ordinary working people to run for office is essential to systemic change. A Congress or state legislature full of the rich will never embrace a labor-friendly agenda challenging the corporate oligarchy. The effort by unions and community organizers to get ordinary working-class and union people to run for office at all levels is essential to the transformation of US politics and to moving toward the creation of a Democratic Party that speaks for the same people whom they represent. Politicians who can best feel and understand the suffering and needs of ordinary working Americans are those born and raised in the working and poor communities that the Democratic Party has largely abandoned.

Meanwhile, beyond the necessity of building for the long term, the anti-corporate and anti-fascist coalitions of youth, workers, women, and people of color, the constitutional changes essential to the deeper labor and popular pro-democracy movements and their anti-corporate and anti-war agendas are already well-known in the US. Many have been embraced by the Democratic Party. They involve the constitutional elimination of the Electoral College and a move to a popular vote for the presidency – one person, one vote. We need new constitutional decisions and urgent laws, starting with a decision fully reinstating the 1965 Voting Rights Act, as well as laws to guarantee universal by-mail voting, non-discretionary certification of votes, and the prosecution of people intimidating voters. Likewise, the Supreme Court must overturn Citizens United as pro-democracy movements work to enshrine in state and federal constitutions provisions that ban the mass buying of the Presidency and Congress by billions of dollars in dark money. New laws banning large private and corporate donations and significantly curbing corporate lobbying need to be passed. Public funds supporting all qualified candidates should be provided, creating a new public campaign finance system and ending once and for all the buying of the President.

Anti-fascist and pro-democracy major laws must include Constitutionally mandated appointment of four new Supreme Court justices and term limits for Supreme Court justices, as well as strict ethical rules banning private gifts and ensuring impeachment of corrupt Justices. The major authoritarian decisions of the Roberts Supreme Court – from the Immunity decision to Chevron to Dobbs – must also be immediately repealed. A Constitutional Amendment making Washington DC a state, with two senators and a Representative with full voting power, should be passed. While Republicans have a slim majority in the Senate and House, Democrats will try to force coalitions with small groups of Republican Senators or Congresspeople courageous enough to stand up against unconstitutional or authoritarian Trump initiatives. Virtually all these anti-fascist and pro-democracy legislative and Constitutional changes already have wide public support and must now be made as part of an emergency pro-democracy Constitutional and Congressional revolution. This form of anti-fascist coalition building from the "inside" of government, including lawyers in the Justice Department who stand up to refuse anti-democratic Trumpist orders to prosecute his enemies or otherwise violate the law, is central to curbing Trump in his second term. Lawyers from pro-democracy groups outside the government - like the ACLU, the Legal Defense Fund, CREW (Citizens for Responsibility and Ethics in Washington), and the Southern Poverty Law Center - likewise will play a major role in fighting fascism by suing Trump for anti-consitutional or other illegal executive orders shutting down free speech, banning books, ordering police violence against street protests, threatening or de-funding media and political dissenters who speak out against him, firing government and other workers, and de-funding schools, universities, and government agencies.

As noted in the last chapter, resistance to Trumpist authoritarianism will also depend in large measure on the resolve and courage of blue states in upholding democratic rights and the rule of law. Democratic governors and attorneys general will operate in their own states and in association with each other to check authoritarian policies in Trump's second term related to mass deportation, freedom of the press, voting rights, and freedom of speech. The same resistance can be organized locally through mayors and counties that help protect local law and elections as well as democratic freedoms. Ironically, "states' rights," long used to protect neo-fascist segregation by Southern states, will now become a bulwark of protection against federal fascism advanced by Trump in Washington.

These constitutional and legislative changes, all opposed by Trump and the MAGA GOP, are part of a long-term anti-corporate, anti-fascist, and pro-democracy struggle that should be taken up – along with broader Green New Deal-style shifts toward a uni-versalizing class politics for American social democracy in the short and long term. It is the only hope for overcoming both sociocide and policide. But as these inevitably long struggles are underway, the government can immediately move in novel ways to combat sociocide. Government is already moving within European nations and some American states in other novel ways to address the sociocidal crisis as central to the pro-democracy transformation. In 2018, Great Britain appointed a Minister for Loneliness, and other European nations are considering doing the same.[36] These officials oversee new govern-ment agencies, usually operating at the local level, that seek to bring people together in shared public gardens, festivals, plays and theater, cafes, and other public spaces. Such public space initiatives are linked to neighborhood anti-poverty campaigns, sustainable energy centers for electric bikes and other public vehicles, safe public spaces in which guns and bullying are prevented, and other community campaigns that build public ties and citizen solidarity. The "anti-loneliness" offices and services are part of a much larger public health campaign in nations responding to the mental health crisis, as well as the economic and political problems that plague people who are isolated and lonely.[37]

These new steps are the cultural expression of broader populist left pro-democracy movements now growing in France, Spain, and other European societies to defeat fascist resurgence. These emergency anti-fascist and pro-democracy coalitions and movements must coalesce nationally and globally in the US and become the foundation of a long-term left populist movement opposing American militarized capitalism.

While opposing MAGA American fascism in Trump's second term and beyond, there must be a continuing and growing universalizing resistance against the Democratic Party's tilt toward corporate and pro-war politics represented by the big wealthy donors and corporate establishment long central to the Democratic Party. The coalition of labor, poor people, women, and anti-racist movements of people of color will have to learn the skills of working with the Democratic Party and against it, always pushing it beyond where the corporate establishment wants it to go. After the 2024 election, the "freedom" movement must move toward joining the Democratic Party to fight MAGA fascism and implement the rights it is willing and able to support, while mobilizing against the corpo-ratism and militarism that will continue to be a threat for decades within the Democratic Party.

Left populism against the sociocide and the policide of militarized capitalism must grow nationally and globally as the core of new universalizing pro-democracy movements. This will require countering the pro-corporate agenda of the Harris sector of the Democratic Party and rebuilding the Democratic Party in the spirit of its progressive caucus led by Bernie Sanders and AOC, who support social democracy and a militant anti-corporate class politics. But such national and global anti-sociocidal politics have to find firm footing in local spaces and people's immediate social lives. You can start at home. Neighborhood communities that share babysitting, bartering, and entertainment services both online and face-to-face operate in hundreds of US cities and towns. These neighborly connections seem small in comparison to the pro-democracy national labor and political movements that are essential to an emergency anti-fascist politics. But such politics are both local and global. Individuals can start by doing everything they can to make new family, friends, and community relations that overcome their own social disconnection and isolation. Such local connections embody the mutuality, social solidarity, and collective good that make possible national sustainable movements for community and deep democracy.

Politics is always personal. This is never truer than in a society facing sociocidal and policidal breakdown. In the face of societal extinction and the looming near-death of social relations and democracy, we must find the humanity to ensure our own personal appreciation of and love for everyone around us. We are all struggling with the same challenges of personal and societal survival. That mindset of appreciation of and love for others, which builds solidarity and caring relations, and which I call the attitude of gratitude, may sound challenging in hard times, but it is at the heart of any prospects for overcoming sociocide and ensuring democracy. Building the social solidarity sustaining our sanity and moving us toward the free communities essential not only to democracy but to our humanity and love of life has now become a survival necessity, not only supporting each of us individually, but all of us together.

Notes

1 Tim Walz cited in Will Weissert and Michelle Price, "Harris Is Pushing Joy." *The Guardian*, August 12, 2024, theguardian.com
2 Mohammad Ali Kadivar, *Popular Politics, and the Path to Durable Democracy*. Princeton, NJ: Princeton University Press, 2022.
3 The National WWII Museum, "The Reconstruction of Justice I Post-Nazi Western Germany." August 11, 2021, nationalww2museum.org
4 Michele L. Norris, "Germany Faced its Horrible Past: Can We do the Same?" *Washington Post*, June 3, 2021, washingtonpost.com
5 Michele L. Norris, "Germany Faced its Horrible Past: Can We do the Same?" *Washington Post*, June 3, 2021, washingtonpost.com
6 Jeremy Rifkin, *The European Dream*. NY: Tarcher, 2004.
7 Paul Hockenos, "Germany's Far-Right Party is Worse Than the Rest of Europe's." *Foreign Policy*, January 26, 2024, foreignpolicy.com
8 Eric Foner, "Why Reconstruction Matters." *New York Times*, March 28, 2015 niytimes.com; Eric Foner, *Reconstruction: America's Unfinished Revolution*. NY: HarperCollins, 1988; Eric Foner, *A Short History of Reconstruction*. NY: Perennial, 1990.
9 Eric Foner, *A Short History of Reconstruction*. NY: Perennial, 1990.
10 Jeremy Rifkin, *The European Dream*. NY: Tarcher, 2004.
11 Jeremy Rifkin, *The European Dream*. NY: Tarcher, 2004; Robert Kuttner, *The Economic Illusion*. Philadelphia: University of Pennsylvania Press, 1987.
12 Jeffrey A. Sonnenfeld and Steven Tian, "The Critics of Bidenomics Are Being Proved Wrong." *Yale Insights*, August 1, 2023, insights.som.yale.edu
13 Charles Derber and Yale Magrass, *Who Owns Democracy*. NY: Routledge, 2024.
14 Anthony Adragna, "Progressives Formally Reintroduce the Green New Deal." *Politico*, April 20, 2012, politico.com

15 Jenny Brown, "2023 in Review: Big Strikes, Bigger Gains." *Labor Notes*, December 15, 2023, labornotes.org

16 Andrea Hsu, Stephan Bisaha, "Are Workers in the Deep South Fed Up Enough to Unionize? We're About to Find Out." *NPR*, May 11, 2024, npr.org.

17 Robert Kuttner, *The Economic Illusion*. Philadelphia: University of Pennsylvania Press, 1987; Jeremy Rifkin, *The European Dream*. NY: Tarcher, 2004.

18 George Orwell, *1984*. NY: Harper Perennial, 2014.

19 Alex Wray, "Gun Violence, Climate Change, LGBTQ Justice. These Gen Z-Led Groups Tackling Our Toughest Challenges." *Reckon*, April 24, 2023, reckon.news.

20 Annie Karni, "House Republicans, Seeing Political Edge Amid College Protests, Spotlight Antisemitism." *New York Times*, April 30, 2024, nytimes.com

21 Alisa Solomon, Marianne Hirsch, Sarah Haley, and Helen Benedict, "Anti-woke Republicans Attacked Columbia University. It Capitulated." *The Guardian*, April 18, 2024, theguardian.com

22 Joseph Konig, "Speaker Johnson Goes to Columbia University to Condemn Pro-Palestinian Protests." *Spectrum News*, April 24, 2024, ny1.com

23 Charles Derber and Yale Magrass, *Who Owns Democracy?* NY: Routledge, 2024.

24 Hafiz Rashid, "UAW President Expertly Skewers Response to University Protests." *New Republic*, May 1, 2024, newrepublic.com

25 Mike Miller, "A Union for All Workers." In Charles Derber, Suren Moodliar, Matt Nelson, Nancy Treviño, eds. *How We Win: Energizing Strategies, Voters, and Agendas*. NY: Routledge, 2024.

26 Ben Manski, "Holding the Fort, Birthing a New World – Why Unions Matter." In Charles Derber, Suren Moodliar, Matt Nelson, Nancy Treviño, eds. *How We Win: Energizing Strategies, Voters, and Agendas*. NY: Routledge, 2024.

27 Ben Manski, "Holding the Fort, Birthing a New World – Why Unions Matter." In Charles Derber, Suren Moodliar, Matt Nelson, Nancy Treviño, eds. *How We Win: Energizing Strategies, Voters, and Agendas*. NY: Routledge, 2024.

28 Katherine Adam and Charles Derber, *The Feminized Majority*. Boulder: Paradigm Press, 2010.

29 Rev. Dr. William J. Barber, "If We Ever Needed a Voice and a Vote, We Sure Do Need Them Now." *The Nation*, October 23, 2024, the nation.com

30 Todd Gitlin, *Occupy Nation*. NY: HarperEnt, 2012.

31 Vivian Gornick, *The Romance of American Communism*. London, Verso 2020.

32 Maura Judkis and Jesus Rodriguez, "The Kamala Harris Meme Decoders Have Entered the Chat." *The Washington Post*, July 23, 2024, washingtonpost.com

33 Chris McGreal, "Trump Voters Hail Controversial Cabinet Picks as the Government They Want." *Guardian*, November 24, 2024, theguardian.com

34 Chris McGreal, "Trump Voters Hail Controversial Cabinet Picks as the Government They Want." *Guardian*, November 24, 2024, theguardian.com

35 Chris McGreal, "Trump Voters Hail Controversial Cabinet Picks as the Government They Want." *Guardian*, November 24, 2024, theguardian.com

36 Ceylan Yeginsu, "U.K. Appoints a Minister for Loneliness," *New York Times*, January 17, 2018 nytimes.com; Rick Noack, "Isolation Is Rising in Europe. Can Loneliness Ministers Help Change That?" *Washington Post*, February 2, 2018, washingtonpost.com.

37 Vivek Murthy, *Our Epidemic of Loneliness and Isolation*. US Surgeon General's Advisory. Department of Health and Human Services, 2023, hhs.gov.

Index

1984 (Orwell) 37, 107
2008 Heller decision 82
2010 McDonald v Chicago 82
2022 Bruen case 82
2024 Chevron decision 31, 104
2024 election 100–101; rhetoric 127–128
2026 Congressional elections 102

ACLU 130
activists, social media 127–129
Adam, Katherine 125
AfD party, Germany 115
affirmative action 93–95
AFL-CIO 17, 123
air traffic controllers strike 16, 91
Alea, Karen 72
alliance, between Silicon Valley and Trumpist Far-Right populist politics 35–36
"alone together" 48
Alphabet (Google) 28
Altman, Sam 31
Amazon 15, 28, 30, 33–34
America First Republicans 94
American authoritarianism, rise of 16
American capitalism 33, 90
American Dream 6, 44, 48
American fascism 100, 106
American militarism 120–121
American neo-fascism 90
American sociocide 9
Andreessen, Mark 26, 39
anti-authoritarian elites 113
anti-capitalist Occupy movement 123
anti-climate policies 67–68
anti-fascist coalitions, rise of 113
anti-loneliness offices 131
anti-racist movements 125–126
anti-Semitism 122
anti-unionism 16–17, 30, 123
anti-war movement 121–122
AOC 132
Apple 28
AR-15 81–82

Arendt, Hannah 7, 19
armed populism 76
artificial intelligence: employment 19–20; regulation 31
assassination attempt on Trump 84, 98
atomization 34, 52
authoritarian leaders 1
authoritarian neo-fascist turn, of the Republican Party 6
autocrats 38
automation 29; and employment 19–20

Baldwin, Richard 18
Bank of America 28
Bannon, Steve 38
Barber, William 126
Barnes and Noble 33
Barr, William 103
Bellah, Robert 7
Bender, Michael 53–54
Bessent, Scott 106
Bezos, Jeff 13, 30, 33, 105
Biden, Joe 23, 92, 100, 107, 119–120
Biden administration 117, 119–120
Bidenomics 119
Big Agriculture 13, 63–65, 69
Big Gas 65, 67, 69, 104
big government 91–92
Big Industry 13
Big Oil 13, 65, 67, 69, 104
Big Pharma 13, 73
Big Tech 10, 28–29, 35, 105; deregulation 31–32; social disconnection 39; unions 119
Big Tech tycoons 13
bird flu 69
Black Lives Matter 124–125
Blacks: affirmative action 93; gun ownership 78
Blackstone 105
Black Voters Matter 125
blue-collar workers 20
Bondi, Pam 103–104
Boughton, Jay 83

Bourdieu, Pierre 8, 13, 51
Bragg, Alvin 103
"brat," Harris, Kamala 127
Brooks, David 77
bullies 108
bullying 84, 109
Bush, George W. 79, 107
Butler, Ronald 83

capitalism 32–33; American capitalism 33, 90;
    Disaster Capitalism 73; fascist capitalism
    114; industrial capitalism 36, 64–65; rise of
    26–27; surveillance capitalism 36–39
capitalist elites 27
Carbon-Industrial Complex (CIC) 65, 68,
    74, 104
Cargill 13, 69
Carlson, Tucker 37, 100
Carnegie, Andrew 12, 29
Case, John 39
change agents 128
Charlottesville, Virginia 98
ChatGPT 31
Chavez-DeRemer, Lori 17
Cheers, Imani M. 41
Chen, Brian 58
Chevron 28, 67–68, 97–98, 104
Chevron ConocoPhillips 65
China 107–108
Christian nationalist movement 78; *see also*
    white Christian nationalism
Christian Right 94–95
Citizens for Responsibility and Ethics in
    Washington (CREW) 130
civic deserts 51–52
civic opportunities 51
civic superheroes 52
civil rights 95
Civil War 79, 90, 112; Reconstruction
    115–116
class, social disconnection 51–52
class politics 112, 126
climate change 63–65, 104–105, 113
climate crisis 66–67
climate denialism 73
climate justice migration bill, New York 74
climate legislation 74
climate protests, Dedham, Massachusetts 65
climate threats 64–65
Clinton, Bill 65, 79, 91–92
Clinton, Hillary 16, 35, 38
Clinton Democrats 92–93
CO₂ 64
Cold War 107
college-educated parents 52
Colt 79
Columbia University 122

Columbine school shooting 77
Comey, James 38
communication 34–40; social media 37–39
community 33, 48–49; break down of 36–40
concealed carry 85
conservative corporate elites 6
constitutional monarchy 116–117
consumer-exploitation 32
Consumer Protection Finance Board 105
consumption 32–33; climate crisis 66–67;
    exploitative consumption 32
contingency, employment 13
contingent workers 13–16
conversational narcissism 56–57
Cooperative Commonwealth 124
corporate Democrats 18
corporate elites 5–6; climate crisis 66–67
corporate high-tech elites 29
corporate neoliberalism 9
corporate oligarchy 104
corporations 105
Coughlin, Charles 94
COVID-19 64, 69–73; remote work 20–21
Cox, Daniel 51
CREW *see* Citizens for Responsibility and
    Ethics in Washington
Crooks, Thomas 98
cults 54

Daniels, Stormy 47
Debs, Eugene 124
decertifying elections, election subversion 97
Dedham, Massachusetts 65
deep democracy leaders 123
"deep democracy" movements 113
deep state 96
defeating Trumpism 114
deforestation 69–70
dehumanizing character of social media 36
democracy 89–90
Democratic Party 10, 19, 130; as
    Establishment 92; Green New Deal 74;
    Harris-Walz Democratic Party 114; identity
    politics 93, 125–126; Jim Crow Democrats
    93; Ku Klux Klan 94; policies of 130;
    rebuilding 132; turn from 35–36
demographic racial tipping points 6
DePape, David 98
Department of Education 105
Department of Government Efficiency
    (DOGE) 105
deregulation 31–32; of fossil fuels 68
de Tocqueville, Alexis 7, 19, 89–90
Dimon, Jamie 13
disaggregating forces 4
disaggregation 3
Disaster Capitalism 73

disempowerment 108–109
Dobbs decision 98
DOGE *see* Department of Government
  Efficiency
Donegan, Moira 98–99
Doubt, Keith 5
"drill, baby, drill" 67, 104
Durkehim, Emile 3–4, 44, 54, 77

ecocide 63, 69
economic restructuring, Magnificent Seven 29
education 122
egoism 4, 45, 53, 55–59, 66
election denialism 99–100
election officials, death threats 99
election subversion 97, 99, 100
Electoral College 130
electric cars 67
employment 12–15; contingent workers
  13–18; remote labor 18–19; remote work
  20–21; technology and 19–20; unions 17;
  workplaces 20–21
environment: climate change 67–69;
  pandemics 69–73
Equal Rights Movement 95
Esper, Mark 84
Establishment 92, 96, 128
Europe: left populist movements 118;
  neoliberalism 71; New Popular Front 117;
  post-World War II 118; universal welfare
  model 120
European colonialism 120–121
European fascism 118
Europeans, values 115
Evangelical movement 94
exploitative consumption 32
extreme American Dream 6, 44, 66
extreme militarism 107
Exxon 13, 65–66, 68
Exxon Mobil 28

Facebook 56
face-to-face social life 33
Fain, Shawn 16–17, 22, 119, 122–123
Falwell, Jerry 94
familiar strangers 33
Far-Right authoritarianism 9, 31–32
Far-Right Christian nationalist movements 78
Far-Right political economy 6
Far-Right populism 1, 4, 35–36, 44–46,
  115, 129
Far-Right populists 8
Far-Right Republicans 108
fascism 94, 100, 102, 104, 106; American
  fascism 100, 106; European fascism 118;
  see also neo-fascism
fascist authoritarianism 114

fascist capitalism 114
Fauci, Anthony 72
fear 104; white fear 6
firing workers 30
Fisher, Mark 8
Fisher, Max 35
Floyd, George 82
Flynn, Michael 38
Ford 28
forgotten man 16
fossil-fuel agenda 68
fossil fuels, deregulation of 68
Foster, John Bellamy 70
France, New Popular Front 117–118
free speech absolutism 38
French, David 52
friendship 48–53; online friends 55–56
Front Row Joes 53–54

Gaetz, Matt 103–104
Galtung, Johan 5
Garland, Merrick 103
gay rights 95
Gaza 107, 121
General Electric 28
General Motors 13, 28
genocide 107
Gen Z 121; activists 128–129; anti-war
  movement 121; guns 86; preppers 81;
  protests 126–127; support for Harris 60–61
Germany 9, 105; societal reconstruction 115;
  see also Nazi Germany
ghost companies 21
ghosted workplace 20
Gilded Age 28–30, 90
globalization 18–19
Goldman Sachs 28, 105
Gornick, Vivian 127
government, combatting sociocide 131–132
Great Britain, anti-loneliness offices 131
Great Replacement theory 37, 100
green energy 65
Green New Deal 74
gun control 86
gun culture 79
gun ownership 76–80, 84–86
gun violence 78–81, 86

Hannity, Sean 104
Harris, Eric 77
Harris, Kamala 2, 9, 23, 40–41, 126; climate
  change 74; guns 86; presidential agenda 113
Harris campaign, social media 40–41, 59–60,
  126–127
Harris-Walz Democratic Party 114
Harvey, David 8
Hassan, Steven 54

Hegseth, Pete 103
Herd, Jeff 21
Heritage Foundation 31
high technology 40
Hispanics, gun ownership 78
Hitler, Adolf 90, 94, 105, 118
Hogg, David 81–83, 86
Homan, Tom 101–102
Howe, Neil 26
human invasion of nature 69–70
The Hunger Games 6
hybrid workplaces 21
hyper-individualistic culture 45–47
hyper-market capitalism 7

identity community 93
identity politics 92–93, 125–126
Ik (Uganda) 1, 4, 44, 63
immigrants, mass deportation of 129
independent workers 14–15
individualism 44–45; during COVID-19 72
Indivisible 114
industrial capitalism 36; climate change
    64–65
industrial factories 12
influencers 34
Intergovernmental Panel on Climate Change
    (IPCC) 64
invisible hand 91
IPCC *see* Intergovernmental Panel on Climate
    Change
Iran 106
isolation 45
Israel 107

Jameson, Fredric 8
January 6 84, 95, 98, 100, 103
Japan, guns violence 81
Jim Crow 79, 90, 93–94, 112, 116
job replacement 29–30; by robots or AI 20
Johnson, Mike 122
journalism 35
JP Morgan Chase 28–29, 105
"The Jungle" 12
Justice Department 103–104, 129

Kamalanomenon 127
Kelly, John 103
Kennedy Jr., Robert F. 73
King, Martin Luther 126
Kiva Systems 33
Klain, Ron 70
Klebold, Dylan 77
Klein, Naomi 73
Koch Industries 65, 68
Kristof, Nicholas 80–82
Ku Klux Klan 79, 94

labor movement 22–23, 123
labor process 12
LaPierre, Wayne 82
League of Women Voters 125
Left populism 16, 113, 131–132; Europe 118
Legal Defense Fund 130
Leonard, Christopher 65
Le Pen, Marie 117–118
Lewis, John 119
libertarian ideology 35
libraries 52
Lindbergh, Charles 94
Lockheed Martin 13
loneliness 7, 45, 49–51, 54; *see also* social
    isolation
lonely society 7
loners 77
look-at-me relations of social media 57
loveless 54
loveless culture 63
loveless society 44
Luttnick, Howard 106

MAGA authoritarianism 19
MAGA politicians 9
MAGA politics 10
MAGA Republican Party 14, 74, 78–79, 95,
    99, 117, 122
Magnificent Seven 28–31
Manafort, Paul 38
Manski, Ben 123–124
manufacturing, automation 19
Marciano, Laura 58
markets 32–33
marriage 46–48
Marx, Karl 4, 7, 12, 36
Marxists 8
masks, COVID-19 71
mass consumption 69
mass deportation 102, 129
mass shooters 77
mass shootings 80–82
McGreal, Chris 128
"me" 5, 83, 91
mental health issues in young people 58
me over the we 5, 55–59, 91
mercantilism 32
Meta (Facebook) 28, 31
Microsoft 28
Milgram, Stanley 33
militarism 107, 120–121
military 102–103; technology and 27
Military-Industrial Complex 13, 105
Military Spiral 106–109
militias 85
Miller, Stephen 96, 101–102, 104
Milley, Mark 103

minority majority 100
mobilization: of Harris campaign 40–41; of ordinary people 130
modernity 7
Moral Majority 94
Morgan, J.P. 12, 29
Morozov, Evgeny 34–35
Murthy, Vivek 48–49, 54, 57–58, 70
Musk, Elon 13, 26, 30, 37–39, 41, 105, 108
Mussolini, Benito 94, 106, 108, 118

narcissism 47–48; conversational narcissism 56–57
National Labor Relations Board (NLRB) 17
National Organization of Women 125
National Rifle Association (NRA) 79, 82–83
NATO 107–108
Nazi Germany 9, 112; *see also* Germany
Nazism 7
neighborhood communities 132
neo-fascism 7, 90, 126
neoliberal corporate elites 5
neoliberal era 6
neoliberal global post-industrialism 21
neoliberalism 6, 8, 56, 65, 91; and Christian nationalist movement 78; climate change 66; ; corporate neoliberalism 9; Europe 71; exploitative consumption 32; globalization 18; pandemics 69–73; virtual communication 34–36
neoliberal market capitalism 5
Neoliberal Spiral 90
neo-Marxists 8
Netanyahu government 107
New Deal 5, 14, 93, 95, 112, 118
New Popular Front 117
New Right 27
new Robber Barons 13, 74
Nixon, Richard 94
NLRB *see* National Labor Relations Board
noise 38
NVIDIA 28

Oath Keepers 85, 95
Obama, Barack 92
Occupy Movement 126–127
Occupy Wall Street 124
online friends 55–56
online sociophiliac movements 129
online world 27
organic solidarity 4
organized labor 124
Orwell, George 107
outsourcing 18–19

Palestine 121–122
pandemics 63–64, 69–73; gun ownership 77–78

parallel lives 59
parks 52
PATCO 16, 91
peace movements 113
Pelosi, Paul 98
people of color 125–126
Pfizer 13
pipelines 65
Planned Parenthood 125
podcasts 41
police attacks on pro-Palestinian student activists 122
police violence 82
policide 1, 4, 89–92, 96, 112–113
policies of Democratic Party 130
political authoritarianism 3, 7–8, 37
political repression 116
political solidarity 116
political violence 84–85, 99–100
politics 73–74
popular mobilizations 113
post-Biden Democratic Party 119
post-industrialism 27
post-New Deal Democratic Party 93
post-New Deal Reagan period 6
post-World War II, Europe 118
Power, Samantha 107
precariat class 13, 95, 127
preppers 81
Presidential Immunity decision 97, 99–100
Presidential impoundment 101
Pressler, Sam 51
pro-democracy coalitions, rise of 113
pro-democracy protests 113
pro-democracy youth movements 122
production relations 13
profit 32
Progressive Caucus 119
Project 2025 31, 68, 90, 96–97, 100–101
pro-Palestinian student activists, police attacks on 122
protests: Columbia University 122; mobilization of ordinary people 130
Proud Boys 85, 95
pro-worker politics 35, 96
public goods 118
public health care 118
public transit 118
Putin, Vladimir 108
Putnam, Robert 7, 48–49, 51

race 93–94
raced-based politics 93–94
racial division 93
racism 90, 93–94; gun ownership 78
rallies, Trump campaign 53–54
Rand, Any 91

Reagan, Ronald 16, 44–45, 47, 91, 94–95, 107
Reaganism 91, 124
Reagan Republicans 18
Reagan Revolution 5, 16, 47, 65, 92, 119
recess appointments 101
reconstruction 10, 115–117
Reconstruction era (US) 90, 115–116
regulation of artificial intelligence 31
relations of production 12, 13
religion, COVID-19 72
remote labor 18–19, 22
remote work 21
Republican Party 74; authoritarian neo-fascist turn 6; climate change 67–68; Establishment 92; identity politics 93; Reagan Republicans 18; *see also* MAGA Republicans
resistance 102, 112, 114; future of 131–132; Indivisible 114
reverse discrimination 95
rhetoric 127–128
Rifkin, Jeremy 115
right to carry concealed weapons 85
road rage incidents, shootings 83
Robber Barons 12–13, 33
Robertson, Pat 94
Roberts Supreme Court 97–98, 130; constitutional monarchy 116–117; gun control 78; *see also* Supreme Court
robots 19–20, 29; Kiva Systems 33
Rockefeller, John D. 12, 29
Rogan, Joe 41, 109
Romney, Mitt 99
ruling elites 6
Russia 108

Sacks, David 26, 39
Sainato, Michael 30
Sanders, Bernie 16, 123, 132
Schedule F politicized employees 96, 101
Schlafly, Phyllis 94–95
Schoen, John 18
school shootings 84
Second Amendment 76, 82–86; *see also* gun ownership
self-interest 44, 55–59, 72
sexism 93
Shaffer, Neil 128
shallow democracy 90
shift from we to me 26
shift-responses 56
Shock Doctrine 73
silent majority 94
Silicon Valley 26–28, 31–32; authoritarianism 38–39; communication 36–40; consumption 32–33; virtual communication 34–36
Silicon Valley Big Tech pioneers, independent workers 14–15

Silkis, Ryan 35
Simmel, Georg 33
Sinclair, Upton 12
single-person households 47
Smith, Adam 91
Smith, Jack 103
Smith and Wesson 82
social capital 7, 51; erosion of 8
Social Capital Survey 51–52
social connection 50–51
social democratic economy 115
social disaggregation 45
social disconnection 39, 49–54; pandemics 70; social media 58–59; of workers 14–15
social glue of society 8
social infrastructure 5
social isolation 49–55, 77; *see also* loneliness
social media 36–39, 113, 126–129; 2024 campaigns 59–60; consumption 34; egoism, self-interest and survivalism 55–59; mental health issues 58; narcissism 57; social disconnection 58–59
social relationships 112–113; employment 13; friendship 48–53; marriage 46–48; pandemics 69; weakness of 8
social solidarity 6, 9, 39
societal reconstruction 115–117
sociocidal Americanism 72
sociocidal culture 39
sociocidal societies 5
sociocide 1–4, 44, 63, 89, 112–113
sociopathic forces 10
sociopathic societies 3–5
sociopathic values 3
sociopathy 3–4
sociophiliac forces 2, 9
sociophiliac movements 117–118
sociophiliac public goods economy 119
sociophiliac social movements 113
sociophiliac values 9
solidarity 6, 59, 116, 120
Sotomayor, Sonia 9, 97
Southern Democratic Party Jim Crow playbook 94
Southern Poverty Law Center 130
Southern strategy 79
Soviet Union 107
Standard Oil 28
stand your ground laws 81–82
states rights 131
Stern, Steve 89
strikes 22, 30
strongmen 4, 108
Stuart, Charles 45, 47–48, 77
students, pro-Palestinian student activists 122
suicide 45, 54
Sullivan, Nancy 70

"summer of strikes" 2023 22–23
support-responses 56
Supreme Court 9; enlargement of 130; gun
    control 78; gun rights 82–86; Presidential
    Immunity decision 97, 99–100; Trumpist
    Supreme Court 10; *see also* Roberts
    Supreme Court
surveillance 129
surveillance capitalism 36–39
survivalism 53, 55–59
survivalists 81

Taiwan 108
tech giants, rise of 28
technological innovation 10; and employment
    19–20
technological solutionism 34–35
technology 26–27; robots 29
tech workers 29–30
temp workers, social disconnection 15
terrorism 107
Tesla 28
Thiel, Peter 26–27, 31–32, 37–39, 105
tipping points 3–5; contingent workers 15–16;
    mass shootings 80–82; Second Amendment
    82–86
transient workers 13–14
Trump, Donald 1, 3–4, 6, 10, 13, 27, 35, 37,
    45–46; 2024 election victory 100–101;
    anti-unionism 123; assassination attempt
    84, 98; climate change 74–75; COVID-
    19 71–72; democracy 90–91; egoism 53;
    firing workers 30; fossil-fuel agenda 68;
    friendship 48; gun ownership 78; guns
    violence 83; marriage 47; mass deportation
    102; military 102–103, 108; narcissism 57;
    policide 96; policies of 129; promises 101–
    103; pro-worker politics 96; Silicon Valley
    37–40; social disconnection 53; unions
    16–17; violence 84–85; white Christian
    nationalism 95
Trump, Melania 47
Trump campaign: Joe Rogan Experience
    41; social media 59–60; *see also* MAGA
    Republicans
Trump girls 53
Trumpism 4, 7–8, 16, 35, 67, 90–91, 114, 124
Trumpist Supreme Court 10
Trump-recession 106
Turkle, Sherry 36, 48, 57
Turnbull, Colin 44, 54

UAW 17, 22, 30, 119, 122–124
Ukraine 107
unions 16, 123; AFL-CIO 123; anti-war
    movement 123; attacks on 91; Biden
    administration 119–120; busting 30;

campaign endorsements 23; "summer of
    strikes" 2023 22–23; UAW 122–124
unitary executive 101
universal welfare model 120
US Agency for International Development
    (USAID) 105, 107
USAID *see* US Agency for International
    Development
US industrial capitalist system 12
US Steel 28–29
US stock markets 105–106

vaccines 71, 73
Vance, J. D. 6, 17, 27, 32, 35, 38, 98
Van Dam, Andrew 18
violence 77, 84–85
virtual communication 34–36
voluntary associations 48–49
"Voters of Tomorrow" 40
voting rights 130
Vought, Russell 96, 101–102
VW plant 119

Walmart 33
Walz, Tim 40, 113
Walzer, Michael 89
warrior board 102
wars 5, 106–107, 120–121; anti-war
    movement 121–122
Watts, Shannon 40
"we" 5, 83, 118
weakening of traditional ties 59–61
white Christian nationalism 79, 85, 92, 94–95,
    100, 103, 126
"White Dudes" 40
white fear 6
white identity politics 95; Great Replacement
    theory 100
white males, gun violence 84
white privilege 92
whites, gun ownership 78
"White Women: Answer the Call" 40
white working people 93
Whitmer, Gretchen 98
Whole Foods 34
wilding 44
Win With Black Men 40
Win With Black Women 40
Wolverine Watchmen 98
women 125–126
worker associations 12
working-class people 2; social isolation
    51–55
workplaces 20–21; role of Magnificent Seven
    in 29

X (formerly Twitter) 37

young people: Germany 115; mental health
issues 58; support for Harris 60

Zauderer, Steven 45
Zeldin, Lee 68

Zoom moms 40–41
Zelenskyy, Volodymyr 108
Zoom meetings, for Harris campaign 40
Zuboff, Shoshanna 36–39

For Product Safety Concerns and Information please contact our EU
representative GPSR@taylorandfrancis.com
Taylor & Francis Verlag GmbH, Kaufingerstraße 24, 80331 München, Germany

www.ingramcontent.com/pod-product-compliance
Lightning Source LLC
Chambersburg PA
CBHW080134270326
41926CB00021B/4475

9 781032 793634